THE POLITICS OF
BRAZILIAN DEVELOPMENT
1930–1954

THE POLITICS OF
BRAZILIAN DEVELOPMENT
1930–1954

JOHN D. WIRTH

STANFORD UNIVERSITY PRESS
STANFORD, CALIFORNIA
1970

Stanford University Press
Stanford, California
© 1970 by the Board of Trustees of the
Leland Stanford Junior University
Printed in the United States of America
SBN 8047-0710-3
LC 71-97918

To my mother

PREFACE

In preparing this study of politics during the Vargas years I want to thank several friends who read and criticized portions of the manuscript at various stages: John J. Johnson, Donald Keesing, William J. Kemnitzer, Ibá Jobim Meirelles, Rollie E. Poppino, and Thomas E. Skidmore. I am deeply grateful to Euclydes Aranha Netto and to Alzira Vargas do Amaral Peixoto, who, in homage to their illustrious fathers, gave access to family papers. In this respect, thanks are also due to Victor Simonsen and especially to General Ibá, friend and mentor. I honor Charles A. Gauld for preserving Farquhar's papers. Professor Johnson guided the doctoral dissertation from which this book grew.

I did much of this research in the Brazilian National Archive and at the National Library in Rio; the staffs were welcoming and helpful. Government libraries were consulted at the Ministries of Finance, Foreign Affairs, and Public Works, and at the National Petroleum Council and the National Department of Mineral Production. The Brazilian press—*Correio da Manhã, Diário de Notícias, Estado de São Paulo,* and *Jornal do Brasil*—graciously placed complete newspaper files at my disposal. Finally, I made extensive use of the United States National Archives, Stanford University Libraries, and the New York Public Library.

The interpretations in this account of the Vargas era are taken at my own risk and responsibility. Working in Brazilian contemporary history is difficult but deeply rewarding in a scholarly and a personal sense. In citing sources, I have tried to strike a prudent balance between my historian's urge to mention everything and my obligation to informants. Anyone working in contemporary history can readily understand this and, I hope, accept it. Brazilian words, proper names, place names, and titles of publications are spelled in the new style (post-1943), except when the old way is appropriate.

Grants from the Foreign Area Fellowship Program and the NDEA Center–Faculty (Fulbright) Program enabled me to spend almost two years researching and writing in Brazil and at Stanford. The content is of course my own. St. John's College in Santa Fe kindly provided office space during the summer of 1968.

Finally, my wife Nancy knows she is my best critic. She made our stay with friends and relatives in Rio de Janeiro a rich sojourn into *a realidade brasileira.*

J.D.W.

CONTENTS

THE POLITICS OF
BRAZILIAN DEVELOPMENT
1930–1954

INTRODUCTION

Getúlio Vargas, in a speech on May 7, 1943, hailed the new Volta Redonda steelworks as the symbol of Brazil's economic emancipation. The scene was a former coffee plantation in the once-prosperous Paraíba Valley, an agricultural region between Rio de Janeiro and São Paulo, which was then known from the short stories of Monteiro Lobato for its "dead cities." With the opening of the steelworks, Brazil would become an independent industrial nation, Vargas said, no longer a mere importer of manufactured goods, an exporter of raw materials. Of course, he hastened to add for the benefit of foreign guests, the new plant was the achievement of all Americans, thanks to the "friendly intervention of President Roosevelt" in securing United States finance. To Brazilians, Vargas offered the new model town of Volta Redonda as proof that higher living standards could come without social conflict. Every Brazilian president since 1909 had aspired to a domestic steel industry. The plant construction was now well advanced, and Vargas stood at the peak of his career.[1]

Behind him lay the depression decade and a commercial policy he now eyed critically. In those years his policy had emphasized increasing exports in which Brazil had a cost and geographical advantage: cotton, coffee, foodstuffs, and certain raw materials. The substitution of domestic manufactures for foreign imports did not have high priority. And though the devalued exchange did give de facto protection to industry, the purposes of Vargas's exchange policy were to keep up debt payments and to cover imports. As the

[1] Superscript numbers refer to Notes (pp. 227–59), primarily citations of sources. Footnotes are designated by asterisks. A list of abbreviations used in the text and the notes is supplied at the head of the Notes section.

decade wore on, payments problems continued, and international politics became increasingly important in trade policy. Thus the trade tangle revealed clearly the problems and dangers of relying heavily on exports. An alternative to the doctrine of comparative advantage was domestic industrial growth. This Vargas expressed well in 1943 at Volta Redonda.

In his second presidency (1951–54), Vargas strongly encouraged State planning to develop power resources. The most important program was the government oil monopoly, Petrobrás. Sending the oil bill to Congress in December 1951, Vargas pictured a bleak future of ever-rising petroleum imports and accompanying payments problems unless Petrobrás was authorized by Congress. That his proposed solution would be, as he phrased it, "a genuinely Brazilian company, with national capital and management," was not inevitable or easily determined.[2] In fact, the decision to found a State oil monopoly was rooted in the 1930's, and Vargas had yet to discover the will of Congress.

This book is a study of policy-making during the long Vargas era (1930–54), when the basic decisions to industrialize were taken. It analyzes three case studies of foreign trade, steel, and petroleum—issues that were hotly debated in the crucible of the 1930's, and that were recast, shaped, and finished into programs after the war, especially during Vargas's second presidency. A discussion of how decisions actually were made may be useful to others than historians.*

The first objective is to tell the story of these three issues and to relate them to the domestic and international political context of the times. To this extent, my book is another small window looking into the Vargas years. In providing chronology and a large core of fact, I have attempted to furnish the raw materials for others who,

---

* The task of theorizing from these Brazilian cases I have left to others, although some generalizations about the Brazilian experience under Vargas may be found in the Conclusion. But though I applied no overall analytical framework, I found that Brazilian policy makers exhibited a capacity for what Charles E. Lindblom aptly called "muddling through." See his by now classic article on incremental policy-making, "The Science of 'Muddling Through,'" *Public Administration Review*, XIX, No. 2 (Spring 1959), 84ff.

like myself, find many assumptions about Vargas and his era to be ill-founded, even mythical.[3]

The second objective is to explain policy-making within the historical context. Who identified problems and goals? Who could enforce his point of view, i.e., who controlled the policy-making machinery? How did the policy makers perceive their opportunities and constraints? Considerable attention is devoted to the uses of nationalism, and to the role and character of Getúlio Vargas, an enigmatic yet influential president who stamped his style on the times.

The emphasis is on the process, rather than on the structure of policy-making.[4] I have attempted to show how contemporaries assessed and justified their actions, as well as how they reached their decisions. Hopefully I have avoided judgments based on subsequent performance. On the other hand, the very selection, relative emphasis, and sequence of the three interlocking case studies indicate my point of view—namely, the attempt to maximize exports had disappointing results, and both Volta Redonda and Petrobrás were success stories. This outcome was by no means inevitable when the policies were being formulated. In fact, the clash of policies, the interplay of personalities, and the uncertainties—all of which will be brought out at length—are a corrective to any sense of inevitability. The principal conclusions I have drawn from the three case studies are as follows.

1. *Foreign Capital.* The withdrawal of foreign capital and/or knowledge of the terms on which capital was offered was a main determinant in policy-making. For example, a continuing shortage of hard currency, coupled with the hope that credits soon would become available, was a major factor in Brazilian commercial policy during the 1930's. Partly for this reason, Brazil flirted with Germany, but did not fall into her economic orbit. As for steel, private foreign capital could have built Latin America's first integrated steel complex (Volta Redonda), but withdrew instead, leaving Brazil and the United States to build it with public funds. Foreign capital, public and private, played a central role in the subsequent development of Brazil's steel industry. The petroleum industry, by

contrast, was developed without foreign capital, since the international oil companies were not prepared to offer enough capital to offset the Brazilians' strong fears about the consequences of accepting any outside assistance. Nor was the United States government prepared to lend the needed funds. The result was Petrobrás, established to allocate over many years enormous sums from a capital-short economy.

2. *The Perception and Analysis of Balance-of-Payments Problems.* In the 1930's, some prominent Brazilians began to realize that neo-colonial status was no longer practicable, and this perception deepened after the war despite the return to an open world trade and monetary system. To be sure, old patterns persisted. It can be argued that the coffee growers were remarkably successful in first securing government aid to diversify their production (1933–40),[5] and then in carrying on after the war (with government price supports) as the major exporters. But rapid growth in the domestic economy focused attention on the fact that exports *cum* foreign credits could not provide for a satisfactory level of imports, and that long-term balance-of-payments problems were in fact limiting growth.[6] This perception helped to identify the steel and petroleum problems and to give urgency to solving them. The actual payments crisis affecting steel imports occurred after 1937 and before a similar crisis regarding petroleum, imports of which did not rise steeply until after the war. This explains, in part, why Volta Redonda came ten years before Petrobrás.

3. *The Patrimonial State.* Government policy makers drew upon old Iberian traditions of patrimonialism, as updated by corporatism in the 1930's, and as revamped into the mystique of technocracy in the 1950's.[7] This was a harmonious model of action, in which ministers, administrators, and interest groups were related functionally, both formally and informally, to a central, legitimizing power focus, the presidency. Several councils were organized along corporatist lines to increase the flow of information between the government and private groups, to allow interest group leaders a role in decision-making, and to legitimize government actions. Professional associations such as the São Paulo Federation of Industries

(FIESP) sought and were granted access to governmental leaders. Urban labor was tied to the State and controlled through paternalistic legislation and government-sponsored trade unions. However informal and incomplete, the hierarchical relation of socioeconomic sectors to the presidency survived largely intact after 1945. During Vargas's second tenure, the role of experts, managers, and administrators, in short, the postwar technocrats, was added, vastly strengthening presidential powers.

It bears repeating that harmony, rather than conflict, was the self-proclaimed style of the Vargas system. That there was strenuous conflict between the various constituencies is of course true. That the Vargas presidency was far from monolithic was obvious to contemporaries. Interest groups, the Army, and the civilian ministers did take the policy initiative, as the case studies clearly point out. Yet time and again these initiatives were muted or modified by an inability to command sufficient resources. The point is not that interest groups were weak, but that in a capital-short economy they could not develop independently of the large resources that only the State could command. Private foreign interests and domestic interests were heavily involved in the calculus of oil policy, but ultimately they could not or would not offer enough capital to maneuver outside the system. This focused attention on the presidency.

4. *The Vargas Presidency.* Despite the growth of patrimonial institutions under his rule, Getúlio himself seemed most comfortable with a contingent system, an ad hoc clustering of groups and personalities around the presidency. With his keen sense of power and personal relationships, Vargas was able to balance and conciliate these groups, diminishing conflict and tension. Volta Redonda is a classic study of the Vargas presidency in action.

Not that Vargas was a man of extraordinary vision; many of his views were conventional and time-bound. Nor did he always use presidential powers to full effect, as the foreign trade case bears out. However, he possessed a sure instinct for spinning a web of influence to key points within Brazil and abroad. Thus, well informed, he acted when he had to on the basis of good information

6 INTRODUCTION

about power and resources. Vargas's presidency was something more than "a rubber breakwater," as one contemporary put it. There was greatness in his capacity to move beyond the role of political broker, the role in which he was most skilled and perhaps most comfortable.

Vargas rarely raised new issues, such as building a steel plant, safeguarding natural resources, protecting labor and thereby managing the "social problem," opening the interior, or beginning an oil industry. But he was quick to identify his political personality with current ideas, and he radiated confidence in Brazil's economic future, promising a bigger pie in which everyone would share without conflict. Ideology interested Vargas little. But insofar as he articulated a mood and an attitude about the necessity for social and economic change without political strife, he was, by instinct, one of the conservative modernizers of developing countries who have attempted to manage change without the class struggles so confidently predicted by Marx.

Halfway through his first presidency, Vargas's superb political instinct informed him it was time to play on nationalistic sentiments. By 1940, he had established the image of both father to the poor and uncle to the rich. But though Vargas added populism to his kit of political tools, he never allowed his labor politics to jeopardize his strong links with more "respectable" groups, i.e., the professional politicians, private business and industrial leaders, the military, and government officials. This essentially conservative approach was challenged by mobilization politics, that is, the promise of a new, radical populism, which appeared with the oil campaign in 1948. In his last years, Vargas failed to capture the new varieties of nationalism, and this was a factor in his tormented second presidency and suicide.*

5. *Nationalism.* The many appeals of nationalism are a politician's delight and a historian's nightmare. Certainly nationalism

* President Juscelino Kubitschek (1955–60) improvised brilliantly on the Vargas score, but underlying political and economic flaws appeared by 1958. For a detailed analysis of this postwar political history, see Thomas E. Skidmore, *Politics in Brazil, 1930–1954* (New York, 1967).

can be defined so as to serve many ends. For purposes of analyzing policy-making under Vargas, it may be differentiated into economic and political varieties and refined by a discussion of who used it and why.

By economic nationalism I mean a policy that has as its goal sufficient national economic power to assure a nation's political independence. Such a policy has two main presuppositions: first, that the nation's natural resources ought to be controlled and allocated by nationals or by the State; second, that there is a value system for determining priorities and evaluating results in terms of the nation's needs—a way of deciding between an emphasis on heavy industry and an emphasis on agriculture, a way of determining the mix of military factors with strictly economic factors, a way of assessing how long the nation can afford to wait for great power status. In asking what weight should be placed upon the future, economic nationalism is revealed as a future-oriented ideology. And while the actual working-out of this policy is highly dependent upon circumstance, it will be shown below when economic nationalism became intense enough in the Vargas years to amount to an ideology of development.[8]

An earlier generation had been concerned with safeguarding natural resources from foreigners.[9] After 1930, however, the depression and a drastic reduction in import capacity forced Brazilians to reexamine their role as a specialized producer of raw materials, and the subsequent postwar expansion greatly strengthened the policies of the 1930's, which aimed toward establishing basic industries in steel and petroleum. In these years, the gap between speculation and action was narrowed to the point where significant new departures were taken. This was not inevitable, as again the case studies point out. But by 1951, with Vargas again in power, the basic decision to industrialize was unequivocal, and economic nationalism was an important influence on policy makers and a central element in popular political culture.

The basically conservative cast of Brazilian leadership in the Vargas years is revealed by the fact that nationalism was rarely used for political mobilization. Economic nationalism was a way of relating group interests to chosen priorities without upsetting the basic social structure. Vargas had little desire to mobilize the lower classes against established groups even when as a postwar populist labor leader he appeared to do so rhetorically. The thrust toward centralism in the authoritarian Estado Nôvo period (1937–45) was remarkable for the absence of a State political party, and for the emphasis on co-option of new social groups, notably the middle classes and labor, into the benefits of employment provided by expanding State services. Technocratic decision-making in Vargas's later presidency was deliberately insulated against populist demands from below. Thus political nationalism under Vargas was essentially benign. But as the 1948 campaign to mobilize support for a State oil monopoly would reveal, political nationalism was a genie that could not forever be kept locked in the trunk of consensus politics.

6. *The Army*. Being the best-organized national institution, the Army impressed its nationalist, reformist, and centralist ideas upon the Vargas years. As a corporation, the Army pressed for better training, higher status, and better equipment for its officer corps. As the paramount military force, it successfully asserted control over regional militias in the 1930's and adjusted its mission to the current situation, whether this was to watch Argentina, send an expeditionary force to Italy, or prepare for some cold war task.[10] As the political arbiter of Vargas's regimes, the Army exercised great influence on policy at every turn of the political wheel.* Moreover, the Army was the main initiating force for economic development projects in the 1930's, and later it retained a key role in industrial planning. The three case studies are in part concerned with the military's role in Brazil's economic development.

Steel and petroleum plans first elaborated in the Army General

---

* In brief outline, the Army allowed Vargas to take power in 1930 as a provisional president, grudgingly let him move from discretionary to constitutional government in 1934, then joined him and in fact pressured him into setting up an authoritarian regime (the Estado Nôvo) in 1937, and finally terminated his long first presidency by a coup d'etat in 1945. In 1950 the Army sanctioned his return after an electoral landslide, but four years later a military ultimatum for Vargas to step down precipitated the dramatic events that led to his suicide.

Staff became realities in the 1930's. Having a centralized bureaucracy and a growing pool of trained administrators and technicians, the Army also took an active interest in transportation, coal, electrical energy, and the central government's regulatory agencies. "The Army is the fulcrum of the nation's defense in wartime," a well-informed industrialist observed in 1940, "but it is also the backbone of its economic reconstruction during the difficult transitional time in which we live."[11] It was during the Estado Nôvo period that the Army emerged as the main engine of economic nationalism and the ideology of development later taken up by technocrats in Vargas's second administration.

Political nationalism interested the Army little. Following the 1930 revolution a group of junior officers and civilians who called themselves *tenentes* (lieutenants) tried to transform the State into an instrument for directing change from above. But they limited themselves to administrative reforms and moralizing, and were unwilling to mobilize the urban masses politically.[12] During the Estado Nôvo, the Army wanted centralized national institutions in order to strengthen the State politically and militarily. Political mobilization was not part of its thinking on development. And with the return to open, democratic politics in 1945, some officers watched uneasily as the 1948 petroleum campaign revealed new possibilities for populism and mass political movements. Thus it bears repeating that the Army was most comfortable with an economic nationalism in which it could act as the main initiator of basic industries.

Having touched upon the main themes, we now turn to a brief discussion of the economic situation in which trade, steel, and oil policies took shape during the 1930's. Beginning in 1929, the collapse of coffee markets, coupled with declining values for Brazilian exports generally (cotton excepted), the falling exchange, and the drying up of British and North American capital markets, created an unprecedented balance-of-payments crisis. Despite government market controls, coffee failed to regain pre-1929 international price levels, and throughout the 1930's it was a weak export. In short, it was now difficult to both service the foreign debt and pay for vital imports—fuel, wheat, industrial raw materials, rails, and industrial equipment—without the favorable trade balance that coffee and other exports had traditionally provided. (The declining trade balance is clearly indicated on Table 1.)

The new Vargas regime, which came to power in 1930, applied conventional remedies to complex economic problems. Wall Street and London bankers wondered if Brazil would honor its commitments; their worries were dispelled, however, by the government's determination to stabilize coffee prices and increase exports. The goal was to mend financial fences, obtain credit, and regain the ability to pay. Hence orthodoxy was the order of the day. "In general, revolutions throughout the world are, and have been spendthrift," as Vargas's Finance Minister Oswaldo Aranha observed to his old boss, Borges de Medeiros. "But ours was the first to economize." Efforts to balance the budget and reduce expenditures "are reasons for Brazilian pride and respect, and for praise from our creditors."[13]

First a traditional British funding loan was tried in 1931, but it failed to stabilize the nation's finances. Then in 1934 Aranha proposed the so-called Aranha Plan based on Brazil's ability to pay. Foreign creditors and governments supporting them agreed to a temporary reduction and consolidation of the debt. But the Aranha Plan was only an honorable expedient intended to allow the continuation of both debt and commercial payments, and by 1937 it failed (see Table 1).

Aranha logically gave debt payments first priority, as a pledge of international respectability. But there were those who favored a moratorium on Brazil's foreign debt, estimated at £250 million in 1933. Capital that might otherwise have purchased new equipment for Brazil's deficient railroads, ports, and shipping, under the Aranha Plan continued to service the foreign debt. Was respectability worth the cost if coffee prices did not rise and the pressure from vital imports continued to force upward the value of foreign exchange and to weaken Brazilian currency, the milreis? These arguments set the scene for Brazilian thinking on foreign and domestic economic policy during the 1930's.

TABLE 1

Exports, Imports, and Foreign Debt Payments, 1928–38
(In thousands of pounds gold)

Year	Exports	Imports	Balance	Debt Payments
1928	97,426	90,668	6,758	16,135
1929	94,831	86,653	8,178	17,390
1930	65,745	53,618	12,127	19,883
1931	49,543	28,735	20,788	17,689
1932	36,629	21,744	14,885	6,682
1933	35,790	28,131	7,659	6,449
1934	35,239	25,467	9,772	7,108
1935	33,011	27,431	5,580	7,494
1936	39,069	30,065	9,004	8,012
1937	42,529	40,607	1,922	9,900
1938	36,337	35,834	523	suspended

SOURCE: Oswaldo Aranha, "O problema da dívida externa," Missão Oswaldo Aranha, Document No. 10 [typewritten], Aranha Archive, Rio.

Aranha, who controlled economic policy from 1931–34, was remarkably successful. Government price supports and export diversification succeeded in arresting the downward slide of coffee prices and in encouraging cocoa and especially cotton exports. Cotton, which commanded high and steady prices in world markets, became the most important commodity. By 1933, domestic prices and industrial production had recovered, largely owing to continuing budget deficits and heavy military expenses for the 1932 São Paulo revolt, which together undercut Aranha's orthodox spending policies.[14] But though there was not a dramatic shift of domestic capital out of agriculture to industry,[15] within Brazil the economic prospects for industry were auspicious. Abroad the world crisis continued.

Brazil's long-range outlook for financial recovery was generally not good, despite the end of internal depression by 1933. The European nations attempted to stabilize their own economies by following policies of self-sufficiency. Competition from the colonies of Britain and France threatened to do to coffee, cocoa, and cotton what British Malaya had done to Amazon rubber twenty years before. Traditional markets for Brazilian products were threatened by the Imperial Trade Agreements (1933) and by aggressive trade policies adopted in 1934 by Nazi Germany. And it was not at all certain that the new Roosevelt administration in the United States would resist the trend toward economic nationalism.

The crisis in traditional foreign markets for Brazilian products contrasted with the expanding internal economy, where industrial output increased by nearly 50 per cent between 1929 and 1937.[16] Stimulated by favorable conditions (reduced export earnings, falling exchange, and the consequent reduction of import capacity), the small domestic iron and steel industry had recovered fully by 1933. By 1940, Brazil was self-sufficient in pig iron and ingot steel, but rolled-products production was still running far behind consumption (see Table 2). And though almost 75 per cent of all light sections and bars were produced in Brazil, the small domestic industry could not provide the heavy steel products, such as rails and plates, on which the railroads, shipping, and the construction industry depended. "We had arrived at the great alternative of nationality," said Edmundo de Macedo Soares e Silva, the Army engineer in charge of Volta Redonda. "Either we would produce those elements basic to our life as a free people, or we would wither away through insufficient exchange resources."[17]

Similar arguments were being made to justify a domestic petroleum industry. Consumption was still low, and petroleum was not discovered in Bahia until 1939. But it was clear to Army General

TABLE 2

Domestic Iron and Steel Production and Consumption of Rolled Products
(In thousands of tons)

Year	Pig Iron Production	Steel Ingots Production	Rolled Steel		
			Production	Consumption	Imports as a Percentage of Consumption
1908–12 (av.)	minimal	0	minimal	272.5	
1927–31 (av.)	27.6	19.9	23.5	514.3[a]	94.2%
1934	58.6	61.7	48.7	343.6	85.8
1938	122.4	92.5	85.7	355.7	75.9
1940	185.6	141.2	135.3	414.5	69.4

SOURCES: For domestic production, Brazil, IBGE, Conselho Nacional de Estatística, *Anuário estatístico do Brasil*, Rio, 1935–40. For figures on rolled-steel products, Werner Baer, "The Development of the Brazilian Steel Industry," unpublished manuscript.
[a] 1929 only.

Staff officers that Brazil ought to develop at least a refining industry for military, economic, and strategic reasons. Acting on these
defense considerations, they wanted to prevent the international
oil companies from moving into all phases of the nascent industry
except distribution, which foreigners already controlled. Thus the
postwar debates over oil policy had their genesis in the depression
decade.

To the nationalist, present conditions are the most intolerable
when opportunities for improvement exist. The Vargas government's experiments with corporatism and centralization attest that
the climate for a new kind of economic nationalism had been prepared by the depression. After recovery in 1933, the issues of commercial policy, steel production, and oil refining became urgent. It
was then that economic nationalism became an ideology of development. Who set priorities in the Vargas system, and who controlled the policy-making machinery? How did Brazilians perceive
the options open to them? To answer these questions, the narrative
turns to the case studies of three issues that were characteristic of
the Vargas years and that were the focus of ideological debate.

PART I · TRADE

1 · BRAZIL AT THE CROSSROADS

In 1934, Brazil was caught between two nations with mutually exclusive trade policies, Germany and the United States; the two countries began a chiefly economic, but also ideological and political competition for paramount influence in Brazil.[1] Sharing between them nearly 55 per cent of Brazil's total export trade, they competed for Brazil's allegiance to their respective economic systems—the managed economy of Hitler's Germany or a free trading bloc of democratic countries under Roosevelt's leadership. Formally, the United States won the first round in 1934–35 when Brazil appeared to reject a German treaty for bilateral trade in favor of a North American treaty based on the most-favored-nation clause; then in mid-1936 the Reich secured an apparent victory with a new trade agreement. In fact, Brazil equivocated. From 1934 until June 1940, when France's defeat by Germany forced a choice, the Vargas government managed to trade with all comers while avoiding the trade-related problem of political alignment. To this extent, Brazilian policy was successful.

But Vargas and his advisers never really faced a crucial question: what kind of trade would best serve the needs of an industrializing Brazil? However skillfully they maneuvered among their major trading partners, the Brazilians failed to elaborate a long-range strategy. Vargas tended to follow, rather than to press, the opportunities opened up by Germany and furthered by German-American rivalry. In short, he did not fully exploit his bargaining position to secure capital goods for the expanding economy. True, he obtained an American steelworks in 1940. But the steel story followed another scenario, to be discussed later.

Understandably, Brazil could not stop trading with either the

United States or Germany, but Brazilians assessed their situation in various ways. Some, like Roberto Simonsen, president of the São Paulo Industrial Federation (FIESP), wanted a nationalist trade policy. Distressed by the wide variations in wealth and purchasing power among regions, Simonsen wished to promote regional exports and industrial development through trade. "We must orient our foreign policy on the basis of our own economic and social indices, that is, from the inside out, and not copy international directives that do not meet our realities and necessities."[2] The logic of Simonsen's position was to travel further along the road to bilateral trade and barter agreements than many government officials were prepared to go. Other people, like Oswaldo Aranha (ambassador to Washington, 1934–37; Foreign Minister, 1938–44), based their hopes on a resurgence of liberalism and the international trade system through United States leadership and credit. However, several of Aranha's colleagues in Rio did not share his optimism.

Supporters of both arguments jockeyed for immediate advantage and position, but Vargas and his ministers had great difficulty in determining which of the interests should take priority. Having only recently put down the São Paulo revolt and presently contending with Flôres da Cunha in his Rio Grande do Sul power base, Vargas did not want to sacrifice any regional export groups, many of which were tied to the German or the American trade. Importers and industrialists also had important interests to defend. To coordinate and reconcile the interests of these groups with national policy, Vargas created the Foreign Trade Council (CFCE) as his own personal instrument in July 1934. Technocrats, administrators, and class representatives met with the President to discuss, recommend, and approve trade and development policy.[3] Vargas thus bypassed the recently revived Congress, channeled interest group pressures, and strengthened his own position. The CFCE became an important policy-making body through which Vargas could exercise his special skills as arbiter and broker.

The ministers, however, retained important countervailing powers, and they presented their own demands. Since the budget and

monetary policy were linked directly to trade, Finance Minister
Artur de Souza Costa, a fiscal conservative, exercised a constrain-
ing role in trade policy. Often Souza Costa's goals conflicted with
the Minister of Transport's demands for modern rolling stock and
ships, and with the military's desire for arms and defense industries. This intra-governmental debate on priorities reflected the
pressures and opportunities from outside Brazil. Commercial policy had traditionally been the responsibility of the Foreign Minister, and in fact the new CFCE was linked administratively to
Itamaraty, the Foreign Ministry, as well as to Vargas.

Decision-making was therefore subject to influences from the
international arena, and to conflicting demands at home. The government was far from monolithic in its response to the depression
decade; diffuseness in policy-making mirrored the internal disagreements within the ministries and among key advisers over objectives. Not surprisingly, therefore, the government stressed exports, a policy on which it could obtain broad agreement. Hence
there was one constant in Brazilian trade policy, and that was to
maintain, expand, and diversify markets.

Traditionally, the favorable trade balance from coffee sales in
the United States market had been used to service most of Brazil's
external debt, commercial payments, and other transfers. In 1934,
the United States absorbed nearly 55 per cent of all Brazilian coffee exports. Largely because of the drop in coffee prices, however,
the trade balance with the United States declined from $99 mil-
lion in 1929 to $51 million in 1934. Furthermore, the relative share
of coffee in total export value declined after 1933 as raw cotton, a
new export crop from São Paulo, reached the British market and,
increasingly, the German market.[4] At the same time, coffee exporters hoped to increase sales to Germany and Eastern Europe.
The overall result of these developments was that between 1934
and 1940 the United States' influence over Brazilian international
trade declined relative to that of Germany.

Whether or not Brazil, still a neo-colonial debtor nation, could
profitably trade with the Reich was hotly debated in the ministries and in the press. That the tentative answer was affirmative is

explained by the fact that Germany was the third (soon second) market for coffee, and the most promising market (with Japan second) for cotton. The two economies were complementary: Germany wanted the fibers, industrial raw materials, and foodstuffs that Brazil could offer in return for manufactures and capital goods. With the United States market apparently saturated with Brazilian raw materials, and with Britain and the European nations turning toward imperial sources of supply, Germany offered an attractive alternative. But there were at least two basic obstacles to Brazil's trading with Germany. The first was that the Reich insisted on trading in nonconvertible "compensation marks." Ostensibly, this measure was intended to "balance" German imports of Brazilian goods with German exports to Brazil of comparable value. In reality, German officials held the trade initiative by imposing quotas, by establishing the value of their compensation marks, and by determining the prices at which they would buy and sell. The net effect was that the volume of trade increased at the expense of nations trading in free currencies, and free-exchange earnings, on which Brazil's balance of payments largely depended, decreased. The second obstacle was that moving into the German cotton market challenged the United States' position as Germany's principal supplier.[5] The compensation marks earned from cotton in turn weighed against United States exports to Brazil. Few Brazilians imagined that the Americans, who supplied Brazil with wheat, petroleum, automobiles, and other manufactures, would tolerate this competition for very long.

Overall, the Brazilian export trade for the 1930's was marked by "the decline in the relative importance of coffee, the increasing significance of cotton, and the increasing importance of Germany as a market for Brazilian products."[6] German exports to Brazil increased from 12.7 per cent of the Brazilian market in 1929 to 25 per cent in 1938. Meanwhile, figures from the same years show that the once-commanding United States lead was reduced from 30.1 per cent to 24.2 per cent, and British exports were nearly halved from 19.2 per cent to 10.4 per cent.[7] What decisions lead to this shift, and what were the consequences?

To protect the coffee market and to promote new export crops were objectives established by the post-1930 revolutionary government. More than forty commercial agreements were negotiated on an unrestricted, most-favored-nation basis. Attempts to increase trade on traditional liberal lines failed, however, because almost all the Western nations moved away from liberalism after 1931.[8] Under pressure from monetary disequilibrium and declining trade, Brazil followed the international trend toward exchange controls, import restrictions, and protective tariffs. But, in mid-1934, following the stabilization of export values in 1933 and arrangements with creditors to make payments on commercial arrears, the government moved to unfreeze the exchange and simplify the tariff. Brazil, which had reluctantly adopted the emergency measures, anticipated a return to more conventional and more "respectable" policies.

Dependence on coffee, however, placed basic restrictions on the government's freedom to maneuver. In 1931, the possibility of bartering surplus coffee for vital imports or debt payments was considered, and some exchanges were made. Eleven Italian flying boats from the flamboyant General Italo Balbo's world tour were purchased with coffee. Later that year 1,275,000 sacks of coffee were exchanged for 25,000,000 bushels of United States wheat. Disposal of large quantities of coffee on these terms was resisted by the exporters, however, and the government itself put a stop to barter when it realized that the commitment of additional stock to an inelastic market might lead to a further weakening of world coffee prices.[9] Two years later, however, the government was willing to try this expedient again. In 1933, during the London Monetary and Economic Conference, Brazilian delegates Valentim Bouças and Assis Brasil sought the Soviet delegation's response to a possible exchange of coffee for wheat and petroleum. They were informed by Maxim Litvinoff that the Soviet Union had no intention of paying the high coffee prices maintained by Brazil's "ultracapitalist regime" of price supports. Moscow was interested only in purchasing on long-term credit (minimum two years), and selling at sight against firm credit.[10]

If the Soviet Union would not trade, perhaps other Central and Eastern European countries with directed economies might exchange products outside the international coffee market. Schemes to reexport Brazilian coffee to these nations, under the aegis of Germany or Italy, were in fact considered. But the Brazilians always had to come back to the realization that the coffee might be exchanged in free markets and thus upset the delicate coffee price mechanisms. Their caution, moreover, was increased by evidence of German profiteering from coffee transshipped to Eastern Europe and the Soviet Union.

En route to the monetary conference in London, the Brazilian delegation stopped by Washington, in part to discuss persistent reports that the United States Congress might place an import duty or some internal tax on imported green or roasted coffee. The State Department was anxious to avoid such a measure, the Brazilians were informed; but it would be in a stronger position to do so if Brazil gave more favorable consideration to United States exporters in furnishing exchange.[11] In fact, the possibility that the United States might impose a "breakfast tax" on coffee so impressed the Brazilians that in July they accepted the United States proposal to negotiate a reciprocal trade treaty.[12] Brazil, so the American argument went, should consider tariff reductions on United States products in return for the agreement to maintain leading Brazilian exports on the American free list.[13] This was the genesis of the 1935 commercial treaty.

By mid-1934 it was still by no means clear whether the United States would follow economic nationalism under George Peek, Roosevelt's trade adviser, or crusade for free trade under Secretary of State Cordell Hull. Even after Hull's victory over Peek (see Chapter 2), it could not be said with certainty whether Roosevelt had by then decided, or if in fact he ever did decide to emphasize United States exports or to promote a general increase in world trade. The tax on coffee was always a trump that might be played at Washington's discretion to protect or promote vital interests. Clearly Brazilians could not know how and under what circumstances it might be used. The conclusion must be that it was a deterrent to any radical nationalist realignment of Brazilian trading policy. The vagueness with which Brazilians perceived the coffee tax threat helped to increase its importance as a major policy consideration. Nationalists, for example, often suggested substituting relatively cheap Soviet gasoline or locally produced alcohol fuel for American gasoline (the latter measure was supported by Northeastern sugar interests). But to import Russian gasoline was to invite the displeasure of Brazil's best coffee customer, as Valentim Bouças of IBM and other suppliers of American equipment pointed out.[14] What may be called the "best-customer argument" was the stock-in-trade of groups in the American economic orbit. Others argued in a similar vein, including Barbosa Lima Sobrinho, director of the national sugar autarchy (Instituto do Açucar e Alcool, an independent government institute). The government, he said, never intended to replace all imported gasoline with more expensive, and inefficient alcohol. Consumers resisted alcohol additives, and the government could not do without tariff revenues from oil and gasoline imports. Furthermore, "the idea of eliminating gasoline imports [by a tariff wall] did not seem prudent, taking into account that we had a favorable balance of trade with the United States, notoriously our largest coffee customer."[15]

The Vargas administration temporized as long as possible on the American treaty—from October 1933 (when the first American draft was submitted) until September 1934. Having returned with reluctance to constitutionalism in July 1934, and politically beholden to the industrial and commercial bloc of class (corporatist) deputies for his election by the Constituent Assembly, Vargas was not eager to risk his authority in a public battle over ratification of the American treaty. This was clearly established in a despatch dated January 4, 1934, from the Itamaraty to the Washington embassy:

The apparent commercial advantage to the United States from our accepting the whole proposal would weaken that nation's political position in Brazil by provoking the same thing that occurred in Argentina over the British treaty, namely, the industries sacrificed would inevitably mount a public opinion campaign against it [the American government] as well as against the Brazilian government for accepting the treaty.[16]

If all the American requests for tariff reductions were granted, the government feared it would lose essential revenues and be a party to the destruction of its own industrial park.

The Itamaraty agreed to send a counterproposal, but there is no known evidence that it was ever sent. Owing to the national political interregnum, the ministry was not prepared to negotiate until a new Chancellor took office under the new government in July. In the meantime, Bouças learned from Hull in March 1934 that Washington was changing its approach. Although he was irritated with Brazil's delaying tactics, Hull said he would let up on the pressure to negotiate until Congress gave Roosevelt full powers to conclude commercial treaties.[17] And when the Trade Agreements Act was passed in June, Rio was ready with a prestigious new ambassador, Oswaldo Aranha. Washington, for its part, awaited Aranha's arrival in the hope that Brazil would be the first of its trading partners to sign.

Aranha, the brilliant young revolutionary from Rio Grande do Sul, was leaving behind the wreckage of his first national political career. As noted above he was Finance Minister from 1931 to 1934, when his austerity program gave way under the pressure from cabinet ministers, the return to politics as usual in early 1934, and the clamor of foreign interests for resumption of commercial payments. Bitter at the post-revolutionary order—"a desert of men and ideas" he called it—Aranha knew his political career had been sacrificed to old-line politicians from the traditional power centers of São Paulo, Minas, and Rio Grande do Sul. What influence he now retained was through Getúlio Vargas, his friend and mentor, and now constitutional President. Their relationship was intimate, but somewhat one-sided. Aranha was fascinated with Getúlio's political skills, while Vargas fondly regarded Oswaldo as a younger brother, sometimes as the heir apparent. Brilliant, able, and articulate though he was, Aranha was impulsive and lacked the older man's political toughness, his coolness under pressure, his analytical self-control, in short, the qualities of power that were hidden by Vargas's opaque personality. Thus Aranha had the President's ear and was influential, but he usually deferred to Vargas's judgment in moments of crisis.

In four years Aranha had moved from the isolated world of Rio Grande do Sul to Washington, where he became an intimate of Undersecretary of State Sumner Welles, a partisan of Roosevelt's Good Neighbor Policy, and the architect of exceptionally cordial relations between the United States and Brazil. As ambassador, Aranha forged the broad and hopeful internationalism for which he is best remembered; in 1947 he served as president of the United Nations General Assembly. Vargas, for his part, could be well satisfied that Oswaldo was uniquely qualified to represent his personal thoughts to Roosevelt. Handsome and gay, Aranha soon was lionized by Washington society, and through a network of friends and cronies, including newspaperman Drew Pearson, he built up Brazil's public image.

How did Aranha deal with the commercial treaty that Brazil found so unsatisfactory? The negotiations began before Aranha reached Washington in September 1934. Cyro de Freitas-Valle, a close relative of Aranha's, began sounding out the Americans in June. As the new *chargé d'affaires*, he talked to New York bankers, whom he found unwilling to advance what Brazil really wanted, namely credit to buy American goods and liquidate commercial arrears. The Americans suggested he approach the newly created Export-Import Bank.[18] But would the Bank under George Peek, an avowed autarkist, be willing to furnish credits? Peek, Freitas-Valle knew, thought American exporters should be guaranteed prompt exchange coverage by attaching Brazilian coffee earnings. In short, the spirit of American trading policy was unclear, and Freitas-Valle was not sanguine about Brazil's prospects. "The important reason for our seeking the commercial treaty is, evidently, the will of this [i.e. the United States] government to carry it out," he wrote on July 19. There was not much in it for Brazil except the guarantee of continued exemption from coffee duties. Furthermore, "one should not forget that any favor conceded to the United States is very small today beside what it will be in a few years" with Brazil's expected increase in purchasing power. Finally, he echoed the reservations of many high officials in Rio when he observed that to him it was a question not of selling more to a market already saturated with tropical products, but of drawing up proposals to limit the expected flood of American goods.[19]

Meanwhile the State Department (which Welles virtually ran on a day-to-day basis) was eager to negotiate. A modified tariff list would have to be sent, in line with Brazil's new tariff law of July 1934. Welles told Freitas-Valle on July 20 that the negotiations would be conducted in the friendly spirit appropriate between nations bound by close political ties.[20] Evidently, however, Welles failed to allay Brazilian fears that economic nationalists held the upper hand in Washington, and that, as Peek said, the Brazilian case was typical of those in which the United States should act with a strong hand. The Americans were going to make large demands, or so the chargé reported on August 10.[21] José Carlos de Macedo Soares, the new Foreign Minister, seemed to share this conclusion; his instructions to Freitas-Valle were to draw out the conversations until Aranha reached Washington on September 13.[22]

By mid-September 1934, with Welles pressing for action, it was clear to Freitas-Valle that further delay was imprudent. The American goal, Welles now informed him, was to strengthen Brazilian credit and purchasing power; but in view of Hull's new concept of reciprocity this would also have to benefit the United States. The alternative was to ask Rio to guarantee payments for importers of American goods, "since the present delay in exchange coverage was hindering the transactions that the treaty would seek to facilitate." However, Welles also said that an Export-Import Bank credit was negotiable.[23] This was a major development, and Freitas-Valle cabled the Itamaraty for instructions.

Concurrently, the government in Rio was rapidly moving away from its public stand in support of trade liberalization toward a nationalist position. With Aranha safely isolated politically, a new ministry was experimenting with the responsibilities, the perquisites, and the opportunities of power. Macedo Soares, a prominent

Paulista with presidential ambitions and a former director of São Paulo's Commercial Association, could be expected to be well attuned to the cotton, coffee, and citrus fruit interests in his state. Marcos de Souza Dantas, another Paulista and the former São Paulo state Secretary of Finance, now held the post of Exchange Director at the Bank of Brazil. Artur de Souza Costa, a Rio Grande banker, was Finance Minister. And Sebastião Sampaio, a career diplomat from São Paulo, served as Vargas's handpicked Executive Director of the new Foreign Trade Council (CFCE).

Under the influence of these men, the entire trade policy was being reviewed, and this was the principal reason why Macedo Soares cabled Freitas-Valle to stall. The President, he said, in coordination with the CFCE was planning "a general solution to the exchange and commercial problems with all other nations before entering into the important phase of negotiations with Washington."[24] Furthermore, Washington should know that each item in the negotiations there had to be referred back to Rio for his (Macedo Soares's) decision in conjunction with the Council.[25] Evidently Aranha's authority to negotiate independently had been circumscribed before he even arrived.

Exchange controls applied preferentially was the measure by which the newly created CFCE hoped to regulate Brazilian foreign trade. This was clear in a letter of August 13 from Marcos de Souza Dantas, Exchange Director of the Bank of Brazil, to the Council. Souza Dantas proposed to furnish foreign exchange by clearings based on the ratio of Brazilian imports and exports with each country. The better Brazil's trade balance, the more exchange would be granted. A special Bank of Brazil clearing account would be established to convert exporters' milreis into exchange for imports. Liquidating commercial arrears, regulating imports so as to avoid more arrears, and treating the problem as a unit were the advantages Souza Dantas foresaw. It was, after all, a "defensive measure" to use Brazil's favorable trade balances to advantage before others imposed compensation or barter in order to achieve a trade equilibrium with Brazil or short-term liquidation of their export letters.[26]

This "credit compensation" plan, approved by the CFCE, was pending the President's decision. Publicly the policy of exchange relaxation was continued.

Not all the evidence needed to assess this covert decision of the CFCE to abandon free trade is available, but numerous factors were important. First, by mid-1934 coffee prices had not risen, and Brazil's imports were increasing. Second, both Souza Dantas and Artur de Souza Costa, the Finance Minister, were on public record against the Aranha Plan,which they considered unrealistic. Did they plan to reinvest the foreign debt in domestic currency?[27] Or did they want to force debt payments with exports, as many nationalists were suggesting? In view of Souza Costa's known conservatism, these possibilities seem unlikely. However, a simple moratorium on debts may have been under consideration, the clearing plan becoming essentially a defense against reprisals. Third, the "sauve qui peut" attitude expressed in Souza Dantas's letter indicates that Rio was following international trends in self-protection. Fourth, and most important, Germany had recently announced an aggressive trade policy, and its expected proposal for a commercial treaty based on quotas and bank-to-bank clearing was received on August 25.

By August 1934 the powers were leveling their economic guns on Brazil; the most sensitive target, as always, was coffee. Since World War I, Brazil's share of the once-large Imperial German coffee market had been declining because of high taxation, substitutes, and Central American competition. Furthermore, it was learned in June that the German market for nearly one million sacks of Brazilian coffee would be licensed for only six more months. Other exports to Germany were affected. From Rio Grande do Sul came word that a backlog of 165,000 hides (*couros salgados*) had built up pending the resolution of exchange difficulties with Germany and negotiations to ease the quotas that the Reich had been applying since April.[28] Tobacco producers, many of whom were of German extraction, sent anxious telegrams to the CFCE from Rio Grande do Sul. Behind these moves and petitions lay the fact that a large German commercial mission under Dr. O. C. Kiep was arriving to sign accords with those Latin American nations which agreed to receive industrial goods in payment for their exports. Also, German private firms had been instructed by the Reichsbank to secure their raw materials against exports of manufactures.

With characteristic élan, the Germans promised fantastic barter deals: railroad equipment, ships, and coal for coffee in August, industrial goods for cotton in September, capital goods and textile machinery for cacao and rubber in October.[29] The prospects for cotton were bright, they said. Offering to take 100,000 bales, Bremen's Otto Behr & Co. wrote that "Brazilian cotton could conquer the German market to a large extent and drive out competition from American cotton, which at present supplies 80 per cent of our textile plants." Specify the industrial goods you want, the government was informed, and a consortium of German cotton importers headed by Behr would fill its requirements.[30] The high-water mark came in January 1935 when German groups including Siemens, Krupp, and cotton interests joined with Monteiro-Aranha, a Brazilian firm dealing in iron ore, cotton, and coffee, in offering to supply a modern steelworks, arsenals, ships, and other capital goods after closing a huge coal contract.[31]

That Germany's industrial economy was complementary to Brazil's, and that the Germans were eager then and later to buy Brazilian products were positive reasons for this trade. But from the outset there was no mistaking the Reich's intentions: if Brazil did not offer cotton and coffee for goods, others would. And until the war, Brazilian officials claimed with reason that there was no way to trade with Germany except on German terms.

Souza Dantas and Sampaio, the chief Brazilian negotiators, argued persuasively for accepting Germany's conditions. In August, Souza Dantas submitted for CFCE approval a provisional accord to govern relations between the two nations' official banks, and he foresaw only advantages in balancing Brazil's trade with the Reich.[32] Vargas himself was understood to be particularly interested in stepping up cotton production and in expanding Brazil's share of the tropical products market.[33] Some CFCE councillors saw in the German proposals the threat of economic colonialism and possible geo-political dangers, notably in those areas of heavy German immigration such as Rio Grande do Sul and Santa Catarina. On balance, however, the government wanted to reach an accommodation with Kiep and the German mission, albeit with certain reservations about the financial risks attendant upon the new compensation trade. As for the public, it knew little of these events until Souza Dantas published an apology three years later, and even then not much was revealed about the policy debates from August through December 1934.

Brazil, the Exchange Director said for the historical record, had faced three alternatives in 1934. It could have stopped commerce, which would have amounted to a trade war, or tried to persuade the Germans to make an exception for Brazil, or (as was decided) conformed "to the accomplished fact, trying to avoid all the drawbacks and extract all possible advantage." Not to trade was out of the question, if for no other reason than that many regions were dependent on the German market. This was in fact the nub of Souza Danta's argument. More than half the tobacco production of Bahia and Rio Grande do Sul went to Germany. Hides and pelts from São Paulo and Rio Grande, at that time unsaleable in normal trade channels, found a ready market in Germany, as did rice, fruits, rubber, nuts, and Northern short-fibered cotton. Most important of all, however, Souza Dantas was dazzled by the possibilities that German industry offered for Paulista cotton.

Brazil, so his argument continued, could not request exceptional treatment. With 40 million marks of German credits frozen in Brazil (28 million RM, and approximately £600,000 in other hard currencies) it was impossible to continue selling on sight and paying with extended credit. Furthermore, Brazil had surplus products to exchange for German coal, manufactured goods, railroad and electrical equipment, autos and other machinery, ships, drugs, and anilines. All these products were needed by the expanding Brazilian economy.

For these reasons Souza Dantas was eager to sign a "modus faciendi" with the Reichsbank to handle the new compensation currency. This was on October 22, nineteen days after the German economic mission arrived in Rio. A large coffee shipment was immediately arranged (722,000 sacks), and German licenses for Brazilian exports were issued. Acting swiftly, the Bank of Brazil paid Brazilian importers holding blocked reichsmarks with the new compensation marks of lower value, a highly profitable move for the Bank which German creditors resented but accepted.[34]

When all was said and done, Souza Dantas believed, the judgment had to be that the Brazilians made the most of a situation the Germans forced on them. Dr. Kiep, writing back to Berlin, referred to the heavy coffee purchases "which, by the way, removed the chief bait for a treaty with the Brazilians and thus did not make the task of the German delegation any easier."[35] But he also emphasized the Brazilians' cooperative attitude, their strong desire for quotas, and their willingness to accept the principle of trade by increased goods exchange.

Behind the Exchange Director's belief that compensation was in the national interest lay his expectation that all of Brazil's trade partners would inevitably move from economic liberalism to restrictive trading policies, if not the German model of economic nationalism. Even the British had accepted barter and quotas, notably in trade with Argentina. And although he knew the United States was attempting to align Brazil with free trade, he was willing to let good opportunities outweigh Brazil's traditionally close relationship with the North Americans. In short, as Freitas-Valle reported, "he had a very exact notion of our interest in acting jointly with the United States, but, on the other hand, he was obliged to weigh equally relevant factors, such as the geographical distribution of exports with its important internal considerations."[36] This criterion covered the power centers—Rio Grande, São Paulo, and Minas Gerais—as well as the economically distressed and politically turbulent North.

Some who were close to the power holders did not agree. "In principle it [compensation] should be viewed with the greatest reserve," wrote councillor J. M. de Lacerda of the CFCE. A debtor nation like Brazil needed trade balances with which to control the balance of payments and to reestablish its damaged credit rating abroad by paying all foreign debts. In normal times, he added, the German trade was favorable to Brazil, thus the balancing proposal was bad. Also to be considered was the "embarrassment the agreement would inevitably cause on the part of other friendly nations."[37] Valentim Bouças considered the treaty "most dangerous," fearing that Brazil would fall under Germany's economic control. Germany, he predicted, would soon control the Central European coffee market while Brazil bought German goods in depreciating currency.[38] To be sure, Bouças had substantial interests of his own in the United States trade, which might well be jeopardized.

These arguments against clearing would be raised often during the remainder of the 1930's. But at this stage of negotiation they did not prevent the CFCE from elaborating a counterproposal to the German offer of compensation or from asking for assured quotas while awaiting the arrival of the German economic mission from Argentina in early October. Caught between two international forces, and divided internally, the Council's policy in September 1934 appears to have been eclectic. It was tantamount to accepting relations with both trading systems. Although the United States interpreted this economic policy as one of opportunism, it was more; it was a policy of compromise, which fluctuated in response to both foreign and domestic pressures. It was, however, consistent with the objective set in 1930: to maintain, expand, and diversify markets.

Shelving the Brazilian clearing scheme of mid-August, the monetary authorities decided on September 11 to cover 60 per cent of the imports at the official Bank of Brazil rate of exchange and require importers to purchase the 40 per cent remainder at higher free-market prices. Exports, except coffee, were liberated from exchange restrictions. Ostensibly, the purpose of these measures was to attract foreign capital, unfreeze credits, and promote exports.[39] Credits from the United States were considered essential by Finance Minister Souza Costa as the basis for a more liberalized exchange.[40] On the other hand, clearing arrangements were under consideration for countries where trade was balanced or unfavorable, notably Britain, Germany, and Argentina.

Meanwhile in Washington, Aranha on October 2 had his first meeting with Undersecretary Welles and Francis Sayre, the chief American negotiators. Aranha reported back to Rio that the Americans would safeguard all United States interests in the treaty, including exchange, debt payments, and company profits. For his part, Aranha asserted that Brazil did not want a new treaty unless it increased trade. Brazil would forswear the general and unconditional most-favored-nation policy it had followed since 1930 for a bilateral treaty with America only if such a shift in policy assured present and future advantages. Concessions would be made to resolve commercial difficulties if the United States sought a treaty in the large sense which, in Aranha's felicitous phrase, "would assure its [the United States'] grandeur, but facilitate our progress."[41] President Vargas agreed: "Either we sign a treaty to improve our economic relations or we'll leave everything as is, which isn't bad."[42]

But the State Department, knowing the German mission had arrived October 3 would no longer converse in generalities. Aranha cabled on the 4th that the Americans would stop the negotiations if any comprehensive clearing accord or government promise to buy a set quantity of German goods was signed in Rio.[43] And on the 5th, at his second meeting with American experts, Aranha was informed that United States policy allowed two alternatives: either Brazil maintained the most-favored-nation clause as the basis for equal treatment, and regulated trade on this basis, or the State Department would demand guarantees for American exports, for payment of commercial arrears, for prompt coverage of new export letters, and for remission of all income and profits on American business—all to be withdrawn from Brazilian exports. Of these two roads, Aranha remarked, "it is clear they want to force us to opt for the first."[44] Large stakes were involved and the State Department was alarmed by news of the modus faciendi with Germany. Aranha reported on October 6: "they think that the clearing agreement with Germany . . . would render it impossible for them to maintain a liberal orientation," since the compensation policy would be considered a success.[45]

Macedo Soares requested on October 6 that Aranha sound out
State Department spokesmen on clearings, since formal negotiations with the Germans were about to begin. He hoped the Americans would keep three factors in mind: first, that 55 per cent of
Brazil's exports were sold to countries other than the United States,
second, that American exports to Brazil were now increasing while
Brazilian exports to the United States were stationary, and third,
that the "perfect synchronization" of Brazilian foreign policy with
the United States in the Chaco War (between Bolivia and Para-
guay, 1932–35) and elsewhere would facilitate the treaty.[46] Thus
Macedo Soares hoped for two treaties, an American one based on
liberalism, and a German one frankly bilateral and exclusive. How
long Macedo Soares could carry out this kind of policy without an-
tagonizing either of the two powers remained to be seen.

Aranha, for his part, replied that there were two currents in
Washington, one trying to force commercial balances, the other to
increase trade. "The accord with Germany based on compensation
will constitute Your Excellency's support for the first current and,
on these terms, you will place us in an inferior, perhaps impossible
position to negotiate." If Brazil had to begin trading on a compensation basis, and Aranha thought that it might, it should first make
an agreement with the United States, the best customer, for the
most favorable conditions.[47] This argument so impressed the Brazilian officials in Rio that Souza Dantas and Sampaio told the Germans they doubted whether a treaty was possible because of
American pressure.[48] Having carried the discussions to the stage
of bargaining over specific products, they were for the first time
becoming alarmed. What leeway, if any, did Brazil have among
the powers?

The only way to proceed was covertly, Souza Dantas wrote Kiep
on October 13, to hide the results in such a way that when questioned by third parties the Brazilians could claim they had not
found it necessary to sign a new trade agreement with Germany.[49]
At the same time, Aranha was instructed to prolong the American
negotiations in preliminary form at least until the Brazilian congressional elections of November 14, and until the CFCE and the

Tariff Council had completed studies of the United States–Brazilian trade. Macedo Soares was confident that Washington would agree to Rio's modus faciendi with the Reichsbank. As he told Aranha, this banking accord involved no formal clearing agreement, compensation accord, percentage or volume-of-purchase declaration, or length-of-payment conditions. The government would neither supervise nor participate in trade (except for coffee) that would be transacted only between private German and Brazilian firms. But it would accept, de facto, the use of compensation marks.[50]

The crossroads had been reached, or so Vargas believed in late October. The Germans were pressing beyond the bank agreement for a formal treaty, while Welles urged that no decision be formalized until the Brazilians heard what credit facilities he and Roosevelt would offer. If the United States in concert with Brazil did not react to German policy, Welles told Aranha, everyone, including the United States, would be forced to follow compensation.[51] On the one hand, said Vargas, there were the impressive arguments of Souza Dantas, and on the other the attitude and opinion of the United States, "to whom we are linked by great interests. It is necessary to ponder with great care the consequences of a separation or estrangement from the North Americans."[52] How Vargas avoided the horns of this dilemma is discussed in the next chapter.

2 · THE NATIONALIST ALTERNATIVE

Should Vargas safeguard the United States coffee market in a new treaty and thus maintain traditional financial and political ties, or should he formally secure the German outlet for regional production in exchange for goods? Early in November 1934, he gave Aranha full authority to negotiate, and he put the Germans off for a few weeks. But Vargas's principal trade advisers still hoped to follow an eclectic policy, if not an outright pro-German one such as Souza Dantas wanted. At home it was difficult to conciliate the regional producers, who clamored for greater access to the German market, and the industrial lobby in Congress which, led by Euvaldo Lodi, President of the National Industrial Federation (CNI), and Roberto Simonsen of FIESP, opposed a liberal treaty with the United States. Until the end of 1935, Vargas temporized; he decided to let events take their course.

Aranha succeeded brilliantly in modifying the United States demands, which were expressed in a memorandum of October 30, 1934, to the Brazilian embassy. This document was interpreted by Aranha to mean that the new treaty was contingent on safeguarding American exports against exchange controls, and declaring, in writing, Brazil's opposition to compensation. In consultation with Welles and other State Department officials, however, it was decided in November 1934 to follow a new formula: if Brazil guaranteed equal exchange treatment, made tariff concessions, and followed a liberal policy *within its capabilities*, the Department would offer credits and let the Brazilians manage their own creditors, the debt, and their trade balance.

Aranha and Welles, in short, had a meeting of minds. Aranha

had quite reasonably pointed out that Brazil could not possibly comply with the demands in the original memorandum without a massive influx of American capital, which was unlikely to be forthcoming in view of the depressed condition of New York's capital markets. Hence Washington would have to wink at some trade in compensation marks. And the State Department, it appeared, had an overriding political interest in securing the bases for a formal, joint liberal policy with Brazil, one that would lead to a free-trade bloc opposed to Germany.[1] In short, it would have to adopt a flexible response to get Brazil's cooperation. By late November, Brazil was no longer in direct confrontation with one of the two industrial powers; unquestionably, this gave the Brazilians more freedom to determine their own trade policy.

In Rio, meanwhile, the decision was made in late October to inform Aranha for the first time of the German negotiations, and also to stall a formal signing with Kiep until the State Department replied via Aranha. Thus on November 8 a de facto trade agreement with accompanying notes between the Bank of Brazil and the Reichsbank was passed between the delegations. The Germans, having signed their note, went off to Chile confident that the trade agreement would be considered in effect once the Bank of Brazil opened a special account in compensation marks. For their part, the Brazilians delayed by alleging that Souza Dantas and Sampaio had no authority to sign for Brazil until the full Cabinet met to discuss and approve the trade agreement.[2]

Furthermore, Rio had in principle agreed to accept the German idea of goods exchange but not an open treaty. Indeed, at the Brazilians' request, the word "agreement," or "treaty," nowhere appeared in the de facto trade agreement of November 8, which was to last one year (and which the Brazilians never did sign). The Germans agreed to take unlimited quantities of cotton, wool, hides, pelts, rubber, tobacco, and other industrial raw materials, in addition to specified amounts of oil cake, rice, and cacao, an export which the Brazilian government was then eagerly promoting. However, they refused to specify quotas for most of these goods, something the Brazilians had requested out of a strong desire for guaranteed access to Germany's controlled economy. Sales would depend on purchasing German goods: the more Rio bought, the more it would sell, on the principle of one-to-one goods exchange. Furthermore, Kiep overcame stubborn Brazilian resistance to tying coffee exports to a percentage of raw materials exports. And he refused to open up the market to meat and citrus fruits, important products from São Paulo and Rio Grande do Sul. In short, the treaty was advantageous to Brazil, but the Germans had ample opportunities to play off her weak export, coffee, against the promising new hard-currency-earning export, cotton, and to bargain over meat and fruit.[3]

The Brazilians were fully aware that the major inconvenience of compensation was that they would be unable to fulfill their financial commitments to free-trading nations.[4] Compensation marks were useless for that purpose; the German trade would produce no disposable foreign exchange. To limit these compensation transactions, Finance Minister Souza Costa insisted on quoting the compensation marks at the higher London free rate, and then in furnishing German exporters with a percentage of exchange (at the Bank of Brazil official rate) pegged to the amounts of free exchange earmarked for other creditors. Seeking to protect himself from charges of favoritism, moreover, he refused to liquidate German commercial arrears in free currencies faster than he paid other creditors.[5] Theoretically, these banking control measures would allow Brazil to limit its trade with Germany in order to keep on good terms with other trading partners. "Since there will be no direct exchange of products," the Foreign Minister cabled Aranha, "there will be no essential reason for a large increase in trade, and even if there were, German goods imported here compete only with European light industry, not with United States heavy industry."[6]

It should be noted that Germany proposed to open a clearing account in ASKI marks (Auslander-Sonderkonto-fuer-Inlandszahlungen) for Brazilian exporters, while the Bank of Brazil furnished milreis coverage in return. Technically, there was no government participation in the so-called ASKI trade, but in South America it operated in the same way as direct government-to-government barter deals. Whatever the form of ASKI's used, the Reich controlled the currency value and goods these marks would buy.* In fact, compensation favored German exporters, who tended to receive prompt exchange coverage while their disadvantaged competitors, waiting for their share of scarce free currency reserves, were forced to raise prices. Pressure on the limited supply of free currency also weakened Brazilian currency, forcing restrictions on imports from free-trading nations, and causing commercial arrears. Because compensation disturbed the Brazilian monetary system, German products enjoyed a trading advantage from 1934 until the war broke out.

No Atlantic nation in the 1930's was immune from compensation, not even the depression-torn United States, now standing in Britain's stead as the principal defender of free trade. Glowing reports from Germany on the Reich's cotton market were appearing in the Rio press just as word reached Brazil of a very large cotton deal, perhaps as many as 1,200,000 bales, that the United States might close with Germany. It was reported that German payments would be 25 per cent in dollars and the rest in compensation marks for industrial goods.[7] Clearly this was the kind of trade in controlled currency that the United States disapproved of Brazil's following. Its volume was comparable to the cotton deals the Germans were proposing to Brazil. Timed for maximum effect, the German offer was made in November 1934, with the support of George Peek. On December 12, President Roosevelt appeared ready to endorse it. Aranha thought the deal would go through, defeating Hull's entire commercial policy and thereby creating a government crisis.[8]

Brazil's independence of Washington could only have been greatly strengthened if Peek won the day. Rio, in fact, recalled the German trade mission from Chile and let the State Department know that if Peek's deal went through, Brazil would follow suit and defer the United States treaty.[9] However, on December 15, Roosevelt vetoed the German cotton proposal, saying the act was in

* Hereafter, the term compensation marks will be used in discussing German-Brazilian trade.

return for Brazil's consideration of the United States in refusing similar transactions. Moreover, he said the new treaty with Brazil would be drawn up as Brazil requested, that is, without reducing its trade with other nations.[10]

The road seemed open to an eclectic policy. Foreign Minister Macedo Soares in fact prepared to sign treaties with Germany and Italy (who offered naval craft on compensation) as well as with the United States. Preparatory to signing with the Germans, the Bank of Brazil began accepting compensation marks on December 12. Macedo Soares now made significant new demands upon Washington, such as a special "New Deal price" for coffee. He also wanted to negotiate credits before the treaty was signed and, among other things, to have the United States limit or prohibit colonial competition with Brazilian exports in the great North American market.[11] With the industrialists and planters pressuring for concessions from the United States and trade with Germany, Macedo Soares evidently felt he had to force the issue.

Tacit United States permission to trade on compensation was not, however, the same as accepting formal treaties with the fascist nations. From Washington, Aranha said as much to Vargas: "If we insist on our present attitude of wanting to make a treaty with compensations when [the United States] does not acknowledge this practice, and to include arrangements for bilateral favors in the shadow of the most-favored-nation clause, we will create bad will here."[12] Before Vargas and Macedo Soares could put this independent trade policy into effect, however, a mounting exchange crisis dating from November 1934 forced the Brazilians in January 1935 to return at least temporarily to a more traditional stance.

Ostensibly, the monetary crisis was caused by imports coming in, on the official rate, more rapidly than coffee sales, which were weak, could provide exchange to cover imports, debt service, and official purchases. Consequently, Souza Dantas had to abandon the policy followed since September 1934 of progressively freeing exchange controls (see Chapter 1). The weakening coffee market compelled him to give Brazil's best coffee customers 85 per cent, or almost all of the available exchange coverage at the official rate.

Designed to limit imports, the new measure favored the United States and France (the best coffee clients) with 46 per cent and 13 per cent of the official funds. On the other hand, British traders were penalized and had to compete with other nations that did not buy coffee for the remaining 15 per cent of official exchange. Many British firms refused to sell on these terms.[13]

Actually, during the fall of 1934 Souza Dantas had followed policies that contributed to the exchange crisis. First, he facilitated Brazilian regional exports (except coffee) on the free exchange, which effectively weakened the exchange confiscation scheme whereby the Bank of Brazil earned hard currencies. He was convinced that Brazil's pledge of liberal intentions, the Aranha Plan, could no longer be fulfilled. Trade, not debt payments, had priority. Second, he gave exchange preference to large foreign companies, such as Brazilian Traction, São Paulo Railway, Standard Oil, and the Anglo-Mexican Company, and this policy placed additional strains on Brazilian currency reserves just as the coffee market weakened. Souza Dantas believed it important to placate the suppliers of fuel, electric energy, and transportation services, who were becoming restive. But perhaps he was also clearing the decks of arrears and frozen dividends before imposing exchange controls in the expectation that Brazil would soon follow compensation. Third, the Germans knew that Souza Dantas was eager to accumulate compensation marks. They interpreted this as a significant opportunity to supply industrial goods, including tankers, ships for the Lloyd Brasileiro shipping line, and arsenal equipment for the Army and the Navy.[14] In fact, the entire question of German military and development project offers discussed in Chapter 1 was coming to a head just as the monetary crisis struck.

The January 1935 exchange crisis placed Brazil in a humiliating situation and sharply curtailed the Brazilians' freedom of maneuver among the powers. In effect, Souza Dantas faced a choice between suspending the debt or freezing all commercial payments. Vargas, Souza Costa, and Macedo Soares decided that neither alternative was acceptable, and a hastily arranged financial mission was sent to Washington and London. Souza Dantas was forced from office.

Crying that the government had sold out to the international bankers, he joined the protofascist Integralist party as its shadow Finance Minister. Souza Costa went to Washington with hat in hand, and on January 14 all official exchange coverage for imports was suspended.

Linked by strong if somewhat strained ties to the free-trading nations, the Brazilian government was not prepared to slip its traditional moorings for uncharted German waters. A radical realignment toward the Reich was not feasible. But the Brazilians did not fully exploit their opportunities to take and hold a middle ground. Why did the Vargas administration move so tentatively among the powers?

Monetary considerations were overriding. To accept large quantities of German capital goods was to take more Brazilian exports, especially cotton, out of the free market. It was impossible to protect the balance of payments while trading on a compensation basis with only one country. Strapped for dollars, the Brazilians continued to ask Washington for credits to unclog normal trade channels. Thirty years later, barter with the socialist nations would seem less radical because conventional credits were often available through the open postwar monetary system.

International political questions were important, since the United States strongly opposed compensation trading. To have concluded large German equipment deals would have made it impossible for Rio to maintain the public fiction that no new German-Brazilian trade agreement was in force, for otherwise, nations such as Britain, France, and the United States could have applied the most-favored-nation clause against the German trade. Souza Dantas had welcomed barter transactions between private firms. However, the once-powerful official cautiously pointed out to the CFCE that his government was not legally empowered to trade directly with the Reich, on a government-to-government basis.[15] In turn, Macedo Soares talked with German industrial spokesmen about a goods consortium (October 1934–February 1935), but he preferred to deal piecemeal, project by project. Individual German firms then and later helped to weaken the thrust of a coordinated approach by jockeying for Brazilian contracts. And while the Germans played skillfully on Brazilian fears of economic domination by the Anglo-Saxons, the Vargas government was also wary of Hitler's economic and political intentions. Clearly Vargas never intended to use the German trade offensive as a means of loosening Brazil's long-standing political and diplomatic ties to the United States.

Brazilian policy makers expressed no marked leaning toward development projects—expanding exports came first. Hence they had no nationalist development ideology to support and sustain an independent trade policy. The Army was not yet prepared to force a decision, as it would in the Estado Nôvo to obtain a steel complex. More quickly than the Americans, the Germans realized through talking with Brazilian business and military contacts that Brazilian nationalism was maturing into an ideology of industrial expansion. They encouraged this development verbally and with offers of equipment.[16] But until the Brazilians had sorted out their priorities, they were not prepared to vigorously explore the German option.

Finally, Vargas and his close advisers were unwilling to turn away from traditional suppliers. Railroad equipment was needed urgently, and Great Britain had the contract to electrify sections of the Central do Brasil Railroad. Vargas was flexible, he was prepared to bargain, but as the next years would show, he held no particular brief for German industry. Rather Vargas kept asking Roosevelt, through Aranha, how he was prepared to top the German offers.

Souza Dantas's resignation as Exchange Director and Souza Costa's visit to Washington in early 1935 left little doubt that the United States held the initiative in the treaty negotiations, which drew rapidly to completion in January 1935. A reciprocal-trade treaty was signed on February 3, after Brazil agreed to furnish sufficient exchange to cover United States imports. Certain sanitary requirements were modified by the United States, and the assignment of more merchant ships to ply between the two nations was encouraged. Souza Costa assured Brazilian agricultural interests

2

that the treaty made no provision for limiting cotton production, as had been reported in Brazil, or for interfering with coffee sales. Finally, both governments expected the Brazilian Congress to ratify the treaty in short order, for until then, discussions about United States credits to free the exchange, stabilize the currency, and pay commercial arrears would be held in abeyance.

This widely heralded treaty had little practical impact on United States–Brazilian trade. The Brazilians reduced duties primarily on light industrial goods, such as radios, some textiles, rubber goods, office equipment, and preserves, and agreed to maintain trucks and autos on the free list. Of these concessions little need be said. Roberto Simonsen admitted in debate that Brazil's depreciating currency wiped out the American list of reductions, which was based on an exchange rate of 12 milreis* to the dollar in November 1934, but which had fallen to 18 per dollar ten months later.[17]

In retrospect, the ideological and political aspects of this treaty stand out sharply, but as a device for containing German economic penetration it was only partially successful. Brazil, to be sure, did return in February 1935 to free exchange as the United States wanted, and this was the reason Souza Costa gave Berlin for breaking off the drawn-out treaty talks in March. The Bank of Brazil obligated itself to purchase 35 per cent of the value of all exports, including those for Germany, on the less favorable official rate. Thus exports were slighted for an expected return to free-market forces. Nevertheless, as the once-powerful Souza Dantas had foreseen, Brazilian exports to Germany in the first half of 1935 rose 50 per cent over the same period one year earlier. And cotton led the list with 65,000 tons.

It can be argued that high Brazilian officials were not unwilling to support the United States treaty, on which financial credits depended. Certainly there were drawbacks to the German trade, and

* Until 1942, the milreis was the currency of Brazil. The conto, or one thousand milreis (written 1:000$000), was the largest monetary unit. On November 1, 1942, the milreis was replaced by the cruzeiro, one milreis (1$000) being equivalent to one cruzeiro (cr$1,00). In 1966, this cruzeiro was in turn transposed into a new cruzeiro (written Ncr$1,00), which was worth a thousand of the badly inflated old cruzeiros.

these soon appeared. The prices of Brazilian exports to Europe, especially for cotton exported to Great Britain, were raised by premium German pricing. Supplies of compensation marks accumulated beyond Brazil's immediate requirements for German industrial goods, and this tended to force the volume of trade upward. Faced on the one hand with surplus marks and on the other with a depreciating domestic currency, the CFCE attempted to outlaw the compensation trade on May 13. The São Paulo state authorities, being fearful of losing the British market, had suggested this themselves.[18]

The CFCE, however, had to face the fact that important pressure groups were dependent upon the German market. Bahian tobacco planters, Santos coffee shippers, and Rio Grande stockmen convinced the Council to raise its ban on June 17. Only cotton remained prohibited from compensation trade, and this aroused the dissatisfaction of growers from São Paulo and the Northeast; if the government wanted to hold and diversify markets, it should not restrict outlets for any products.

A combination of German threats and blandishments also persuaded Vargas and Souza Costa to revive the compensation trade. Having pressed again for a formal treaty in early May, the Germans were shocked by the May 13 decision, which they said meant a break in trade relations. Souza Costa was impressed sufficiently to begin negotiating a new compensation agreement in which the Germans would take new products, such as meat, but this time the Germans insisted on pegging coffee to cotton. Their formula was 800,000 sacks of coffee for every 50,000 tons of cotton, and thereafter 50,000 sacks for every 5,000 tons. Souza Costa in turn said the cotton quota must be kept as low as possible, while coffee and other products not in great demand elsewhere could be increased.[19] Berlin threatened to stop coffee imports unless its demands were granted, to which Souza Costa replied that Brazil had to earn sterling in the Liverpool market. Thus the talks seesawed until June 17. Soon thereafter exporters to Germany were allowed to put up their 35 per cent (at the official rate) in compensation marks, instead of free currency, which the German banks in Brazil had been protesting since the February currency decree. And the Germans eased off, confident that they had driven the best bargain possible, and that sooner or later the Brazilians would have to trade cotton.[20]

The American treaty, meanwhile, was bogged down in the Brazilian Congress. Passage had been expected in the Chamber of Deputies by late April 1935, but the bill was delayed for months in the Agriculture and Finance Committees and did not emerge for floor debate until September 4. Then Brazilian industrialists made an all-out effort to block ratification. Not surprisingly, the government did not wish to antagonize the industrial class deputies mobilized by Euvaldo Lodi against the treaty.[21] Since Vargas and Macedo Soares were not pushing the treaty bill, it might have been repudiated.

The industrialists argued injured rights, but clearly the tariff concessions were not going to harm three hundred Paulista industries as Roberto Simonsen's FIESP claimed. Nor did Lodi have a very strong argument when he told a United States embassy official that "the treaty . . . lowered Brazilian duties on a number of tariff items in a manner so prejudicial to Brazilian industries that many of them would be seriously crippled" if the treaty were not modified.[22] In view of the actual tariff concessions and the falling currency, these views were only tactical exaggerations. It was not the immediate effects the industrialists feared as much as the precedent this treaty would set.

They disliked not having been consulted, as American interests were by the State Department, when the treaty was being negotiated. This neglect violated the spirit of corporatism, which they eagerly embraced in order to influence economic policy. Clearly the CFCE had not acted as a full-fledged policy-making organ. Rather, the real decisions in late 1934 had been made behind closed doors, in the small circle of intimates with whom Vargas liked to make decisions, and in the Cabinet. Access to the President was through his cronies, instead of through the strong associational links that the industrialists attempted to forge throughout the thirties. Thus the CNI under Lodi and the FIESP under Simonsen were not as directly involved in commercial policy-making as they would have liked.

The precedent of breaching tariff walls also concerned them. An advanced nation, they reasoned, wanted Brazil to reduce the tariffs protecting infant industry in return only for guarantees that the long-standing American policy of free entry for noncompetitive tropical products would continue. Their ideas on this issue were greatly influenced by Mikail Manoilescu, the Rumanian economist who believed every nation had a "natural right" to industrialize behind protective tariffs.[23] In short, the industrialists admired the United States for knowing what it wanted, but in their opinion, free trade was disadvantageous for Brazil. Simonsen summed up the debate: modern governments defend their economies; "the existence of the independent State presupposes the coexistence of an independent economy."[24]

Groups for and against the treaty conducted information campaigns. When the Paulista bankers and industrialists mounted a press offensive against the United States treaty in June, Valentim Bouças, the pro-American importer and international go-between, organized a counterattack. Bureaucrats whose usual job was to study the foreign debt under Bouças in the Finance Ministry's Technical Section were put to work by him drafting pro-treaty articles for the *Correio da Manhã* and sending mimeographed material to influential congressmen and journalists. Bouças, using 22½ contos (22:500$000) of department funds, had good results in the Paulista press and won support from the Sociedade Rural, organization of the coffee planters.[25] Vargas and Macedo Soares, however, were not stirred into action in support of the sinking treaty bill until they heard via the United States ambassador that American domestic interests opposed to the treaty and to duty-free coffee were arranging a showdown in the United States Senate.[26] Lodi backed down under presidential pressure, and the treaty was voted in September, passed by the Senate in November, and finally ratified one month later.

Roberto Simonsen, throughout the debates, remained opposed to a treaty that he thought disarmed Brazil without either solving the problem of colonial competition from abroad, or promoting industrial growth at home. To him, a "dangerous principle" was at work, according to which the Americans got the raw materials they needed while Brazil agreed to let in goods from the United States that were already produced in Brazil.[27] In fact he thought the nation's entire trade and financial structures had to be reorganized on lines completely different from the liberal United States treaty.

Simonsen's reasoning was based on what were for him three irrefutable facts. (1) The Aranha Plan did not work, and Brazil could not continue both debt and import payments. (2) Colonial competition increased, but the prices paid for Brazil's tropical exports did not. (3) Trade was not growing fast enough in value to pay for ever-increasing imports. In short, Brazil faced a prolonged and worsening balance of payments problem that expedients like the Aranha Plan, or more foreign loans, could not solve. This early analysis of long-term economic problems was elaborated further by Simonsen in later years, and after the war it came into fashion among his young protégés, a new generation of economists and technocrats.

Simonsen's solution to the capital shortage in 1935 was to increase Brazil's share of the world tropical products market. Normal trade channels, he said, should still be used, but in addition Brazil would secure special quotas from its foreign creditors. In turn, the creditors would accept debt payment in "excess" goods valued on a ten-year average of pre-1929 price levels. Simonsen proposed a national export institute, with representatives from the main exporting states, to be charged with promoting exports, negotiating quotas with other governments, and making foreign payments with products along the lines of the German trade, but on a much smaller scale. Enlarging Brazil's share of the world market, and diversifying exports were two additional objectives. The differential export tax (35 per cent) would be eliminated to encourage exports. At the same time, the institute would balance imports against actual cash on hand, and by controlling the exchange it would give priority to essential imports, such as wheat, fuel, industrial equipment, and raw materials. Sweeping planning powers were foreseen. The institute would coordinate the many measures to protect and expand production already taken by the CFCE, the sugar autarchy, the Bahian Cocoa Institute, the National Coffee Institute, São Paulo state, and industrial groups. Finally, Simonsen suggested that this sprawling regulatory and planning agency could coordinate plans of the Ministries of Finance and Agriculture to rationalize industrial and agricultural production, and consumption in the domestic market.[28]

Simonsen asked the Chamber of Deputies to accept what was perhaps the most sweeping proposal for economic reorganization and planning that any responsible Brazilian proposed in public during the 1930's. Clearly nationalistic, it was ingeniously designed to expand trade and at the same time protect industry and limit nonessential imports of the kind Brazilians themselves might produce. However vaguely worded, it was a proposal to associate interest groups directly in the planning process. Thus Simonsen was groping toward a theory of development that would fit Brazilian conditions.

At least for the public record, he did not elaborate on this sweeping scheme. Several key points remained open. What was the "normal" volume of Brazilian exports? Were creditors likely to accept the goods payment plan? How could Brazil, under such an institute, escape reprisals from the industrial nations that controlled the tropical products market? With these essential questions left unanswered, the institute could not have appealed to Vargas and his ministers, who looked for more respectable solutions to the monetary crisis and its adjunct, the imbalance in foreign trade.

In December 1935, the CFCE rejected Simonsen's plan and chose instead to follow a new trade policy based upon the United States–Brazil treaty. The principal agricultural groups were in fact strongly opposed to Simonsen's suggestion because they wanted fewer government controls, not more. A national export institute, they felt, would soon control all commerce, set up rigid export-import quotas, and benefit the industrialists, not them. Restoration of the international free market, not its restriction, was their goal. And as if to underscore this characteristic pre-1929 outlook, the Curitiba Chamber of Commerce (Paraná) observed that differing regional interests ruled out any overall plan for foreign commerce. These arguments were weighed in the CFCE decision.[29] In reporting to the Council, Valentim Bouças summed up the case against Simonsen with a liberal argument: the course of Brazilian development lay not behind protective tariffs and exchange controls, but through expanding its international trade. Thus the Council adopted the United States liberal model for its trade policy.[30]

President Vargas accepted the Council's proposal to renegotiate all commercial agreements then in force (except with Portugal, Uruguay, France, Argentina, and the United States, all recently negotiated), and to sign bilateral treaties based upon reciprocal most-favored-nation treatment. The full Brazilian duty reductions would be exchanged only in return for guaranteed market access and low tariffs. Would the new policy work? The answer was not long in coming.

3 · TRADE AND FOREIGN POLICY

A combination of German pressures, the urgings of prominent Brazilians, and sheer opportunism on the part of the Rio government led in June 1936 to a Brazilian trade agreement with Germany. Brazilian trade policy in the next four years was not based on an economic program; no coherent and logically developing design existed. But at least the government consistently took advantage of whatever commercial opportunities arose. To expand and diversify markets was to follow a policy of de facto neutrality toward the German and the United States trading systems. The process by which Brazil sloughed off the new liberal trade policy of January 1936 and moved toward a covert accord with the Reich six months later has never been adequately explained. An account of these negotiations with Germany, therefore, is important, if only to illustrate the pressures and constraints on Brazilian policy makers.

German policy toward Brazil had three objectives: the first and most urgent was to secure raw materials; the second to weaken and disrupt United States influence; and the third to use the German embassy for purposes of propaganda and subversion, notably among Southern Brazilians of German ancestry. For both economic and political reasons the Germans asked Argentina, Chile, and Brazil, in September 1935, to raise their legations and the Reich's to embassy status and to exchange ambassadors.

Brazil, however, was not so eager to establish closer political and economic relations with Germany. Three times Berlin asked the Itamaraty to discuss the issue before notes were exchanged in November 1935. Although the Germans claimed their motive for having an embassy was administrative, not political, the Brazilians sensed that the real purpose was to facilitate new commercial treaties with the ABC countries.[1] After installing their embassy in Rio, the Germans learned, to their annoyance, that José Moniz de Aragão, the new Brazilian envoy, would not be accorded ambassadorial status by his government until the Senate approved sometime in May 1936.

Hitler, in conversation with Moniz, enthusiastically explained the mutual advantages of increasing trade. And perhaps, he mused, Brazil might want to join the projected Anti-Comintern Pact.[2] To underscore its diplomatic verve, the Reich—decisive and impressively certain of what it wanted—backed and probably sponsored a proposal made in early January by a German-Brazilian consortium to exchange coffee for armaments, merchant ships, and railroad and heavy industrial equipment.

The ostensible purpose of this consortium, incorporated in Rio as the International Commercial Society, Ltd. (SOINC), was to fulfill Brazil's military and industrial needs. It was founded in late 1935, and was represented in Brazil by Monteiro-Aranha, Inc. One recalls that in 1934–35 Olavo Egydio de Souza Aranha, a prominent Paulista with interests in cotton and coffee planting and iron ore export, had promoted a large coal syndicate as the basis for a special bilateral contract with a German industrial goods consortium. In his capacity as international go-between, Souza Aranha was to the German authorities what Valentim Bouças was to American officials—a bearer of notes and information, a negotiator with semiofficial Brazilian government status, and an active promoter of trade involving large personal interests. He was also the representative of the Krupp industries in Brazil, an association not unrelated to the SOINC proposal. The German connections were managed by two bankers, Conrad Donner of Hamburg, who had interests in São Paulo cotton, and E. R. Lauber, who was willing to finance iron ore exports and equipment for a Brazilian steel plant.[3] The main purpose of this consortium was to act as intermediary and purchasing agent in special large transactions between the two governments, and to take a leading role in the Paulista cotton and coffee export trade.

Through SOINC, the German government took the initiative in January 1936: the National Coffee Department of Brazil was invited to supplement the then low German quota of 800,000 sacks with an additional shipment of 300,000 sacks for the German Army and Labor Corps. Perhaps, as SOINC said in a memorandum for the Brazilian legation, a whole generation of young Germans would in this way come to prefer the taste of Brazilian coffee. Coffee from this special account would not be reexported. The German government would open a special account in compensation marks with which the Brazilian government could purchase the goods it wanted, and SOINC would handle the transaction.[4]

Berlin was eager to facilitate the SOINC operation, as Moniz observed, and other offers were likely to follow as the Germans built up a coffee stockpile for strategic (i.e. war supply) purposes. The Reich wanted an immediate reply from Brazil, and if the SOINC memorandum was turned down, it planned to approach Brazil's competitors in Colombia and Central America.[5] If Brazil accepted SOINC's proposal, would it be bringing in a Trojan horse? Although the Germans agreed not to tie their demands for cotton to the coffee quota question (despite Rio's refusal to trade cotton on compensation from May through November 1935 and again in January 1936), the threat was implied. The weak coffee market was vulnerable to pressure. And tying a substantial part of Brazil's exports to Germany was fraught with economic, financial, and political dangers.

The international situation was complex. For one thing, the United States considered Brazil to have declared itself opposed to direct intergovernmental transactions of the SOINC kind. For another, Washington one year earlier had viewed unfavorably any possible barter of commodities (cotton especially) for armaments that might displace United States cotton exports.[6] Now Germany intended to force these issues.

The SOINC proposal was unfolded with finesse to meet Brazilian needs, specifically those of the Finance, War, and Foreign Ministries. In February, the Germans showed interest in manganese, rubber, and cacao, which they would pay for exclusively in merchant ships and arms.[7] In March, the German Economic Ministry authorized Souza Aranha to negotiate, through SOINC, the liquidation of old frozen German credits totalling between £500,-000 and £600,000.[8] And in April, Berlin offered to take 1,600,000 sacks of coffee if SOINC handled 500,000 of these sacks in return for arms, and if Rio freed substantial amounts of cotton for sale. Finally, in May, the Germans granted substantial increases in the quotas for tobacco, oranges, meat, bananas, and other products in return for cotton and the special coffee quota.[9] These, in brief, are the steps Germany took from the original consortium offer to the trade agreement of June 1936.

Meanwhile, acting independently of the secret SOINC proposals, regional export groups in Brazil pressured the CFCE to expand the German trade. In fact the old Souza Dantas thesis was still relevant, and controversial, as was shown by the case of Northern Brazil. It could be argued that the Northern states depended on Germany only because of inertia, poor quality control, and inadequate communications with other nations, especially the United States.[10] Nevertheless, there were strong positive arguments for continuing and expanding the German trade. In November 1935, Northern cotton growers had sent over three hundred telegrams to the CFCE urging that the German trade be renewed. It was renewed briefly—until the announcement of the new liberal trade policy. Telegrams sent to the CFCE by Northern commercial groups in 1937 reveal the extent of concern. From Amazonas to Bahia, the fact was that the principal export crops could only be sold to Germany.

To Paraiba cotton planters the case was clear. Eighty per cent of their state's treasury revenue depended on cotton sales. Some 65–70 per cent of their production was low-grade, short-fibered, and generally poor quality cotton that found no market in Liverpool, the British cotton emporium, whereas 19,000 tons were bought by Germany, in 1936, at premium prices. The growers ominously mentioned the agonizing situation of 1935–36, when the German market was closed. In early 1936 they had protested collectively to the President. In 1937 they scarcely had to spell out the threat, namely that a depressed region that had seemed on the brink of revolution in 1935 might still be subverted by communists and leftist politicians. Moreover, they added, the North ought to be treated equally with other regions and had a right to export its cotton.

The Amazonas Commercial Association pointed out that Germany absorbed nearly 75 per cent of its rubber production, the low-grade types, whereas the United States and Britain limited their purchases to the premium Acre type. The small tobacco growers of Bahia claimed they were "mortally vulnerable" to any decrease in the German trade. Similar cables poured in to the CFCE from Rio Grande do Sul tobacco producers, Paraná lumbermen, São Paulo citrus fruit growers, and other Northern agriculturalists.[11] As for cotton, Britain and Japan could not take all the Paulista production, which increased from 98,000 tons in 1934–35 to 170,000 tons one year later. As for coffee, Souza Aranha said, "compensation marks are worth much more to us than ashes."[12]

Pressured by the Germans and well-organized groups at home, the CFCE decided in February 1936 to open general discussions on trade in Berlin. Vargas, however, personally instructed Sebastião Sampaio, the Brazilian representative, not to discuss anything more binding than a "provisional modus vivendi" with Germany. Brazil could readily denounce it, or so Vargas hoped, in the event of trade discrimination.[13]

In April, Sampaio presented Berlin with a memorandum based on the United States guidelines for reciprocity and unconditional most-favored-nation treatment. But the Germans never treated this document or its bearer seriously. As Moniz learned in early May, the Sampaio memorandum would be an excellent basis for negotiating a permanent accord sometime in the unspecified future; for the present, however, the Germans wanted to make a temporary agreement around the SOINC proposals.[14] In fact, the serious talks were taking place in Rio, between the President, his Ministers of Finance and Foreign Affairs, and Souza Aranha.

Throughout March and April 1936, Souza Aranha worked to unfreeze Brazilian cotton policy, the key to trading with compensation marks.

I moved heaven and earth in order to achieve this and to persuade these gentlemen that although the Reich government now urgently needs our cotton, we will be growing a great deal of cotton in the future [for a more competitive market]. I called their attention to the new extensive plantings in Turkey, Persia, Argentina, Chile, etc.; I gave exact statistics on the Paulista harvest [then just coming in]; I got interested circles in São Paulo to support our position, which was quite necessary, since . . . there are still many influential people who are against cotton export for compensation marks. Thanks to these efforts, however, I succeeded in persuading the critical people that the Brazilian government must oblige the Reich government in cotton.[15]

Impressed by Souza Aranha's argument, Finance Minister Souza Costa agreed to trade cotton in return for a larger coffee quota and arms, to be handled through SOINC. On April 17 the CFCE officially approved the forthcoming negotiations in Berlin for the signing of a "provisional commercial accord" with specified import and export quotas.[16]

Souza Aranha continued to talk with private businessmen about coffee, cotton quotas, and the SOINC deal. For his part, Foreign Minister Macedo Soares said that he was willing to increase trade with Germany, but that as soon as possible he wanted to sign a provisional accord based upon the Sampaio memorandum. Thus on April 30 he suggested substantial increases in the German quotas for coffee (to two million sacks), cotton (52,000 tons until end of the year), and other exports, including frozen meat, oranges, bananas, and Brazil nuts. He accepted the SOINC proposals as negotiable in return for the large coffee quota.[17]

On May 12 Berlin agreed to exchange notes covering SOINC and the quotas for one year. But for their purposes Macedo Soares's coffee quota was too high, the cotton quota too low. So they suggested quotas of 1,600,000 sacks of coffee for the year ahead, including 500,000 through SOINC, and 70,000 tons of cotton. Although no formal agreement was signed, the two governments had reached an "understanding" to trade on compensation. The Brazilians were informed they had nothing to lose in separating the two accords, because Brazil could always use the most-favored-nation clause to obtain greater advantages in future negotiations.[18] In short, Brazil had to accept trade with the Reich on German terms. The upshot of these complex negotiations was that by the end of May, Brazil had a new trade agreement but not a formal treaty. In fact, the new Brazilian trade policy proclaimed on December 31, 1935, had been bypassed completely. The benefits for Brazil, however, were substantial. Restrictions on all major products in the export list, cotton excepted, were liberalized or removed, as indicated in Table 3.

With this new agreement Berlin engineered a victory for its trade principles based on compensation and intergovernmental trade controls. Rio limited cotton exports (to 62,000 tons) in order to hold down the supply of compensation marks and to placate Washington and London. The interests of Northern and Paulista growers were balanced by dividing the quota equally between them. Coffee would not be reexported. For its pains, SOINC was allowed to handle a special cotton quota (10,000 tons) to redeem old sterling credits; in addition it obtained the special coffee allotment, and received German permission to transact 25 per cent of the regular Brazilian cotton quota. Soon it became the largest exporter of Paulista cotton to Germany. Thus Brazil's liberal policy was compromised; the nation's economic needs were put before

TABLE 3

Quotas for Brazilian Products in the 1936 Accord and the 1935 Trade

Product	1936 quotas	1935 trade
Coffee	1,600,000 sacks	871,000 sacks
Cotton	62,000 tons	83,000 tons
Tobacco	18,000 tons	17,000 tons
Frozen meat	10,000 tons	50 tons
Bananas	4,000 tons	102 tons
Brazil nuts	4,000 tons	3,000 tons
Oranges	200,000 cases	16,000 cases

SOURCE: Telegrams 139 and 140, The Ambassador in Brazil [Hugh Gibson] to [Cordell] Hull, May 30 and June 1, 1936, *Foreign Relations of the United States, 1963*, V, 257, 261 (Washington, 1954).

Note: Products for which no quotas were set were cereals, rubber, cacao, mate, oleaginous seeds, skins, hides, wool, oils, minerals, honey, and all raw materials destined for German industry.

international respectability. However, few impartial historians today would gainsay that decision.

This eclectic policy was awkward to explain at home, but the most immediate problem was to conciliate Washington. The Foreign Minister's approach to the United States was based upon three assumptions: first, that the German-Brazilian agreement could stand if the wording were changed; second, that the United States would be mollified if Brazil imposed explicit quotas on German imports; and third, that the United States would permit large shipments of Brazilian cotton to Germany.

In May the Germans had first proposed two sets of notes, one openly setting quotas, the other covertly recognizing compensation and SOINC. On June 1, Welles went on record against systematic compensation, but his memorandum failed to convince Macedo Soares to abandon the German accord.[19] A modification of the wording was hastily arranged with Berlin, and on June 8 the Brazilians decided officially to view the accord as an expedient for maintaining trade with two nations whose trade systems were incompatible. Most-favored-nation treatment was declared for the public record. But in Berlin, only an oral agreement on Brazilian quotas for German industrial goods was exchanged, and in Rio the notes regarding SOINC were signed but not published.[20]

On June 13, Macedo Soares released the open provisions of this German accord in a circular telegram to the state governors. Unfortunately for him, he used the term "provisional accord" instead of "commercial understanding." The United States, the foreign and domestic press, the Brazilian Congress all requested clarification. Macedo Soares, embarrassed, was hard put to explain how no treaty in the conventional sense had been signed. To be sure, the accord was advantageous and the Brazilians had calculated, correctly, that the United States even when aroused would not apply sanctions. But there were doubtful aspects, and the achievement of eclecticism could not be explained as a diplomatic triumph. Macedo Soares, in fact, fell back on the argument of irresistible German pressure.[21]

The Brazilian quotas on imports of German trucks, autos, typewriters, and calculating machines were based upon the 1935 trade in these items, plus 10 per cent, in order to protect other suppliers of these goods, or so the Brazilians maintained. The Germans attempted to escape these limits; under pressure Brazil changed the quota basis from 1935 to the previous twelve months' trade. British and American officials noted that the quotas in fact extended the Reich's commercial gains of 1935 at their expense and that despite Brazil's assurances Germany would soon become the leading exporter to Brazil.[22] Table 4 shows that their fears were well founded.

The failure to establish effective quotas, however, does not suggest that Brazilian officials were eager to reorient their entire trade toward Germany. Clearly, Vargas and Macedo Soares did not want to abandon a middle ground between the industrial powers. From 1936 to 1939 the Bank of Brazil made sporadic attempts to limit its supplies of compensation marks and so control the import volume; but the Control Board set up at Euvaldo Lodi's suggestion to supervise compensation was ineffectual. Organized in July 1936, the Board brought together interest groups and officials in the Ministry of Finance. Souza Costa, being indulgent toward the trade, handpicked the Board members, and as a result it had no autonomy and no regulatory powers.[23]

Throughout Brazil the accord itself and the quota issue were controversial, but only a few insiders had the facts with which to defend or attack the government's dealings with Germany. The nub of conflict centered on cotton, a product Germany badly

TABLE 4

Value of Brazilian Imports, 1935–37
(Thousands of pounds gold and per cent of total trade)

	1935		1936		1937	
Supplier	Value in thousand £	Per cent of trade	Value in thousand £	Per cent of trade	Value in thousand £	Per cent of trade
Germany	5,608	20.4%	7,065	23.5%	9,697	23.8%
United States	6,406	23.4	6,651	22.1	9,337	22.9
Argentina	3,534	12.8	4,941	16.4	5,675	13.9
United Kingdom	3,409	12.4	3,385	11.2	4,909	12.0

SOURCE: Great Britain, Department of Overseas Trade. *Report on Economic and Commercial Conditions in Brazil, 1938 and 1939* (London, 1939), pp. 63, 103, 140.

wanted. Macedo Soares, like Souza Dantas before him, was impressed by the possibilities for Paulista cotton. Moreover, the growers were pressuring him to release cotton for compensation currency, and many responsible Brazilians saw cotton as the key to escaping their dependence on coffee, with its low prices. Others feared, however, that to flood the German market with cotton was to invite United States cotton dumping or retaliations on coffee. In the words of one prominent manufacturer, it was impossible for Brazil "to light one candle to God and another to the Devil."[24]

The cotton issue became critical in late May 1936, just as negotiations with Berlin were ending. Macedo Soares favored agreeing to the German demands for a large quota of 70,000 tons. However, the Germans settled for 62,000 tons after President Vargas himself urged a smaller quota.[25] Rightly or wrongly, Vargas believed that the United States would not tolerate a larger quota, and so he imposed a compromise. Evidently the Germans were willing to accept his conciliatory gesture, at least until the accord was completed, for on June 16, Moniz was informed that additional German purchases could "easily reach 150,000 tons."[26] But the growers were bitterly disappointed at the smaller cotton quota.[27]

Harmony reigned during the CFCE's public session to examine the new accord. On June 18 exporters of coffee, fruit, and other products joined with German bankers, the president of the German-Brazilian Chamber of Commerce, and embassy officials to hear Sampaio and Macedo Soares explain how free-trade principles had been squared with the economic necessities of the two nations.[28] On June 22 the controversy over cotton climaxed in closed session. At stake was not the cotton market alone, but the future course of Brazil's trade policy. Since February 1936 Vargas, Souza Costa, and Macedo Soares had followed a devious course to eclecticism. Could Brazil in fact trade with whom it pleased, as Macedo Soares contended, or did it have to make a choice between two incompatible trade systems, as Aranha argued from Washington?

With Vargas absent, Macedo Soares and Valentim Bouças spoke their minds freely to the Council. The Foreign Minister argued as follows:

One must realize that, fortunately for us, Brazil is not a United States colony that must bow to the impositions of the Americans, who seek only to obstruct the sale of our cotton to Germany. Nevertheless, I affirm to you that at this very moment we have received a German proposal to buy not 62,000 but 150,000 tons of cotton, and that should it be necessary for marketing our cotton production, I shall certainly make the transaction, however displeasing to the United States. And in saying this I should also add that it is sad to have Brazilians attacking this policy in order to put themselves at the service of the Americans.[29]

This was a direct reference to Aranha, the man Macedo Soares considered to have been instrumental in limiting the cotton quota through his influence with Vargas. Bouças, in reply, roundly attacked compensation. "Though we are not worried about German imperialism," he concluded, "we should realize that when the Americans adopt a defensive position we will call it Yankee imperialism."[30]

The policy thrust of their positions was clear. That both Macedo Soares and Aranha were presidential hopefuls added a note of personal bitterness and rivalry. To be sure, they had different styles and vantage points. Macedo Soares, a Paulista politician, looked toward Brazil's traditional trade and cultural ties with Europe. Aranha, a gaúcho revolutionary, was infatuated with Roosevelt and the New Deal. The one would follow trade opportunities; the other would point to Brazil's vulnerability in a dangerous world. Macedo Soares, in short, argued that trade and politics were separate, whereas Aranha said they were not.

Macedo Soares's actions in the German negotiations had been consistent with his beliefs: "Brazil should emancipate itself from monoculture and should likewise avoid the 'single customer,' the 'large client'; otherwise it cannot face any economic problem with the necessary freedom of action."[31] Thus it can be argued that eclecticism was a form of economic nationalism. However, Macedo Soares did not promote economic development by systematically exchanging raw materials for German industrial goods—exports still came first. Nor did he carry out the proposed arms exchange through SOINC. As a practical politician, he was receptive to current ideas of national independence, but he stopped short of articulating an ideology of development through trade. Indeed it would have been very difficult to go beyond eclecticism as long as the policy focus was outward, to world markets, instead of inward to development projects.

Eclecticism was consistent with Brazil's general trade guidelines: maintain and diversify markets. It was also based on keeping trade interests separate from international politics. Thus eclecticism appealed to those who stood somewhere between the economic nationalists, who looked toward German planning methods and markets, and the free traders, who accepted the United States guidelines of reciprocity and most-favored-nation treatment. Percival Farquhar, an old Brazil hand, summed up this point of view in March 1939: the intention here is "to trade what the country has to give in the best market, keeping free from too close entanglements." As a Brazilian friend told the Yankee promoter, this was "to carry on flirtations even to advanced points, but to marry no one or to give oneself to no one."[32]

In 1936 Brazil moved closer to eclecticism, and the nation continued this policy until the German market closed in 1939. Despite another crisis in 1937 with Washington over the renewed German agreement, the policy was maintained. It survived even in 1938, when the Estado Nôvo ushered in an epoch of statism under the military, imposing exchange controls and a moratorium on the Aranha Plan. And after a temporary break in diplomatic relations with Germany (1938), eclecticism returned.* An export mentality

---

* The German trade was not all smooth sailing after 1936, but it bears repeating that the economic advantages were sufficient to outweigh Brazilian doubts and divisions of opinion. Understandably, the government was reluctant to pass judgment. Twice the CFCE set up special commissions to assess the costs and benefits, only to temporize in mid-1937, and again in 1939. Its first report, dated June 4, 1937, was vague and general, perhaps because this commission was charged with responding to American expressions of alarm over the increasing German competition. It was decided to extend the 1936 modus vivendi for three months while the German problem was being studied. See CFCE, Processo 575, "Ajuste comercial Brasil-Alemanha," AN, and "Comércio exterior do Brasil," *O Observador Econômico e Financeiro*, Ano II, No. 18 (July 1937), pp. 15–21. This accord was extended every three months thereafter, until 1940. Alarmed at the growing volume of German imports, in 1938 the Bank of Brazil imposed temporary restraints on compensation trading, and in August 1939 Leonardo Truda, the Bank's Director, asked the CFCE to reevaluate this trade with a view to limiting and restrict-

still reigned. But as the Army pressed for a steelworks, oil refineries, railroad equipment, and arms, and as first Germany (in 1936) and then the United States (in 1938) began stockpiling Brazilian raw materials, a new mixture of personalities and pressures influenced the policy-making process. Brazil's increased bargaining power was more and more conditioned by the fact that the two major powers were moving beyond economic competition to war. Aranha's alternative trade policy depended on close political and economic ties with the United States. Colonial competition and Germany's search for territory and raw materials (which Brazilians took seriously) were the two great dangers against which Aranha erected his policy of building a rapprochement with the United States, beginning in 1934. Brazil needed capital, credit, and skills from the United States. "My opinion," he wrote to Vargas, "is that this is our century, as the first Roosevelt said, and that it is incumbent upon our generation to use this opportunity to develop our economy and make our country strong."[33] Aranha, therefore, opposed the 1936 "understanding" with Germany for high policy reasons.

Vargas appeared to go along with the broad outlines of the policy Aranha was formulating in Washington, even as he hoped to continue good trade relations with Germany.[34] As a realist and a skeptic, however, Getúlio must have asked himself, "What do the Americans have in mind, and when will they deliver?" To be sure, the possibility of Export-Import Bank credits for railroad, mining, and steel equipment was discussed on an exploratory basis in the fall of 1937 (see Chapter 5). And in Washington a small circle of officials became increasingly enthusiastic about Brazil's enormous potential and wanted to help it along economically. While purchasing raw materials they came to realize that Brazil was an important and enjoyable political ally. Bonds of self-interest and genuine warmth produced a special enthusiasm toward Brazil, which Ambassador and Mrs. Carlos Martins furthered after busi-

ing it. A second CFCE commission so resolved, but following the plenary session's failure to reach a decision in December, Euvaldo Lodi moved to table the report "until a more opportune time for further study." CFCE, Processo 979, "Importação e exportação, Brasil-Alemanha," AN.

ness sessions broke up for drinks and samba music.[35] Roosevelt felt benevolent toward Brazil, but though he was keenly interested in bringing Brazil into American defense plans, it cannot be said that he had grasped the possibilities and responsibilities of foreign aid in the late 1930's. He did not become specifically committed to economic development loans until the dark days of 1940. Until the fall of France, Roosevelt's private hints of aid to Aranha went well beyond his legal and political authority from Congress to grant it. As negotiations in Washington for old American cruisers fell through (1936), followed by Argentina's successful torpedoing of the destroyer lease plan with the United States (1937), the practical results of Aranha's policy were not spectacular. For his part, Vargas welcomed close relations with the United States, but he was careful not to commit himself or Brazil irrevocably to his Foreign Minister's position.

On the other hand, President Vargas did not follow the lead of economic nationalists at home who urged him to negotiate large exchanges of goods with Germany. Personally, the President preferred to conciliate those who held different points of view on trade policy rather than follow a direct course of action that might limit his freedom of maneuver with domestic groups or lead to difficult political choices abroad.

After the coup d'etat of November 1937, some military officers and administrators in the Estado Nôvo appeared eager to expand trade with Germany, despite the political risks. They argued reasonably enough that Brazil should accept the best terms possible. Trading Brazilian products for German capital goods such as a steelworks was especially attractive to them, because it would not force the nation to shoulder an additional burden of foreign debt. Though these elements distrusted Aranha and his policy, Vargas urged his old protégé to stay on as ambassador in Washington, since his prestige would be helpful in arranging United States military and industrial credits. Such assistance, Vargas said, would enable him "to avoid offers from other countries, such as I am resisting and intend to continue resisting."[36]

If trade with Germany was essential, so were the political and military lines to Washington, and Vargas tried to maintain them both.[37] Thus when the military signed a large artillery contract with Krupp in March 1938, Aranha had already agreed to become Foreign Minister. Aranha was brought in to balance nationalists in the armed forces—certain officers who, in their eagerness to obtain equipment for railroads and a steel plant, might have strained Brazil's traditionally close relations with the United States.

Vargas succeeded brilliantly in his role as the broker among factions and as the conciliator among policies. But his political stance was based on the strategic superiority of the United States in the Western Hemisphere; for when the "colossus of the North" was challenged militarily by German victories in Europe, it was impossible to maintain a middle position in trade and aid. In June 1940, a choice impended that was perhaps one of the most fateful Vargas ever faced. At any moment the British fleet might be captured or sunk, rendering Brazil militarily defenseless. Moreover, the Germans were threatening that unless Brazil joined in the new German-dominated Greater European market zone it would be punished economically after the war, which few believed would last long.

Swinging like a compass to the new power pole, Vargas issued first one enigmatic (but pro-German) speech on June 11, aboard the cruiser *Minas Gerais,* and then another to military officers on the 28th. Aranha publicly reassured Washington of Brazil's continued faith in the Inter-American system. Vargas privately asked the German ambassador how trade might be increased. There are many interpretations of Vargas's stance at this critical juncture.

Was the President reorienting Brazil toward Germany? Aranha, who was well informed, thought so as he passed this poem around among friends:

> A bordo do *Minas Gerais,*
> Houve um discurso turuna:
> —O nosso chefe Getúlio
> Entrou pela quinta coluna.*

---

* Aboard the *Minas Gerais,* / There was an incredible speech: / —Our leader Getúlio / Has joined the Fifth Column." Anecdote courtesy of Professor Hélio Vianna.

The Germans thought Vargas was unequivocal. Ambassador Curt Prüfer telegraphed the Foreign Office, "The speeches mean . . . a rejection of North American policy by the Federal President in anticipation of England's defeat and the resultant weakening of Roosevelt, and the orientation of Brazilian policy toward trade with Germany and Europe."[38] In short, Vargas had almost but not quite committed himself to Germany.

But perhaps he merely hedged. Vargas was famous for landing fish in rough waters, and so the *Minas Gerais* speech could have been his protection. If the Germans had won in Europe they could not then have said that Brazil was on the Allied side and have used this pretext for sanctions or conquest.[39]

Or was he warning Washington to provide immediate economic support and industrial credits? The well-informed editor of *O Imparcial* believed so. The United States, he said, must understand "that Pan-Americanism cannot and should not be a mere doctrine. It ought to be an economic system . . . or it will not resist the coming conflict."[40] Some persons who were close to Vargas still maintain that the June 11th speech was delivered to line up full United States government financial support for a government steel plant.[41]

However difficult it is to balance these viewpoints, the conclusion must be that Vargas's speeches marked the end of eclecticism as an effective policy. As Germany failed to defeat Great Britain, and consequently could not develop her vaunted continental market, Brazil moved rapidly toward the United States. Closer ties followed logically from negotiations over air bases and the steelworks in 1940 to raw materials agreements and a wartime alliance in 1942. The German-American trade rivalry had always been linked to larger political and strategic factors. Now Brazil's options were forced, and Vargas chose to strengthen the traditional North American alliance.

Brazilian commercial policy before the war brought mixed results. In the plus column, Vargas maintained and increased trade with two competing, hostile systems. If favorable credit terms and market opportunities enabled Berlin to gain at Washington's ex-

pense, Rio was reluctant to make a final decision. Vargas muddled
through with his Foreign Trade Council, which was useful as a
sounding board and as a legitimizing body, but which never developed into an important policy-making organ in its own right.
Attempts to shape a more coherent commercial policy were frus-
trated by monetary pressures, by the crosscutting demands of pressure groups and prominent officials, and by policies of the major
powers.

Given the Vargas regime's internal divisions over trade objectives, the emphasis on exports was sound. The results, however,
did not meet expectations. By 1940, prices for Brazil's major exports were still disappointingly low. Imports, however, were increasing rapidly as the domestic economy grew impressively. From
this standpoint, Vargas had done little to promote industrialization
through trade.

Development planning through a more imaginative approach to
trade remained a largely unexplored idea partly because the policy-making process was too diffuse to support, or even to identify,
such an objective. Roberto Simonsen's plan for a national export
institute, in 1935, departed too radically from current policy, and
was too narrowly based, to be influential or politically relevant.
More important was the fact that until 1937 no group or coalition
had emerged to impose a modernizing ideology. Thus Vargas
failed to follow up German heavy equipment offers with sufficient
vigor after 1934. And aside from procuring railroad equipment and
safeguarding vital imports, the government did not develop a
schedule of priorities or discipline imports in line with the requirements of an industrializing society. Thus Vargas and his
ministers picked their way through the trade thicket without benefit of a future-oriented trade policy more nationalist than the one
eclecticism provided.

When the Brazilian Army impressed its own sense of urgency
and priorities upon the new authoritarian State in 1938, German-
American rivalry was becoming overtly political and strategic.
Poised for conflict, the powers responded when Vargas pressed

for a steel plant. It was this combination of a changed international environment and the emergence of a forceful, initiating group of Army officers that distinguished the final phases of decision-making about steel from the diffuse policy process regarding foreign trade.

PART II · STEEL

Santos Dumont and his flying machine were the talk of Brazil before 1910. The pioneer aviator was imitated by so many compatriots, it is said, that upon meeting a Brazilian one would ask, "How's your airplane?" In the 1930's, the question was "What's your steel plan?," and a serious answer was expected.[1] In government commissions, in Congress, in the press, and in the armed forces, people were talking about "our steel problem." Finally, in 1940, having ripened as a national issue for two decades, it was resolved.

Steel policy did not emerge full blown, as some technocratic master plan of Vargas and the Estado Nôvo; rather, several strategies had been worked out and opinions formed long before the Army pressed for a modern steelworks in 1938. This chapter surveys the basic conditions of Brazilian iron and steel production, then reconstructs the development of policy between 1918 and 1938. Chapter 5 discusses in detail the period 1938–40, when private foreign solutions and nationalist solutions were advanced in a setting of great urgency. The personalities, groups, and ideologies at play in this period are surveyed in the context of both foreign and domestic affairs. Then Chapter 6 analyzes the final phase, in which the Brazilian government took over the steel project abandoned by the United States Steel Corporation, and chose Volta Redonda as the site for its steel complex.

In market size and in iron ore supply, Brazil clearly fulfilled two preconditions for successful steelmaking. This had been well known since World War I. The basic obstacles to establishing a large-scale steel operation using coking coal were technical and economic. Brazil lacked important elements of the standard formula for successful steelmaking: cheap, good quality metallurgical coal, abundant capital, and inexpensive, reliable transportation. In addition, administrative goals, nationalism, and politics were important factors, for the final Volta Redonda solution was determined, in part, by those who controlled the planning operation. The complex steel issue was neatly summarized by a contemporary entrepreneur. "For me," he wrote Vargas, "the steel problem is primarily a simple technical problem, secondarily an important economic problem, and finally a very delicate political-military problem. But there are those who, perhaps rightly, would invert the order."[2]

There were two predominant attitudes in the discussions over steel. Many Brazilians argued that the steel plant could not succeed without foreign capital, management, and coal. But others, including leading nationalists, believed that a key industry like steel should not be controlled by foreign concessionaires in any event, or be dependent on imported coal, in case of war.

The outlines of the steel problem, being well known, need only to be summarized briefly before we turn to the hitherto obscure main lines of policy and policy-making.[3] As noted in the Introduction, Brazil's small domestic iron and steel industry flourished after 1931. Under the stimulus of falling exchange rates and a high tariff, the industry prospered and kept out less expensive foreign construction steel and pig iron. It expanded both by using existing capacity more fully and by creating new capacity, but these gains, though impressive, did not keep pace with demand. Thus in 1940, about 70 per cent of all rolled-steel products, including rails and plates, were not yet manufactured in Brazil. Imports of steel as an industrial raw material were heavy and increasing. With the demand for basic steel products increasing to 600,000 tons per year, Brazil's steel consumption was already larger than that of some European nations.[4] Brazil had enormous iron ore reserves to draw on (thirty billion tons today), and the experts knew also that their ore, being high in iron content and low in impurities, was well adapted to use in the then current blast furnace and open-hearth steel furnace technology. Their problems, as mentioned, lay elsewhere.

Brazil's metallurgical coal from Santa Catarina state in the Far South, is high in ash and sulphur content. Being difficult to mine, expensive to treat, and far from the steel plants, it is more costly, as well as of lower quality than the imported coals with which it must be mixed. Until 1939, the characteristics of Santa Catarina coal were so poorly understood that many experts doubted whether it could be used in modern blast furnaces. Poor coal remains the dominant raw-material cost in Brazilian steelmaking today. Charcoal, although successfully used in Brazil for reducing ore, is less efficient and requires very large forest reserves and cheap labor. In the 1930's, moreover, many engineers and jour-nalists shared an almost ideological bias against charcoal and small-scale electric furnaces. Coke, in short, was the most efficient fuel, and the best suited for modern methods of steel production.

Rail service in the metallurgical heartland, a triangle sketched from Belo Horizonte to São Paulo and Vitória, is overloaded and unreliable today. Volta Redonda still must contend with high transportation costs for assembling its raw materials and for de-livering finished goods to Rio and São Paulo, the principal mar-kets. Thirty years ago the major rail link for this Center-South re-gion was a brake on development; the Central do Brasil Railway (EFCB) was severely undercapitalized and could not meet all the requests for freight cars. One must not underrate the importance of poor railroad service in the calculus of Brazilian steel policy. In the 1930's and 1940's the Central do Brasil was a formidable obstacle. The same government railroad also served the Paraopeba Valley mining region in Minas Gerais, from which small shipments of iron ore and manganese lumbered down the steep mountain grades and on to Rio for export to Europe and the United States. The only alternate rail route, from Minas to Vitória on the Espírito Santo coast, was controlled by Itabira Iron Ore Company, a Brit-ish syndicate under Percival Farquhar. Known as the Vitória a Minas, this inefficient narrow-gage line had to be completely re-

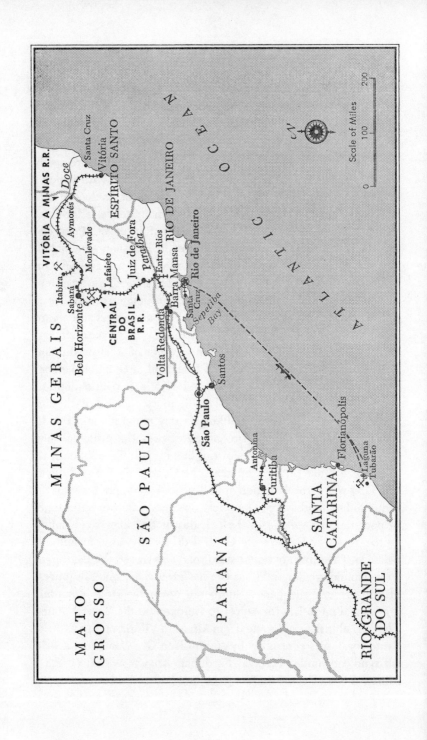

built, widened, and supplied with heavy rails. But many Brazilians echoed Farquhar's view that the Vitória a Minas, not the EFCB, was the only practical rail route. It led by easy grades into the undeveloped Rio Doce ore zone in Minas Gerais, one of the world's richest iron ore reserves, and the future site, some thought, for a Brazilian Ruhr.

Domestic financing of highly capitalized steelworks has been difficult at best for Brazil since 1950. In the 1930's there was scant capital at home for such a large enterprise; financing had to come from abroad in some form, and from either the United States or Germany, since Great Britain was exporting little capital to Brazil. Foreign bankers and their governments knew that a modern plant of at least 200,000 tons of annual capacity could survive in the protected domestic market. With domestic recovery in 1933, the Brazilian government again sought foreign finance for the steelworks, as it had intermittently since 1910. Growing domestic demand threatened to outrun available foreign exchange for steel imports. In this setting of growth and exchange crisis, the problem, again, was not one of markets, but of how to arrange for coal, capital, and transportation.

The story of steel, from a Mineiro blast furnace called "Hope," built in 1891, to the large integrated works of today is well known, although a good historical survey of the post–World War II industry is lacking.[5] Until Volta Redonda began operations in 1946, domestic iron and steel production was based on charcoal-fueled blast furnaces in Minas Gerais and electric furnaces using scrap in Minas, São Paulo, and Rio de Janeiro state. The large Monlevade works excepted (see pp. 87–88), high cost and low volume were the two characteristics of this small industry. Hence every President after 1909 promised to find a more economical solution based on coke. The governments of Nilo Peçanha and Hermes da Fonseca offered monopoly privileges, duty-free imports, and subsidies as inducements to found a modern industry. However, all plans were curtailed with the closing of foreign capital markets during the Balkan Wars and World War I. Thanks to the tariff and subsidies, Brazil's embryonic steel industry survived foreign competition in the 1920's, but that was all. The solution that overshadowed all others for twenty years was devised in 1919 by Percival Farquhar, the American entrepreneur.[6]

Farquhar's plan was grandiose but well conceived. After consulting with President Epitácio Pessôa, who was eager to initiate steel production and oil exploration in Brazil, Farquhar proposed to export iron ore from Itabira and simultaneously to establish a modern steelworks that would produce basic steel products. The American wanted to mine up to ten million tons a year of high-grade hematite and to ship this ore via Santa Cruz, a sleepy fishing village in Espírito Santo that was to have become both the port and the site for a steelworks. Rails, shapes, sheets, and bars led the list of imported manufactures that the new 150,000-ton plant would replace. Returning Farquhar ore boats would carry high-quality American and European coal for the steelworks. This was the famous Itabira Contract of 1920.

President Pessôa signed, thereby accepting Farquhar's terms: Itabira Iron Ore Company would supply everything, from a modern industrial railroad, to port services, a shipping line, and the steel plant, which Pessôa wanted badly; in return, Farquhar's syndicate would receive monopoly rights over its private railroad from the Rio Doce ore region to its private port at Santa Cruz. This so-called Itabira solution was sound because it fulfilled the requirements for good coal, enough capital ($80 million), and cheap, reliable transportation.

Farquhar captured the imagination of the Brazilian political and industrial elite, which tended to regard Itabira as a "king solution" to the entire iron and steel problem. This term, as used by the Brazilian geographer Hilgard O'Reilly Sternberg, describes a grandiose scheme that appears to solve a complex problem in one stroke.[7] Farquhar's supporters tended to regard the Itabira Contract as the only means of solving Brazil's problems of steel and iron ore export. His detractors were repelled by the enormous scope, and said Itabira endangered national sovereignty. Psychologically, Farquhar's king solution obscured more modest plans. Until Vargas revoked his concession in August 1939, there seemed to be only two options in the minds of many Brazilians: develop the nation's key heavy industry with Farquhar, or nationalize the Itabira plan without him.

Itabira ran into political difficulties from the start, and remained controversial. The plan first had to be approved by Minas Gerais, where the mining would take place. Minas was a "sovereign state" in the regionalistic federal system before Vargas. Under Governor, and later President (1923–26), Artur da Silva Bernardes, the Mineiros dreamed of establishing a new Ruhr within their state boundaries and of stemming thereby the flow of economic and political power to rival São Paulo.* In an attempt to placate Bernardes, Farquhar reluctantly offered to establish his plant at Aymorés, within the Minas frontier, although he argued correctly then and later that a seacoast location was more economical for transportation costs. But Bernardes would not agree to Itabira on any grounds. And aside from his intransigence, there was the issue of divergent aims. Farquhar was first and foremost in the ore exporting business, whereas Minas and the federal government were committed politically to the steelworks.

Farquhar argued reasonably enough that mining and steel manufacturing were different enterprises and that it was therefore economically wrong to treat them as one. Ore exports were affected by cyclical demand in the European and United States markets; hence the profits were very good in some years, but lean in others. In pricing, shipping costs, and demand, mining had different requirements than steelmaking, which depended on a steady supply of cheap raw materials, long-term financing, and domestic market conditions. Thus Farquhar believed the steel plant logically should follow completion of economical rail and shipping services, especially a first-class railroad. To him, the Brazilian steel problem was primarily a "railroad problem." Mining therefore took priority over the steel plant; but much as he tried to escape the steel plant obligation, Farquhar was plagued by the king solution mentality.

Mineiro nationalists claimed that Farquhar had hoodwinked

---

* Throughout his long political career (1904–52), Bernardes exemplified *florianismo*, a nationalist attitude stressing authority, nativism, and confidence in the nation's economic future. This he inherited from Carlos Vaz de Melo, his father-in-law, a regional political leader in Minas who in the early 1890's supported Marshal Floriano Peixoto, the nationalist President.

Pessôa to get their ore, that he would never willingly found a steel-works. As his biographer has shown, Farquhar was indeed a rugged individualist of the old school—secretive, tenacious, and fully able to manipulate the corrupt politics of the Old Republic.[8] But he was also something of a dreamer, and his papers in the Biblioteca Nacional contain several work sheets for steel plants ranging from 150,000 to 300,000 tons of steel capacity. Doubtless he did originally use the steel plant as bait in order to get the ore concession, where the real profits lay.[9] But he probably would have built the plant eventually. The problem was less one of motivation, as the nationalists charged, than of finance.

From 1910 to about 1937, foreign financial interests connected with the international steel industry were concerned primarily with obtaining Brazilian iron and manganese ores for steel plants in Europe and in the United States. The construction of new steelworks in underdeveloped nations did not interest them. Moreover, the large established industries seem to have acted in collusion to discourage the founding of new plants in steel-importing countries that, in their opinion, did not enjoy "natural" conditions for a steel industry.[10] Brazil, with poor coal and bad railroads, was not at that time able to counter the argument, based as it was on the international division of labor thesis. Not surprisingly, Farquhar's backers in the United States and Europe strongly objected to building a steel plant. Thus in 1928 Farquhar gladly renegotiated the Itabira Contract, surrendering monopoly transit and port rights in return for relief from the steel plant obligation.

The obvious question is, was the Farquhar option—with or without the steel plant—a reasonable one for Brazil? Domestic political problems aside, Farquhar faced three serious difficulties, which in the end were largely responsible for wrecking his plans.

One may assume that if Farquhar had been able to obtain the financing, any administration after Bernardes left federal office (1926) until the Estado Nôvo (1937) would have accepted Itabira. In 1929 Farquhar almost launched the venture, only to see it wrecked in the Wall Street crash. Backed by international bankers, European steel interests, and a United States equipment consortium, Farquhar had planned to raise $55 million (without the steel plant); the United States would subscribe 55 per cent, Britain 30 per cent, and Germany the remaining 15 per cent. But then the New York capital markets closed, and until the United States rearmed in 1940, there was little chance that the American financial keystone would fall into place for Farquhar.

Another problem was that Europe needed Brazilian iron ore, but the United States did not. In 1929, British and German steel companies were ready to take ore contracts, and again in 1936 they were prepared jointly to contract for yearly shipments of four million tons over the next ten years. This time financing was to have been divided almost evenly among the British, German, and United States capital markets.[11] Bethlehem Steel Company, with its coastal steelworks at Sparrows Point, Maryland, was the logical American outlet, but the company told Farquhar it was reluctant to launch his scheme for fear that a competitor might establish another coastal plant using Itabira ore.[12] Wrapped up in Itabira as he was, Farquhar discounted the fact that in 1933 Bethlehem and U.S. Steel both negotiated large Venezuelan ore concessions on liberal terms. His hopes for Bethlehem lingered on until just before the war, when that company began to develop its Venezuelan mines for export to Sparrows Point.

The steel plant was therefore an added financial burden, on top of Farquhar's already massive capital needs. As noted before, his backers had objected to the plant in the early 1920's. Would they object again after 1937, when the Brazilian government again insisted on treating ore and steel together in a king solution (see Chapter 5)? That Bethlehem's hesitancy would create a serious obstacle for him was considered likely by Farquhar. Since German interests reluctantly agreed to include the plant, however, in 1938 his financial planning shifted more toward German participation.[13]

Farquhar's dealings with Fritz Thyssen of the giant Vereinigte Stahlwerke were mysterious to Brazilians, some of whom sensed therein a threat of German imperialism. Few knew that in 1936 Thyssen, with his government's backing, was prepared to furnish railroad, port, and mining equipment to Itabira in return for ore shipped to Europe in German bottoms.[14] Farquhar's correspondence shows that in 1938 the two men were considering an exchange of German railroad and steel manufacturing equipment for four million tons yearly of Itabira ore. Foreign Minister Aranha was sufficiently alarmed to block Farquhar's plans in 1938.[15] Ever hopeful, Farquhar tried to balance German equipment with Export-Import Bank finance, but his financial prospects in Washington were never bright. Ironically, the Yankee speculator had become involved in the very kind of international intrigue that the nationalists always said would threaten Brazilian sovereignty.

Itabira polarized public opinion for so long that to discuss it was in a very real sense to discuss the entire future of Brazil's heavy industrial development. His many partisans believed that Farquhar alone had the contacts and experience with the foreign financial and industrial centers to obtain the requisite foreign capital, management, and technology. His enemies of many kinds thought his plans were dangerous. If the railroad for transporting ore took priority over the steelworks, as Farquhar said it should, the nationalists accused him of dodging the steelworks obligation. If steel manufacturing and ore exports were joined in a king solution, which he tried to avoid, they accused him of grasping sovereign powers. Thus the Itabira controversy was a focal point for ideological dispute. Since in the minds of many Brazilians the two problems of ore and steel were combined, the following discussion of Itabira's enemies will also touch upon the iron ore issue.

Various economic interests attacked Itabira in the name of nationalism. Domestic manufacturers of pig iron and steel claimed that the new plant would certainly ruin them. Ore exporters along the Central do Brasil line thought that a new, efficient industrial railroad into the Rio Doce region would permit Farquhar to undersell them. Foreign and domestic owners of ore deposits near Itabira charged Farquhar with operating a transportation monopoly. The domestic coal producers in Southern Brazil feared that Farquhar's ore boats would return with cheap foreign coal. Even armaments importers felt threatened by any large steelworks that might supply steel for artillery and projectiles to the Brazilian Army.[16] The fact that all these interests had close connections with the state and national governments added force to their chorus of protest.

To better his public relations, Farquhar always emphasized the obstructionism of these pressure groups rather than the desire of some Brazilians to find a viable alternative to Itabira. Convinced that ore-rich Minas could become an industrial power, the Belo Horizonte business community opposed Farquhar even as it welcomed the opportunity to invest in Belgo-Mineira, a steel company controlled by interests in the Low Countries (see p. 87). The Mineiros also backed President Bernardes in his fight against Itabira, and they supported his proposal in 1924 that the government subsidize two small plants of 50,000 tons capacity in Minas, and a third in Santa Catarina.* After 1936, Farquhar discovered yet another source of opposition—national financiers who, like the banker Guilherme Guinle, were attracted by the profit potential of a large steelworks and had capital to invest. The conclusion must be that regional and interest group pressures were deeply involved in the controversy regarding Itabira and the entire steel issue.

Itabira also generated a less specific brand of nationalism than the defensive acts of special interests. Between the wars, Brazilians increasingly discussed the larger question of direct foreign investment in developing their natural resources, especially iron ore and petroleum. In part, they exhibited the natural xenophobia with

---

* The Bernardes steel plan (Decree 4,801) exemplified planning by the patrimonial state; legislators, industrialists, and technicians were invited to confer together on the steel problem. The result was an interlocking of government and private goals: rails production to refurbish the railroads, subsidies (up to 80 per cent) to encourage private investment, national coal to benefit the Santa Catarina coal interests and to further the Army's objective of self-sufficiency. Instead of using one efficient 150,000-ton plant as some engineers had urged, production was to have been divided among three small plants to benefit regional interests in Minas and Santa Catarina. Too small for efficient operations, and badly located, these plants were never built. For his part, Bernardes tried then, and later in the 1950's with petroleum, to carry out ambitious nationalist goals on a shoestring. See the critique by Ferdinand Labouriau, a Farquhar partisan: *O nosso problema siderúrgico* (Rio, 1924). As for the Mineiros, several other steel projects were proposed and abandoned over the years, until 1956, when a joint Brazilian-Japanese consortium founded USIMINAS, the first coke-based steel complex in the Rio Doce Valley. For the Mineiro viewpoint, see Dermeval José Pimenta, *Implantação da grande siderurgia em Minas Gerais* (Belo Horizonte, 1967) and Athos de Lemos Rache, *Contribuição ao estudo da economia mineira* (Rio, 1957).

which elites on the Latin American periphery of the Atlantic world viewed the industrial powers. Farquhar himself lamented "a certain strain of chauvinistic antiforeign sentiment," which was easily aroused against him.[17] In part, it was the desire to modernize, to secure bases for eventually attaining economic and political independence. In fact, there were two waves of nationalism, which moved from antiforeignism to a modernizing ideology of development. The first nationalistic current began around 1910 and had two main aspects: antiforeignism and regionalism.

Antiforeign nationalists articulated the frustration and unease that many Brazilians felt about the foreign iron ore rush, which followed predictions of diminishing world ore resources.[18] By 1918, British, United States, German, French, and Belgian interests controlled most of the best deposits in Minas Gerais. Artur Bernardes and his compatriots felt strongly that Brazil must not repeat the colonial experience of two hundred years before, when Portugal had taken most of the gold in the Minas mining rush. Now, foreigners like Farquhar would leave only "empty holes" behind unless their plans to export iron ore were stopped. Eventually, the industrial powers would be forced to deal on Minas's terms when their own reserves ran low. Until then, the Mineiros should obtain the maximum benefit from their rich patrimony by forcing mining interests, by means of differential ore export taxes, to build a steel plant. As for Itabira, it was unthinkable. Brazil, in short, had the iron ore resources to become a great power, and Minas had the means at hand to be the new industrial power center.

The dream that ore would soon do for Minas what coffee was doing for São Paulo was shattered in the late 1920's. New surveys showed that in Minas alone the known reserves of high-grade iron ore, estimated at 3.5 billion tons in 1910, were actually about 13 billion tons. Bernardes clung to what might be called "the fabulous resources argument" long after it ceased to have statistical validity, but a whole generation of Brazilians was educated by him and other nationalists to preserve this great wealth from foreigners. The argument against foreign capital in iron ore mining is an enduring tenet of Brazilian economic nationalism.

Thirteen billion tons of high-grade hematite was indeed a treasure, and most of the best deposits were not owned by Brazilians. Even with the spread of national consciousness among certain elites after 1918, however, the nation's political, business, and industrial leaders did not accede to attempts by nationalists in Congress to restrict foreign mining activities. Farquhar and his monopolistic contract were criticized, but he agreed to modify his aim in return for abandoning the steel plant. In fact, nationalists in Congress could not effectively challenge the long-held liberal ideal of free access to raw materials until 1929, when Brazil's capacity to import was drastically reduced. Nevertheless, the opinion was growing that natural resources should not be left undeveloped and under foreign ownership, and that Brazilians should share in the benefits of ore exportation.

The tenentes, who led the second wave of nationalism after 1930, were concerned primarily with moralizing the nation's politics and administration. But insofar as they had a program for economic development, it was to centralize legislation and regulate concessions. Thus Juarez Távora (Minister of Agriculture) placed prospecting, licensing, and statistical services under the newly created National Department of Mineral Production (DNPM), and José Américo de Almeida (Minister of Transport) investigated the Itabira Contract and attempted to nullify it.

The direction of *tenentismo* was toward some form of State-regulated economy. Yet the nation's political and industrial elite did not share the young reformers' belief in the efficacy of government economic enterprises. Roberto Simonsen, the industrialist, stated unequivocally that the State should be a regulator, but not a producer.[19] The new Vargas government ignored José Américo's call for a State steelworks.[20] Távora hoped to nationalize natural resources and mining under legislation modeled on the 1927 Italian mining code, but the 1933–34 Constituent Assembly watered down his proposals by providing only that all ore beds and water power sources not then being "worked" belonged to the State. As a result, many foreign mining properties including Itabira escaped, despite the 1934 mining code restricting foreign ownership.

Following the Paulista revolt in 1932, the tenentes declined as an effective national political force. They left a legacy of centralism, however, and they gave an impetus to reorganizing the country that their senior officers continued for purposes of military and economic defense. Thus in 1931 Minister of War Leite de Castro organized a National Steel Commission to study the entire problem of iron and steel.[21] In 1933, he led a mission to study European steel plants. The recently founded Army Engineering School began to train metallurgical engineers, and many Army officers received specialized training abroad. And in 1934, General Pedro Aurélio Góes Monteiro, a former tenente leader, urged Vargas to place the small existing national steel industry under government ownership.[22] Few senior officers were prepared to follow the talkative Góes down the road to statism; nevertheless, the military establishment, by the early 1930's, had assumed a prominent though not yet predominant policy-making role in the government's steel plans.

Here was the source of national regeneration, military preparedness, and government intervention in the economy, which gave impetus to economic nationalism as a modernizing ideology within the armed forces. By 1937 the Army in particular, as a national institution, was determined to find a realistic alternative to small-scale domestic steel production and to build a base for national economic self-sufficiency in the event of war or blockade. And though the military officers concerned with industrial development were not united in opposing Farquhar, they did agree that an immediate solution was imperative.[23]

In the meantime, Farquhar argued effectively for his "railroad solution," and from 1931 to 1935 his views were upheld in four of the five official reports on Itabira and the steel problem that reached Vargas's desk.[24] In 1935, the President appeared to sponsor Farquhar's program—he at least submitted it to Congress as a government bill—but he did not press for a resolution, and the debates dragged on inconclusively until the Estado Nôvo coup closed Congress in November 1937. So long as Farquhar had no financial backing, there was no need for Vargas to link his name with the controversial project.

Therefore, in 1937 Itabira still dominated Brazilian thinking on the iron ore and steel problems, but Farquhar was far from being able to line up the massive financial backing that might have won over the nationalist opposition. However, one more facet of the complex steel issue remains unexplored: How did Brazilian entrepreneurs themselves propose to solve the problem?

Many plans were drawn up after 1930, but all of them depended on large government subsidies, which were not available and/or were based on uncertain technical processes. Both these drawbacks defeated José Bento Monteiro Lobato, the publicist, who hoped in 1931 to interest Brazilian private capital and the government in a new American process for direct ore reduction. Spurned by the government, Monteiro Lobato turned to an even riskier industry: petroleum exploration. The usual problems of coal, capital, and transportation remained unsolved, even in the more important proposals.

How to reconcile a large modern plant with existing iron and steel interests was a major part of the steel problem. Spokesmen for the domestic industry claimed that an efficient operation based on coking coal would ruin them. The issue was neatly posed by Alexandre Siciliano Junior, a Paulista coffee grower with interests in metallurgical plants based on scrap. Itabira, Siciliano wrote Vargas, was "a state within a state," and a threat to all existing interests that did not meet the military requirement of self-sufficiency. The alternative to Farquhar was government intervention. Siciliano proposed the establishment of a 150,000-ton government plant at Juiz de Fora, Minas Gerais, to produce steel ingots for existing rolling mills in Rio, Minas, and São Paulo. The government cokery he projected for Entre Rios (Rio de Janeiro state) would use imported coal initially, then Brazilian coal to supply coke for the steelworks, illuminating gas to neighboring cities, and by-products for explosives. There was no future in steel manufacture based on charcoal, he concluded. Nonetheless, the government plant would not compete with existing blast furnaces; these might produce high-grade iron for special steels. In effect, the State's role was to coordinate and expand on, but not supplant, the existing industry.[25]

Siciliano, in short, placed the burden of producing coke from Santa Catarina coal and of building the steel plant on the government. German interests, as mentioned, examined Siciliano's plan in 1934–35, but nothing came of it. Aside from financial problems there were other weaknesses in the plan: the separation of coking facilities from the steel plant, which ran against the modern concept of integrating all operations at one location, and the dependence on a notably inefficient branch line of the Central into Minas Gerais.

Henrique Lage, the coal and shipping magnate, proposed a private solution based on what he called the formula "coal-ore-ships." In August 1923, he sent President Bernardes a memorandum setting forth a plan to form a national steel consortium from five member companies of his industrial group. The consortium would build two steel plants, one of 120,000 tons capacity for rolled steel at Gandarella (Santa Barbara, Minas Gerais), the other of 30,000 tons for special steel at Niteroi, across the bay from Rio de Janeiro. Both plants would use coal from the Lage mines in Santa Catarina. In return for establishing the plants Lage wanted regal subsidies, which amounted to having the Treasury modernize his coal operations and develop his extensive but as yet untapped Gandarella ore deposits. Furthermore, both areas required extensive railroad construction with federal funds. "By carrying out the consortium's entire plan," he claimed, "the Brazilian government will do a great deal to favor economic independence and national defense, and without any monopoly or ore export."[26] One year later he readily adjusted his aims to Bernardes's steel program.

In 1936, Lage revived the consortium plan, only this time the capital for equipment was to come from iron ore exports. Thus he proposed to the National Security Council a small charcoal-based steelworks at Gandarella, a larger plant at Antonina, Paraná, using local ores and Santa Catarina coal to produce initially 150 tons a day of rails, plates, and sections, and another works on the Ilha da Vianna, at his shipyard in Niteroi, using electric steel furnaces and pig iron from Gandarella. He foresaw a combined yearly steel production of 150,000 tons. However, capacity could easily be expanded up to 500,000 tons to meet defense needs. Lage claimed he had found an "entirely Brazilian solution," and in 1938, after informing Vargas and the Security Council once again of his plans, he began building at Antonina.[27]

However ambitious, Lage's plans were not economically well founded, for they were based on coal of unknown quality, they were undercapitalized, and they depended on poor railroads. Furthermore, the Antonina site was far from consumer markets, and the ores there were unstudied. Yet the Lage program was important, if only as an example of the way industrialists tried to operate within the State. Not only were his existing coal and shipping operations already subsidized, but also the Gandarella mine along with his entire industrial empire was heavily mortgaged to the Bank of Brazil. Further evidence of his power is seen in the fact that Euvaldo Lodi, president of CNI, was director of the Gandarella Company, and Lage himself owned nearly 80 per cent of the Santa Catarina coal fields. When this flamboyant entrepreneur died in 1941, he willed his industrial empire to the nation that had so generously subsidized it.

The only practical alternative to Itabira between the wars was proposed and carried out by Belgian representatives of a Belgo-Luxemburgian holding company known as Aciéries Réunies de Burback-Eich-Dudelange (ARBED). In 1921, they informed Governor Bernardes that a large plant could be founded in Minas with charcoal fuel, thus avoiding the logic of Farquhar's plan to export iron ore for foreign coal. Their site at Monlevade, between Belo Horizonte and the Vitória a Minas terminus near Itabira, was well located in the midst of large forest reserves and near the ore, but construction was delayed until rail service was completed to Belo Horizonte in 1934 by the federal government. In the meantime, they formed the Belgo-Mineira Company with some local capital participation, and during the 1920's they operated a small plant at Sabará. Efficient and well-directed, Belgo-Mineira cultivated excellent relations with Bernardes and the Belo Horizonte business community, which was represented on the company's board. After 1931, the Army supported Monlevade as an essential self-sufficient defense industry and asked Vargas to complete the rail link. And in 1938 production began at the 100,000-ton plant, which is still the world's largest charcoal-based integrated steelworks.

By 1940, Belgo-Mineira dominated the Brazilian steel industry. In that year, Sabará and Monlevade together produced 85,655 tons of ingot steel out of a total national output of 141,201 tons, and in rolled steel Monlevade alone turned out 95,556 of the 135,293 tons domestically produced.[28] Monlevade, however, was at best a partial answer to rising demand, for it did not produce the heavy steel products on which shipping, the railroads, and the construction industry depended.

Although preeminent, Belgo-Mineira was careful to unify its objectives with the other Brazilian iron and steel manufacturers, which also expanded in the 1930's. It controlled substantial ore reserves in its own right, but was concerned primarily with steel production rather than ore exports. Thus, from 1921 to 1938 the company fought tenaciously against the Farquhar railroad plan to develop the Rio Doce Valley. To protect the Monlevade plant against a more advantageously located coastal steelworks was a long-standing objective.[29] Together with the other small producers, Belgo-Mineira joined with Euvaldo Lodi to form an industrywide association in 1931 to set prices and regulate competition. That this constituted a steel trust was denied by the industry: "The most that can be said is that an accord exists among steel plants to protect the industry by means of common sales prices and production quotas."[30] Yet the association also lobbied against Itabira and paid some blast furnaces not to operate. The growing steel industry was an important national resource in depression times and in the event of war, but it could not keep pace with domestic needs. Nor was the new Monlevade plant an alternative to the old, expensive domestic steel producers; rather it was fitted into the overall objectives of the whole industry.

In 1937, therefore, a new formula for large-scale steel manufacture was still elusive. Looking forward to the day when Brazil would become a steel-exporting nation and an industrial power was a national pastime, but the basic options remained the same as in 1920. Ore and steel could be joined in a king solution, or the Farquhar railroad plan could be followed in order to create the right economic conditions for founding a steelworks in the Rio Doce Valley. Farquhar counted many well-connected businessmen, financiers, and publishers in his camp, but many powerful interests, including several military officers, opposed him. Still undecided in 1937, the Vargas government was under mounting pressure from the public and from the armed forces to "do something."

Beyond the welter of opinion and argument, however, one assumption predominated in the highest administrative councils. Regional solutions based on using charcoal fuel were inadequate; the steel problem had to be solved as a national problem. Moreover, the situation had recently been altered by boom conditions in the European ore market. Beginning in 1935, European rearmament was creating a strong demand for Brazilian ore. Thus conditions were ripe for a new solution, and the Army was determined to establish a steelworks as one of its primary goals in the Estado Nôvo.

Placing the steel problem in State hands was central to the administrative program by which Vargas and the military hoped to achieve economic progress under a regime of political order, the Estado Nôvo. Even before the November 1937 coup d'etat, Vargas had decided that in order to avoid choosing among competing interests, he favored a government steel solution.[1] But it was one thing for the President to set guidelines, quite another for the government, which had barely started to coordinate its new powers, to implement them. Until 1940, moreover, there was no single policy; rather there were many possible lines of action, and the ministers followed up their own leads, each attempting to find a solution.

In February 1938, Vargas publicly announced three possible approaches to the steel problem. A steelworks might be built by the State, either with foreign capital or with earnings from ore exports; by the State and Brazilian private investors; or by private Brazilian companies with their own and foreign capital, under State control. Furthermore, Vargas called pointedly for a simultaneous solution to the ore export tangle and to a steelworks that followed German or North American lines. Thus he revived the old dream of trading ore for a steel plant, and he left no doubt regarding the most probable bidders. Ostensibly, he opened up the issue to public debate and solicited advice from all interested parties. This was good politics. In fact, he waited for some foreign steel company to tip its hand.[2]

Overseas, there was an improved industrial climate, marked by European recovery, rearmament, and industrial expansion. Military requirements and self-sufficiency were being stressed in locating and developing steel industries, and the older liberal arguments of economic specialization and the division of labor lost ground. Noteworthy in the State-sponsored steelworks of Germany, Turkey, Japan, and the Soviet Union were the emphasis on defense needs and the prominent role assigned to military managers and engineers. Closer to home, the military in Argentina, Colombia, and Chile were calling for national steel plants. Now the Brazilians joined this world trend.

Brazil's bargaining position was greatly strengthened as a result of these events. Until 1937, steel companies were generally reluctant to disturb established markets or to assist in developing "unnatural" industries among steel-importing nations. Now projects like the Brazilian steelworks were becoming internationally respectable. Moreover, the steel companies were backed by governments that were experimenting with the new and unfamiliar politics of foreign aid. German and United States firms were attracted by Brazil's large internal market and ore reserves; their governments were prepared to bolster strategic and political interests with industrial credits.

But although this situation allowed Vargas freedom to maneuver among the great powers, he was not concerned with foreign policy initiatives. Rather, his political skills were engaged in balancing factions within his own government. The economic nationalists, especially the Army, wanted to trade iron ore to Europe—principally to Germany, on compensation—for a steel mill and railroad equipment, whereas Foreign Minister Oswaldo Aranha, with the support of pro-American business groups and a few key individuals such as Valentim Bouças, tried to combat German economic and political penetration by lining up United States credits for the equipment. Aranha's domestic position was weak, but he appeared to have the President's confidence and his support for the traditional policy of close relations with the United States. Largely because of Army pressures, but also in part because of the new opportunities being presented in the United States and Germany, and surely because of his own growing interest in the steel question, Vargas had committed himself politically to resolving the problem. Which domestic faction would win out? Which steel policy would attract the best foreign offer?

As ambassador to Washington from 1934 to 1937, Aranha had discussed Brazil's iron ore and steel problems with American government officials and industrial leaders. These informal talks convinced him that American interest existed and could be encouraged. Aranha must have discovered the real state of Farquhar's financial prospects, and he must have communicated his misgivings to United States officials. For as early as 1935 he reported to Vargas that an American group (unspecified) wanted to carry out the Farquhar plan, after "reducing it to reasonable proportions."[3] And by late 1937 conversations had begun with the Export-Import Bank on ways to end the Itabira impasse. In October, the Bank's president (Warren Lee Pierson) informed Aranha that he wanted to begin a major effort in Brazil, that is, to greatly increase credits for American industrial goods, including long-term financing for equipment used in Brazilian public works projects. Writing home his impressions, Aranha advised: "I think the steel problem can be solved with these people's help, once our government takes charge of the matter and assumes responsibility for the projects."[4] But the abrupt imposition of an authoritarian government in November, the suspension of Aranha's own debt plan, and the renewal of world depression caused a temporary cooling of United States interest. Aranha had made a promising start, however, and Vargas incorporated his findings into the aforementioned February 1938 speech.

In 1937, a study of the Brazilian steel problem carried out by United States engineers in behalf of DuPont interests, who had $20 million they wanted to invest abroad, yielded favorable results.[5] Analysis of the Brazilian market revealed that a plant of 200,000 tons capacity could produce all the $48 million worth of steel, raw materials, and simple manufactures then being imported. Furthermore, a modern, coke-based plant could easily produce the 75,000 tons of rails that Brazil needed immediately, as well as structural steel for construction, steel plates for the Navy, and tinplate to start a national canning industry.

Consistent with United States practice, the experts advised a plant location close to water supplies, good transportation, and consumer markets. Thus the economic indicators pointed to a site on the coast, perhaps at Rio or Vitória. Surprisingly, it was decided that the Central do Brasil, when improved, could support a modern steel mill at Rio and, in addition, haul enough ore to compensate for having to buy coal from abroad. (Most Brazilians, it should be noted, agreed with Farquhar that the Central could not economically service a large plant; the Vitória a Minas route was far superior.) Disappointingly, Brazilian coal was declared unsuitable, and though the experts realized that imported coal endangered the goal of self-sufficiency, they saw no alternative; standby charcoal-based blast furnaces could be built for use in the event of a wartime cutoff. Private Brazilian capital participation was strongly recommended. In fact, total cost estimates were modestly set at $18 million, with $10 million in dollars for equipment, and the remainder in milreis for the plant, the industrial town, rail connections, and mining operations.[6]

Except for the problem of coal, the DuPont report was remarkably optimistic on every aspect of Brazilian steel manufacture. The study embodied modern location theory and reflected the current nationalistic concern for self-sufficiency, defense needs, and Brazilian capital participation. But it obviously did not satisfy those nationalists, chiefly in the Army, who demanded government control, if not an outright statist solution.

The DuPont Corporation, Aranha, and Warren Pierson of the Export-Import Bank may have been exploring ways to finance the Rio Doce Valley solution (without Farquhar) just as Vargas and the Army were planning the Estado Nôvo coup. Whatever the location—Rio on the Central do Brasil or Vitória on the Vitória a Minas—elements in the military were opposed to turning over control of a key industry like steel to foreign interests. This was another reason why Vargas, even before the coup, wanted to place steel under State control. Clearly, the President was under heavy pressure from the Army for a government plant, for on December 6 he told Aranha that Pierson would be welcome to discuss any large public project, as for example expropriation of the Farquhar-controlled Vitória a Minas in conjunction with a State steelworks.[7] It seems probable that DuPont was not sufficiently interested or was not prepared to accept these terms; in any case, the project fell through.

In the early years of the Estado Nôvo, the nationalists were divided ideologically between those who would regulate the investment of foreign capital and those who would eliminate any direct foreign participation in mining and metallurgy.[8] Since the building of the steel plant depended on foreign finance and technology, the entire steel problem was affected by this cleavage. Several conflicting laws were passed, raising doubts at home and abroad about the legal status of foreign companies, the government's intentions, and even Vargas's ability to manage his Army-backed regime.

The nationalization of mines, power resources, and "industries considered basic or essential to the economic or military defense of the nation" was an important provision of the new constitution promulgated in 1937. This was interpreted to mean ownership by Brazilian nationals, and possible government control of the steel industry. All usage of subsoil wealth was reserved for Brazilians, or companies with Brazilian shareholders. However, in Decree Law 66 (December 14, 1937) the legal definition of "Brazilian" was modified almost immediately. International legal practice was followed in order to declare that foreigners could be considered juridically Brazilian; thus aliens could hold stock in and direct mining companies that were organized under Brazilian laws. Here, in short, was a basis for foreign investment in a steelworks.

The extreme nationalists, however, would not tolerate investment by outsiders in critical areas like steel and mineral production. Throughout 1939 they gained headway, until the 1940 Mining Code prohibited foreigners from owning or investing in subsoil resources or steel companies using domestic raw materials. This Code, in turn, was softened sufficiently by decrees in 1941 to allow foreign capital back into these areas. However tangled, the mining laws were in general less rigidly conceived than the laws passed at the same time barring foreigners from the fields of petroleum exploration and refining (these are discussed in Chapters 7 and 8). More was at stake than slogans or aspirations. The conflicting legislation reflected a basic struggle to determine whether the nation should develop its heavy industry in cooperation with private foreign capital, principally from the United States, or, for defense purposes, take the road to an iron ore and steel autarchy.

General João Mendonça Lima, the Minister of Transport, was the leader of those who favored statism. This career officer from Rio Grande do Sul had fought for Vargas in 1930, then was active in the tenente movement, and later had the thankless job of directing the problem-ridden Central do Brasil. Without having been supplied any new equipment, rails, or adequate spare parts since 1929, the railroad, except for its recently electrified suburban lines, could not meet the increasing demands for service in Brazil's economic heartland as well as haul ever increasing tonnages of iron ore and manganese after 1934. In desperation, Mendonça Lima allowed ore exporters to furnish their own private rolling stock in exchange for reductions in freight rates, which were already below cost. But in 1937 the railroad carried 400,000 tons of ore with difficulty, and it was estimated that the Central's users daily requested 500 to 800 more cars of all types than it could supply. Thus in September 1937 the harassed director advanced his own king solution to ore exports, steel, and the Central do Brasil.

Mendonça Lima estimated that to meet current demands the railroad needed a minimum of 500,000 contos in new equipment and improved trackage. Although he agreed with Farquhar that the Rio Doce route was best suited for large exports of ore, he did not think that Brazil could wait any longer for the Itabira solution. Therefore, he proposed to export iron ore over the Central to Rio for shipment to Europe on a crash basis in return for coal, railroad equipment, and a steel plant.[9] The mechanics of this proposed operation, which would be State-run, were left to Paulo H. Denizot, an iron ore exporter in his own right. Denizot's plan for a government ore monopoly was ready in January 1938, and soon thereafter Mendonça Lima, the new Transport Minister, made overtures to German steel firms. In effect, this policy was also represented in Vargas's February speech.

The guidelines established by Mendonça Lima and elaborated by Denizot were based on government ownership of all ore reserves along the Central, and eventual yearly exports of 15 million tons. From surveys of the three largest properties, Denizot concluded that the as yet undeveloped Itabira and Gandarella (Lage) deposits were less immediately useful for expropriation than was Casa da Pedra, an efficient mine on the broad-gage Central with reserves of one half billion tons. The German owners, A. Thun and Company, controlled the largest ore-exporting operation in Brazil, and in 1937 Thun shipped 300,000 tons in its private fleet of 300 cars. Mendonça Lima urged Vargas to make Casa da Pedra the nucleus of a new Mining Service under the Transport Ministry. For good measure, he added, the Mora da Mina manganese deposits ought to be acquired from U.S. Steel; the manganese would thus be secured for the future Brazilian steel industry and foreigners would be prevented from making fantastic profits on Brazilian ore.[10]

The Transport Minister was not alone in thinking that great revenues would almost immediately accrue from the European ore market and that the State should take the profits. Juarez Távora, the old tenente leader, supported Mendonça Lima's position, as did many other nationalists in and out of the military. However, implementation of the project hinged on an initial currency or bond issue of 100,000 contos, which Artur da Souza Costa, the orthodox Minister of Finance, would not support. Paulo Denizot claimed this amount would be amortized within six years, leaving 80 per cent of the profits (814,000 contos total) for electrifying and double-tracking the Central to Belo Horizonte; the steel plant might be financed with the same profits. Denizot's profit margin for acquiring this equipment was projected from estimated earnings on exports, which were to increase from one and a half million tons in 1939 to seven million tons in 1944. If forty thousand tons were exported each month in 1939, he argued, then the profits on ore, which brought 64$000 a ton f.o.b. Rio, would be 31$000 a ton. Mining, transport, and loading costs were calculated at a low 33$000 per ton. But as Pedro Rache of the Bank of Brazil pointed out, this large profit margin depended on lowering the Central's freight rates from 44$ooo to 18$ooo a ton. Denizot was asking one government agency to subsidize another's operation. Hence the project was economically unsound.[11]

Had a European steel company accepted Mendonça Lima's plan, it is problematic whether opposition from Souza Costa, a fiscal conservative, Rache, a Farquhar ally, and Aranha could have stopped it. Mendonça Lima held the policy initiative, and in January or February 1938 the German firm of Demag received an enquiry from the Brazilian government. Was the firm interested in constructing steelmaking, rail, port, and mining installations valued at 200 million reichsmarks in return for long-range payments of one million tons a year in iron ore?[12] Was the German government prepared to participate directly?

Demag decided to explore the offer. The German Economics Ministry considered the project "of great economic importance for the future relations of Germany and Brazil," but the Reich's terms were not so generous as to indicate that the plan at that time had high political priority. The German government would not appear as a partner in the contract. And although 50 per cent payment in ore was acceptable, the other half had to be in raw materials of the Ministry's choosing (i.e. cotton), and on a short-term basis. Finally, the project would have to be split into separate parts to give Germany an out or a means of pressuring Brazil in the event of payment problems.[13]

In late March 1938, Demag contacted the Vereinigte Stahlwerke, the largest German steel combine, whose subsidiary, Stahlunion, exported sixty thousand tons of ore in 1937 from its modest Brazilian holdings. Stahlunion was well informed on Mendonça Lima's ore monopoly plan, Souza Costa's opposition, and the fact that the project involving Demag hinged on expropriation of all private properties, including Stahlunion's own deposits.[14] Nonetheless Demag formed an informal consortium with Stahlunion and Krupp. During armaments negotiations with the Brazilian Army in March, Krupp had been willing to build the steelworks in conjunction with shops to service and fabricate artillery. Demag was in fact the leading German contender, but Krupp was well connected in Brazil through its local representative, Olavo Egydio de Souza Aranha of SOINC, whose activities in the German trade are by now familiar.

Any hopes for immediate negotiations with Brazil were dashed in May when the Stahlunion withdrew from the consortium. "According to the unanimous opinion of people familiar with Brazilian conditions," Stahlunion reported, "the political and economic situation in that country is such that this project cannot be pursued from our side." Moreover, the project was considered financially unsound. Since the Central could not carry more than a million tons of ore a year, the profit margin on this amount would not be enough to support interest and amortization payments in a reasonable period of time.[15] The fact that Fritz Thyssen of Vereinigte Stahlwerke was working independently with Farquhar may have influenced the Stahlunion report, although by now Demag itself felt that the whole project was not yet ripe for negotiations. For in the meantime, Mendonça Lima's project had lost headway within Brazil, and the Denizot plan was under fire.

Vargas, in the February 1938 speech that suggested so much but specified so little, had also encouraged a full-dress public debate. He ordered the Federal Technical and Financial Council (CTEF) to examine the issue openly, away from "closed conference rooms and more or less self-interested groups."[16] Organized in the Ministry of Finance, the Council was the counterpart of the once powerful but now defunct Senate Finance Committee. Commercial interests strongly entrenched on the CTEF made it the voice of private enterprise within the corporatist-leaning Estado Nôvo system. The first report was delivered by Pedro Rache, an ally of Farquhar. Thus Itabira was to be debated once more, this time among friends.

Mendonça Lima's crash export project had been based on the assumption of quick profits, but he also believed that until Santa Catarina coal was proved to be both economical and adaptable to blast furnace operations, there was no alternative to exporting ore in return for foreign metallurgical coal. However, recent experiments in the Ministry of Agriculture made the technical outlook for domestic coal seem brighter. Farquhar himself shipped a sample to London, where his long-standing engineering associate, Herman Brassert, returned a favorable verdict. And the CTEF banked heavily on these new hopes for Brazilian coal in its well-publicized report.

Following debates in May and June 1938, the Council reversed recent government guidelines by separating completely large-scale ore exports from the steel plant in their planning. Although Itabira was approved as the best long-term solution, a coastal plant of 200,000 tons capacity was recommended to meet current market needs. This was no victory for any of the recognized king solutions, whether liberal or nationalist; rather, the three current plans for massive ore exports in exchange for imported coal were set aside for an intermediate solution based on both domestic and imported coals.

Both the leading nationalist plans depended on foreign credits but rejected direct foreign investment. One, the Denizot plan, has already been discussed. The other, by Raul Ribeiro da Silva, envisioned a Brazilian company, formed with mixed capital, to export ore, operate a large steelworks in Rio, and modernize the Central.[17] Ribeiro, like Denizot, enjoyed support among the military, but his credentials were weak, and his plan called on the government to participate as a minority partner with private Brazilian groups. Pedro Rache, the CTEF reporter, as much as called the two plans economic monstrosities that were dependent on subsidized freight rates, large government credits, and unrealistic projections of present boom conditions in the European ore market.

However, Rache's own efforts to revive the Itabira king solution (this time with Mineiro equity participation) were rebuffed. Guilherme Guinle, an old foe of Farquhar with steel plans of his own, led the nationalist attack. Itabira would do for Brazil's sovereignty what the Suez Canal had done to Egypt's independence, he said. With their international outlook on business, however, the CTEF councillors did not respond to Guinle. But they had scant expectations for the rapid completion of Farquhar's railroad, the key to Itabira with or without the steel plant; they knew Farquhar's financial prospects were weak. Therefore the Council separated Itabira once and for all (it was thought) from the steel plant, just as it had abandoned ideas of massive ore exports on the Central do Brasil.

Having decided to rely as much as possible on domestic coal, the Council could now logically view the steel plant as a separate operation from ore exports and railroad construction. However, the decision to use domestic coal was still controversial, and there was also disagreement over the plant locations proposed by Rache. He favored a site in Santa Catarina or Paraná, near the southern coal fields, and this was in effect an invitation to Henrique Lage to go ahead with his Antonina steel plant. The majority of the CTEF, however, supported Major Macedo Soares e Silva (the Army technical expert), who suggested a market-oriented site in Rio. In the final report, all three sites were recommended for the immediate solution. However, the Council accepted Rache's judgment that the Rio Doce Valley would have to be developed first, with private foreign capital, before the right economic conditions to support a really large steel industry would prevail.[18]

The chorus of objections from many sources was immediate, the clamor of adverse publicity was prolonged. Separating ore from steel was highly controversial: "Why should we abandon our trump card?" Souza Aranha, Krupp's representative, wrote to Vargas. Domestic groups like Souza Aranha's own were circling the Itabira behemoth like sharks near a dying whale.[19] The steel plant issue was now a *cause célèbre*, public opinion was fully mobilized, and Vargas sensed political danger in a false step. In August 1938 he tabled the CTEF report, announcing that he had first to hear from the Foreign Trade Council (CFCE), and then the military-dominated National Security Council before making up his mind. The Rache report was a political, not to mention psychological, dead letter. Yet the bypassed CTEF had been a useful sounding board. "Now that all the interests have shown themselves in public," Vargas said privately, "we can move on to a real solution."[20]

Meanwhile, in Minas Gerais, the Itabira controversy broke out anew. Although Rache had suggested that Mineiros might take a 40 to 50 per cent interest in Farquhar's mining company, this idea was repugnant to those Mineiro nationalists in the Bernardes tradition who in general rejected any foreign profiteering from the ore, and who in particular opposed Farquhar. Their old dream of industrialization through ore exports, of a steel plant at Aymorés, and of Brazilian control over the Rio Doce Valley had been kept alive since the 1920's. In June 1938, the Commercial Association of Minas Gerais, under banker José de Magalhães Pinto (later UDN leader, Governor of Minas, and Foreign Minister), commissioned a project in which these old ideas were adjusted to new realities.

Mineiro business and industrial leaders wanted a simultaneous ore and steel solution, in which almost all the capital (700,000 contos) would come from government subscription, but the goal was private control through a small issue of common stock. This pattern of private groups relying upon government support is by now familiar. However, in reviving the old Rio Doce Valley king solution, the Mineiros added some new elements. Especially noteworthy was their direct appeal to the Army General Staff to order a national solution, and their justification of the Aymorés site on strategic grounds, such as the nearby forest reserves for emergency charcoal fuel, and the remoteness from air attack. But even more important was their proposal to tap the new federal Pension Funds and Social Security Institutes for investment capital. This revived Rio Doce project found little favor outside Minas Gerais, but it indicated current thinking.[21]

In criticizing the Mineiro project, one engineer wrote Vargas that the ore export problem was essentially an international one, and could not be considered narrowly from a supposedly Brazilian point of view. Nor did this critic believe that the armed forces had a role in heavy industry.[22] To be sure, the appeal to the military for assistance in the steel problem was controversial among private groups. However, the German example of rapid steel expansion under the Army was compelling. Assis Chateaubriand used the columns of his influential *O Jornal* to discuss the rapidly built

Hermann Goering Works at Linz, Austria. Goering did not lose time hearing commissions or collecting reports, he said. "How many times has Mr. Getúlio Vargas shown Goering's powers of decision in matters of such overriding importance as steel?" Brazil should heed the German lesson, he concluded—Vargas must close the debate and solve the iron ore and steel problem.[23] Chateaubriand's argument was not lost on the Brazilian armed forces. Though important decision makers in military and business circles did not agree on the extent and form of government intervention, they called on the administration to "do something" without delay.

The idea of tapping the semipublic Funds and Institutes appears to have become current among several important groups by mid-1938. Souza Aranha, for example, mentioned it to Vargas in August. This was a "brilliant solution," said one member of the Rio de Janeiro Commercial Association. The State might draw off some capital from the Funds (i.e., de-capitalize them) without jeopardizing the security for which the workers paid low dues. Their indirect and involuntary participation could be justified as a patriotic act.[24] In short, a new source of public finance had been discovered.

Finally, the Mineiro report echoed the widely held conviction that iron ore exports and the steelworks were unalterably linked together in the industrial destiny of Brazil. In turn, this sentiment lent validity to the nationalists' position, according to which Brazil must control, if not prohibit outright, foreign participation in the ore export sector.

Yielding to the inevitable in July 1938, Farquhar offered once more to construct a steelworks at Santa Cruz. Tenaciously, he continued to fight against increasingly unfavorable odds and a worsening image. His semi-secret ties with Fritz Thyssen appeared sinister to those who feared an imperialist take-over of the iron ore deposits; German statements of colonial ambitions were taken seriously by Brazilians. Aranha, for his part, used Farquhar's German ties as his reason for blocking Itabira, and some military officers genuinely feared Farquhar's railroad would be used by an invading German army. Many writers picked up the theme: "Mr. Farquhar is an intelligent, cultivated old Gentleman," said one critic.

"He could go to Europe. His first class ticket on the most luxurious boat would be paid for him. He would be entrusted with a letter to his superiors saying that he had fulfilled his duty, and that if he had not been successful, it was because Brazil, unfortunately, is not a nation of cretins."[25] If the language was excessive, the fears it expressed were real. Farquhar hoped to allay these apprehensions by forming a Brazilian mining company and by balancing German participation with British and Export-Import Bank funds.[26] However, his financial prospects in the United States still were not bright, and his plans were strongly opposed by the military, who now took direct command over steel policy.

General Mendonça Lima coordinated the next, most directly military phase of the decision-making process, which lasted from late 1938 to February 1939. The Foreign Trade Council, where the steel question now rested at Vargas's request, acted as an administrative cover for the Army. After minimal debate, the Council supported Mendonça Lima's plan to solve the ore and steel problems simultaneously, and upheld his poor evaluation of domestic coal. One year before, in March 1938, the councillors had assembled in full plenary session to sanction the Army's petroleum plan (see Chapter 7). Vargas himself had manipulated the CFCE to build a consensus for the government's trade policies. Now he called upon the Council's technocrats, bureaucrats, and interest group representatives to legitimize the Army's steel plan and thus to share political responsibility for it. As with petroleum, so with steel: again the councillors were asked to approve a special report drawn up secretly by men acting formally under the President but in fact responsible to the military.

General Amaro Soares Bittencourt and Admiral Ary Parreiras, an ex-tenente leader, presided over the CFCE's special commission on steel, which in February 1939 voted to monopolize ore exports as the precondition to founding a State steelworks. Like the National Petroleum Council, which controlled the oil industry, a new Brazilian Steel Institute would regulate as a public utility the domestic steel and mining sectors, with the latter passing under State ownership. Within these general guidelines, the special commission's immediate objective was to establish the steel plant.

The aims of their project were (1) to export two million tons of iron and manganese ores yearly via the Central and a government ore fleet, in payment for European coal and equipment, (2) to found a plant in Rio de Janeiro, based on coke, that would produce 180,000 and later 300,000 tons of iron and steel, (3) to condemn all foreign ore concessions, including Itabira. As for location, the Commission seriously considered the Paraíba Valley, an alternate to Rio de Janeiro that lay beyond the effective range of naval gunfire and midway between the large Rio and São Paulo markets. In fact, several government-controlled steel parks were envisioned. To clear the air, they disavowed both the Ribeiro and Lage steel plans, as well as a plan proposed by the old steel pioneer Trajano Saboia Viriato de Medeiros. Foreign steel concessions also were condemned.

This project, for what amounted to military operation of the steel plant and State ore company, was vulnerable at several points, however. It depended on large exports over exposed sea lanes; it depended on foreign coal and could not be self-sufficient in the event of war; and it depended on long-term ore exports to finance major equipment purchases. Furthermore, the domestic capital base was still uncertain. To be sure, in January 1939 it was announced that at least 50,000 contos yearly from the new five-year development plan would be set aside for the steel plant. Outright public ownership was preferred, but with capital in short supply, the commission recognized that the venture might have to be organized with the state governments, or as a semipublic mixed corporation, with 51 per cent government control.[27]

Understandably, Vargas and the administration as a whole were reluctant to commit themselves to the Army's solution, and in April 1939 Vargas passed the CFCE report on to the National Security Council for further study. Farquhar, whose own vital interests were at stake, was a keen observer of the opinions that divided the government. Thus in May he wrote his New York associate:

In general the rank and file of officers in the Army and Navy . . . want to use [their] control of all iron ore exports to give the Government funds to build a military steel plant. . . . Some higher officials especially in the Navy accompany these views. The Minister of Finance, the majority of the cabinet do not wish to have the Government involved in expense of building or troubles of operation of the Steel industry with the incidental management of ore exports. Those favoring the Government plant point to Germany, which with [its] own capital and own raw materials goes ahead so fast, and maintain that Brazil, with raw materials, certainly can do the same without foreign loans by trading raw materials for equipment.[28]

This accurately described nationalist viewpoints, especially among the armed forces. Within the highest governmental circles, Farquhar observed, the nationalistic current was considerably stronger regarding the steelworks than regarding the ore monopoly scheme backed by the Mendonça Lima faction.[29] In short, the steel plant had priority over any ore export project.

Farquhar worked out another plan, which included a plant of 150,000 to 300,000 tons (designed by his friend Brassert) using imported coal, a rebuilt Vitória a Minas, and mining operations. This time the entire Brazilian operation was to be run by a national company, but financed by an American counterpart company. In February 1939 Farquhar sounded out the Army Chief of Staff, General Góes Monteiro, who was encouraging, and then he drew up a formal proposal.[30] Little did the persistent Yankee realize that in the meantime the government had decided to offer Itabira to the highest bidder. Though they were still divided on the wisdom of seeking German or United States financing for the steel plant, Aranha, many military men, and some state interventors (governors) agreed that Farquhar had to go. Did they know that Farquhar through Alexander Malozemoff, his New York partner, was also sounding out the Argentines on purchasing Itabira ore? Evidently the ministers agreed among themselves to discuss Itabira with potential foreign investors as long as it was clearly understood that the controversial mines would be operated under government control. In its eagerness to solve the steel question, however, the government was prepared to discuss ore exports via the Central line as an equally feasible alternative to Itabira. This Aranha informed Washington in February 1939.[31] Once more, Brazilian ore was being used as bait.

Suddenly the range of options broadened as it had not since President Epitácio Pessôa's visit to New York in 1919. The course of Brazil's future steel industry was being decided not in Rio de

Janeiro but abroad, where government missions under Major Macedo Soares e Silva and Oswaldo Aranha were visiting foreign capitals and the big steel companies.

Having left for Europe under Mendonça Lima's orders in January 1939, Macedo Soares studied local ore markets and solicited proposals from several steel companies to design, finance, and operate the Brazilian State steelworks along lines established by the Army-sponsored CFCE report. In Germany, he renewed his former contacts with Demag, and also talked with representatives of Gutehoffnungshuette, Stahlunion, and Krupp. The first two firms drew up plans and cost estimates for a classic, integrated plant at Rio. Krupp, on the other hand, insisted on an experimental direct ore reduction process, the Renn method, requiring little coke and no blast furnaces.[32] But it was Brassert, the British engineer then also dealing with Farquhar, who made the most attractive offer.

On the basis of Brassert's experience in building State plants in Turkey, Italy, and German Austria (the Hermann Goering Works), the firm was well qualified, in Macedo Soares's view, to design— and to run initially—Brazil's own plant. He thought the government should first contract with Brassert, then organize a steel company, including leading Brazilian financiers on the directorate. The capital, all public, was to come from two sources: the domestic stock in paper milreis, drawn from the Pension Plans and Institutes, and a hard currency loan raised abroad. Turkey had borrowed from British banks to finance its steel plant; so might the Brazilian company borrow the $15 million needed for imported equipment as estimated by Brassert and the Germans. Having no direct foreign investment, the company would avoid the foreign payments burden once it retired the loan, and Brazilians could control the new industry.[33]

By training, outlook, and experience, Macedo Soares preferred to do business with a Western European firm. In late April, however, as he prepared to recommend this program, he received new orders from Mendonça Lima to break off talks in Europe and to begin substantive negotiations in New York with the United States Steel Corporation. As a direct result of Aranha's own mission, Vargas and his cabinet had decided to look toward the United States for the long-sought steel solution.

Having been invited by President Roosevelt in late 1938, Aranha left Rio in February 1939 to discuss a wide range of topics having to do with Brazilian–United States political and economic relations. Among other things, such as financial and debt problems, Aranha brought up the possibility of United States government credits for raw materials development and the steel plant. Aranha informed the Export-Import Bank of his government's probable intention to cancel the Itabira concession and to build a State steel plant. Brazil, he said, was counting on United States assistance in founding the steelworks. Otherwise, it would be forced to turn toward Germany, which it did not wish to do.[34] This line of argument was effective. Aranha won a tentative commitment from the Export-Import Bank to finance equipment for a national iron and steel solution; in May, Macedo Soares sailed for New York to confer with U.S. Steel.

As far as can be determined, Aranha attempted to rekindle DuPont's interest in the steelworks, but finding that company reluctant to participate, he turned to U.S. Steel. Valentim Bouças, writing to Vargas in March, confirmed that corporation's interest in Aranha's proposition and in obtaining ore from the Rio Doce Valley.[35] Apparently the giant American company soon lost interest in anything so grandiose as Itabira, despite the Brazilians' willingness to nationalize Farquhar's properties and options. For as Farquhar learned in April, U.S. Steel was willing to explore possibilities for furnishing foreign exchange and equipment in return for Brazilian ore, but it advised Aranha against a State steel plant and expensive railroad construction in the Rio Doce Valley. Instead it proposed a joint American-Brazilian company to operate the steel plant and to develop Brazil's resources.[36]

U.S. Steel's experts exhibited a fresh approach to the old problems of coal, capital, and transportation. The corporation had been impressed with the DuPont studies, and its own engineers reported that Brazilian coal was adequate for blast furnace operations. Following technical discussions with Macedo Soares in May, U.S.

Steel decided to send an eight-man technical mission to Brazil under Heman Greenwood, president of its export subsidiary.

Brazilian policy shifted toward U.S. Steel, accordingly, but not without causing some friction between Aranha and the military. Aranha, who reported directly to President Vargas, favored an American private company. Macedo Soares, who was in New York and had limited authority, was skeptical: "It is possible that we will derive some benefit from this collaboration, but we must be cautious."[37] An entire year would be lost if, after making its technical study, the corporation decided not to go ahead. And while the Army Major talked to the Americans about limiting U.S. Steel's equity participation to a maximum of 30 per cent in a State company, he was uneasily aware that U.S. Steel probably wanted to run its own operation in collaboration with some private Brazilian groups. "If this is it," he wrote Mendonça Lima, "our objectives will be defeated. Collaborating to found a key industry is admissible, but it is imperative to safeguard Brazil's economic future by limiting this collaboration to the bare minimum, and by avoiding complete domination."[38]

Thus Aranha returned to Brazil brimming with optimism; Macedo Soares was less enthusiastic, but he too thought the steel project was about to begin. Aranha, who had Vargas's support, was confident that American capital, management, and technical expertise would crown the long-held dream with success. For his part, Macedo Soares pointed out that there was an alternative to U.S. Steel; he was prepared to go ahead with the technical aspects, if Vargas thought the plant could be financed. Various interests, as always, would be opposed to it, but "we have every means to neutralize those groups which, until now have blocked a rational solution." Above all, he concluded, "it is time to build."[39]

Arriving in June 1939, the U.S. Steel experts under Greenwood studied ore resources, the Santa Catarina coal fields, possible plant locations, and transportation and market conditions. Macedo Soares coordinated a group of Brazilian experts with the American engineers, and in October a joint report was issued, providing a comprehensive solution to steelmaking under difficult Brazilian conditions.* In its economic and technical aspects, the United States Steel project was well conceived. Brazilian coal was thoroughly studied and found suitable for blast furnace operations. This conclusion was important. Although the Greenwood mission originally recommended using only foreign coal at first, and then mixing in domestic coal when the right balance was determined, it was decided that Santa Catarina coal might be used alone. Thus in the event of war, continuous steel production, though expensive, would be assured; the primary military goal of self-sufficiency was attainable.

After a comprehensive study of railroad conditions, the experts decided to base the U.S. Steel project on the Central rather than to rely on the Rio Doce route. An improved and better managed Central, they reasoned, could carry all the 650,000 tons per year of inland raw materials required by the steelworks, and at the same time the railroad could handle enough ore from the Paraopeba Valley to compensate for foreign coal. Furthermore, it was established that the money was better spent on the vital Central as a matter of national policy than it was in reconstructing the Vitória a Minas line. That Belgo-Mineira was already operating a large plant in the Rio Doce Valley region was considered another good reason for relying on the Central. In short, the two steel operations would not compete.

* At Mendonça Lima's request, Vargas created the National Steel Commission on August 5, 1939, under Macedo Soares, with João Baptista de Costa Pinto, Plínio Reis de Catanhede, and Joaquim Miguel de Arrojado Lisbôa, a Mineiro engineer, as members. Charged with studying the steel question, they primarily facilitated studies by Greenwood's U.S. Steel experts. Macedo Soares arranged for the Americans to consult with federal and state officials, including representatives of the domestic steel and coal interests. The Mineiros, under State Secretary of Transport João Kubitschek, were apparently very cooperative. After issuing the joint report with Greenwood on October 20, Macedo Soares waited impatiently for U.S. Steel's decision. When this was delayed, his Commission issued its own report on February 29, 1940; it called for implementing the plant designed by U.S. Steel, creating railroad, machine tool, pipe, and boiler plants, and for modernizing the existing mining and coal industries under a National Mines and Metallurgy Council. The Commission did not act on its report, however, since it was soon absorbed into the National Steel Plan (see Chapter 6), with Macedo Soares as Technical Director. Brazil, Comissão Nacional de Siderurgia, *Report* to Mendonça Lima, Feb. 29, 1940, in Presidência Archive, 20327, 1940, AN.

Thus the Federal District near Rio was selected as the best site for construction of the plant. There, at Santa Cruz on the Sepetiba Bay, sea and land transportation services would meet midway between the Santa Catarina coal fields and the ore mines in Minas. The site was market-oriented, it had abundant fresh water, and it was ideally suited for iron ore exports as well as coal return. Furthermore, the production program of basic products, such as rails, shapes, plates, sheets, and tinplate, was carefully drawn up to give minimum interference with existing domestic production. With proper tariff protection, an initial production of 285,000 tons would give a net profit return of 14¾ per cent on invested capital of $35 million.[40]

This solution fulfilled all the economic requirements of large-scale steelmaking. It was designed to conciliate existing producers, to meet military requirements, and to improve existing transportation routes. Furthermore, the steel plant was not necessarily tied to iron ore exports in return for coal and capital. So superior was this solution to Farquhar's most recent plan that, in August 1939, the Itabira concession was cancelled to clear the air.* Henceforth, the problems of steel and iron ore exports were considered by the Brazilian authorities as completely separate.

A company would be organized in Brazil to manage the steelworks, but U.S. Steel would in fact control the operation through the $5 million worth of common stock it would receive in return for equipment. Brazilian private interests, notably Heitor de Carvalho of the Paulista Railway and the Guinle group, planned to subscribe the remaining common stock. Capitalized at $35–40 million, the

---

* Cancellation was a public gesture only, to end support for and rumors about the embattled Yankee speculator's controversial king solution. Farquhar's protests to Brazilian and United States officials obscured the fact that he retained control of the railroad and his option on Itabira properties, the key holdings on which his twenty-year dream to export iron ore was based. In 1942, however, British and American insistence on developing these properties for the war effort led to expropriation. With Export-Import Bank finance, the government's new Rio Doce Valley Company opened the mines, rebuilt the Vitória a Minas, and became the principal ore exporter. Farquhar, though stunned, soon recovered his enthusiasm for Brazilian development and founded a small company, Acesita, to produce special steels in the Rio Doce Valley.

operation required, in addition to common stock, $20 million in equipment loans from the Export-Import Bank and the remainder in bonds from the government Pension Funds.[41]

By November 1939, the proposal was well regarded in the highest Brazilian government circles, and the Greenwood mission returned to the United States for a final decision from the corporation's Finance Committee. President Vargas was enthusiastic about the prospect. It might take Brazil ten or twelve years to carry out the project by itself, he told Greenwood, and the operation would be costly and inefficient.[42]

Nonetheless, the Greenwood mission's proposal did not satisfy those economic nationalists in the armed forces who since 1937 had insisted on government control of the steelworks. They were neither prepared to tolerate U.S. Steel's mining operations in Brazil, nor to accept the fact that the steel plant would be financed in part with foreign equity capital. Within the government, controversy continued. First, in early November, the Minister of Finance turned down an Army suggestion for a one million conto note circulation to finance the steel plant.[43] And then in January 1940—just as the U.S. Steel Finance Committee was making its decision—the Mining Code prohibiting foreign investment in mining and metallurgy was promulgated. U.S. Steel had already made its participation conditional upon substantial modifications in nationalistic Brazilian laws: apparently the corporation insisted that it control the operation, that Brazilian legislation on subsoil rights be changed to protect the corporation's mining properties, and that United States technicians be allowed to work permanently on the steelworks.[44]

The nub of conflict centered on the main purpose of the projected steelworks. Clearly, the nationalists wanted to preserve all development in the metallurgical and mining sectors for Brazilians. Just as clearly, U.S. Steel was attracted by the growing South American steel market and wanted to establish a Brazilian base of operations. Perhaps, like the Hanna Mining Corporation after World War II, it was interested also in large-scale ore exports over the Central to Sepetiba Bay. (As mentioned, the corporation

owned substantial manganese reserves in Minas Gerais.) More
probably, it may have already decided to limit future iron ore export operations to its extensive, but as yet untapped Venezuelan
holdings.

Vargas evidently thought he could satisfy if not reconcile the
two positions. Mendonça Lima, for his part, was willing to accept
the cooperation of U.S. Steel on condition that it was limited to
technical, financial, and managerial assistance. On January 7, 1940,
the Transport Minister publicly supported the plan. Vargas was
willing to discuss the conditions stipulated by the corporation and
there is little doubt that he would have accepted many of them. On
December 30 he announced his approval of the project, leaving the
details for later discussion. Having thus committed himself, Vargas
was shocked to learn in mid-January that the corporation's Finance
Committee had decided to abandon the Brazilian venture outright.

Several explanations for the company's withdrawal were current.
(1) There was a conflict within the company between liberals interested in Brazil's economic potential and conservatives concerned
with preserving existing export markets; for instance, in 1939, U.S.
Steel shipped rails and plates to Brazil which were alone worth $5
million. (2) The Russian invasion of Finnish nickel properties
owned by the company pointed out the dangers of investment
abroad during wartime. (3) The company was financially over-
extended; having recently carried out a vast expansion program at
home, it thus decided to continue its usual policy of not investing
in steelworks abroad. (4) Political considerations intervened, despite the very favorable interest of Vargas, the State Department,
and President Roosevelt.

While the reasons for withdrawal have never been fully clarified,
there was a direct relationship between the corporation's reluctance to invest and the appearance of new exclusionist mining legislation. U.S. Steel must have thought its future plans for steel and
(possibly) iron ore and manganese development in Brazil were
thereby jeopardized. Herbert Feis, the State Department economist, assessed this political aspect as follows: "In part it is the
sense that any large project in Brazil involving important foreign

interests will inevitably sooner or later come under fire, in part the sense of the great uncertainties in Brazilian affairs: these seem to create too great a risk compared with the possible profit."[45] In effect, U.S. Steel voted no confidence in a regime which Washington was most eager to assist.

For once, Vargas's skills for balancing and conciliating differences failed him. Even in the austere Estado Nôvo there was room to maneuver among the laws, and Vargas probably intended to grant most of U.S. Steel's demands. And although officers under Mendonça Lima maintained their nationalist aims, one may speculate that they would have acceded to a compromise in order to secure U.S. Steel's participation. By pulling out, the American company confirmed Macedo Soares's 1939 prognosis, causing Brazil to lose valuable time. Vargas and the Army were indignant. Washington soon learned that Rio expected the United States government "to do something, in light of the Good Neighbor Policy."[46] As Vargas instructed his ambassador in Washington: "Following our traditional policy and trusting the United States, we want to strengthen the Brazilian economy; and we always prefer American capital collaboration. But if we do not find aid in that country, we will take advantage of other possibilities as they arise."[47]

Stung by this setback, the Brazilians were now prepared to take decisive action. In the previous two years, many elements of a successful steel solution had fallen into place: Pension Fund capital, domestic coal, and the Central route. The once dominant king solution mentality was replaced by an overriding desire to establish the steelworks; ore exports were separated definitively from steel manufacture. And though economic nationalists in the armed forces had worked at cross purposes to Vargas and Aranha during the U.S. Steel episode, the military's role in heavy industrial planning was well established. Soon the Volta Redonda plan was to reconcile nationalist demands for State control with the requirements of a modern steel plant.

Volta Redonda was a wartime solution to a complex industrial, political, and defense problem. The U.S. Steel Corporation study of 1939 had pointed the way to a definitive solution. Building from this, the new Brazilian plan included ideological and military considerations. Two primary goals were set for the government steelworks: to attain substantial independence of imported steel products, and to produce steel as economically as possible, given Brazilian conditions. An important secondary aim was to provide a model for developing a new, industrial society. Thus the decision to locate in a decadent coffee region, the Paraíba Valley, was not based on strategic and economic reasons alone—the model industrial town was clearly intended to symbolize State-sponsored social and economic change.

Direct government action did not immediately follow U.S. Steel's withdrawal. Indeed, for several months thereafter Vargas still hoped that an American steel company would contribute capital, know-how, and management, thereby giving Brazilian entrepreneurs the confidence to invest. U.S. Steel, at the urging of Vargas and the State Department, came back into the picture at least three times—in February, July, and December 1940—before hopes for cooperation with it were finally abandoned by the Brazilian authorities.[1]

Other steel companies and engineering firms were invited to study the steel problem. Brassert, Arthur G. McKee, and Wenner-Gren, the Swedish steel and armaments manufacturer, all sent representatives to Brazil in the spring of 1940. Ford, Bacon, and Davis, the American engineering firm, and Bethlehem Steel were approached by the State Department. Even Farquhar considered himself back in the running. In March, Krupp was reported in the Brazilian and American press as eager to construct and finance the plant, but though Krupp was the major arms supplier to Brazil it was not a front runner; Macedo Soares preferred the classical methods of Gutehoffnungshuette and Demag to the direct reduction process Krupp promoted, and his opposition was decisive.[2] So there were several possible lines of action. Vargas and Aranha insisted on first exploring the United States option; the military still leaned toward doing business with Europe.

Vargas was under heavy pressure to get results. European steel imports were halted by the British blockade, and the President's prestige was at stake. To keep things moving, he announced in late February that the Brazilian government would organize a steel company; and on March 4, an Executive Commission under Guilherme Guinle was organized to prepare a definitive national steel plan.* Financing was arranged with Caixa Econômica, the Government Savings Bank (400,000 contos or $20 million), the Pension Funds (50,000 contos or $2.5 million), and the Special Public Works budget (50,000 contos) for a total of $25 million in domestic currency. The Export-Import Bank was approached about the possibility of financing $17 million worth of United States equipment. For its part, the State Department asked the Brazilians to wait while it tried to line up some American private company. In case this approach failed, however, it would discuss support for the Brazilian State plan.[3]

As the spring of 1940 wore on, Vargas's hopes that his government might not have to bear the financial and managerial burden began to fade. Nothing definite was coming from the State Department's effort to interest American firms, and in May he could wait no longer. Having been caught short once before, with U.S. Steel, Vargas now layed Brazil's case on the line to Washington. The gov-

---

* The Executive Commission of the National Steel Plan, with Guinle as president, included two technical experts (who were also the dominant personalities), Ary Frederico Tôrres and Macedo Soares, two engineers, Oscar Weinschenck and Navy Captain Adolfo Martins de Noronha Torrezão, and the Paulista financier, Heitor Freire de Carvalho. The idea of associating prominent financiers with a government company went back at least to 1939 and the Army-sponsored special commission of the CFCE. Guinle and Carvalho had expected to participate in the U.S. Steel venture.

ernment steel plant was described as the key to Brazilian economic development and as the test of Brazilian–United States cooperation under the Good Neighbor Policy. Apparently, some basis for foreign private investment was still negotiable,[4] but the government declared its intent to exercise full control. On May 31, Washington responded by agreeing in principle to commit the Export-Import Bank to invest up to $17 million for equipment, and Vargas agreed to send a negotiating mission shortly.[5]

Vargas and Ambassador Martins succeeded in lining up official United States government participation almost two weeks before Vargas's famous speech of June 11 aboard the *Minas Gerais* (see p. 65). But events had moved rapidly. The lightning German victories in Europe raised again the possibility of German finance for the steelworks, and the President found himself in an awkward position. In June and July he invited the Germans to make a definite offer, but at the same time he pressured the United States for an immediate pledge to finance all necessary equipment. Washington, in turn, wanted to discuss its aid in conjunction with military and political objectives, notably the stationing of United States Army troops at strategic Brazilian air bases in case of war. With Germany's prestige at an all-time high, Western Hemisphere defense planning was controversial among leading Brazilians. For Vargas to accept military cooperation with the United States at this juncture, the Americans knew, he had to drive a good bargain. Probably, if he did not obtain more concessions from the United States he would be under heavy pressure to cooperate with Germany. It was less likely, though possible, that he was waiting for the expected German victory in Europe before making a definite commitment to the Reich. The evidence is not entirely clear; in his usual style, Vargas, as long as possible, avoided committing himself. At stake was nothing less than the economic, political, and military orientation of Brazil.

By midsummer, 1940, the United States was fully aware that unless it offered credits for arms and the steelworks immediately, the Germans would furnish them. During June, the Brazilian case had been forcefully presented to Washington, and by late July the preliminary negotiations were under way. The Brazilian mission with Guinle, Macedo Soares, and Tôrres arrived in Washington July 25, only a week before President Roosevelt decided to give Brazil and Mexico first priority on military and economic aid. Skeptical of Latins, Federal Loan Administrator Jesse Jones was paternalistic and at times sharp with Guinle, who was courtly and phlegmatic, and with Macedo Soares, the dynamic, competent, and ambitious technical expert. "The great problem in Washington," Macedo Soares reported, "was to convince Jesse Jones that we could construct a steel plant that would not be owned by, or associated with a large American steel company."[6] These talks bore fruit; the Export-Import Bank pledged $20 million in late September to a wholly Brazilian-owned plant.[7] Thus the financial keystone finally fell into place. In effect, the Germans were outbid. Not only were they unable to guarantee immediate equipment delivery, but their terms were less favorable than those of the Americans. The Reich had demanded that half of the payments in Brazilian raw materials be in German hands before the equipment arrived. And when the German steel firms, at their government's urging, finally ceased to compete with each other for this project and formed a consortium, it was too late.[8]

For both Brazil and the United States, the steel plant agreement was more than a mere trade of economic aid for access to strategic Brazilian real estate. The State Department thought that "it assures for many years to come a close and useful cooperation between the two countries and sets up . . . [an economic] barrier against Germany." A rising living standard for Brazil, and an expanded market for United States goods were other long-range benefits envisioned by Washington.[9] Official Washington now confirmed what the Germans and some American policy makers had been saying since the mid-1930's, namely that an industrializing Brazil would be a better trading partner.*

* Lloyd C. Gardner, in his stimulating *Economic Aspects of New Deal Diplomacy* (Madison, Wis., 1964), pp. 129–31, sees the steelworks as an updated form of American economic penetration via sales of heavy industrial equipment. By contrast William L. Langer and S. Everett Gleason, in *The Challenge to Isolation; 1937–1940* (New York, 1952), stress security aspects. I

At the cost of substantially committing themselves militarily, the Brazilian armed forces approved the agreement. Thus the immediate opportunity to establish a steelworks took priority over aspirations for complete financial and political independence. If Brazil had insisted on total national financing then, as the *Diário de Notícias* pointed out, there was no solution in sight. The journal endorsed United States aid as a practical alternative to Farquhar's schemes.[10] Furthermore, the essential Army demands for foreign loans and technical aid, not direct investment, were realized. As one mining authority observed, "We are receiving limited financial and technical aid without promising our metallurgical riches to foreign powers."[11]

Meanwhile, Colonel Macedo Soares had completed his investigations of possible locations for the steelworks, and in July 1940 the Executive Commission officially selected Volta Redonda, an abandoned coffee plantation six miles east of Barra Mansa in Rio de Janeiro state. In early 1939, the Army's special commission at the CFCE had given serious consideration to a site in the Paraíba Valley; but this plan, which would have joined ore exports with steelmaking, was soon supplanted by the U.S. Steel study. Why, then, did Macedo Soares decide to reject Santa Cruz on Sepetiba Bay, the site recommended by the latest Brazilian, United States, and German studies?

Defense requirements were overriding in view of the war and the dramatic effectiveness of submarine warfare. Volta Redonda lay fifty miles inland, behind the Serra do Mar mountains, well beyond the range of naval gunfire. Other reasons were also impor-

---

prefer a broader interpretation that takes as its theme the ambiguities of politically inspired foreign aid projects. This question of mixed motives notwithstanding, Volta Redonda has proved to be a highly successful, ongoing loan project. Among the Germans' motives for wanting to expand their economic bridgehead in Brazil may be counted political prestige, trade, and access to strategic raw materials. Following the successful conclusion of the Guinle–Macedo Soares–Tôrres mission, German interests in Brazil, acting on Berlin's instructions, reportedly made "every effort to gain control of the Belgo-Mineira steel plant" but were blocked by the Brazilian government, which in cooperation with the company called in all outstanding bonds. Despatch 3638, Burdett to Secretary of State, Rio, Sept. 25, 1940, DS 832.6511/167 and Memorandum, State Department, Sept. 30, 1940, DS 832.6511/177.

tant. Once the government had decided that the site must meet defense requirements, it then projected the optimum economic, social, and political conditions. The addition of these new factors to the generally accepted criteria for site selection—assembly costs, transportation, and markets—changed the balance of factors that previously had favored Santa Cruz. To further explain this unexpected choice, the Commission affirmed that sites at Antonina, near Lage's defunct project in Paraná, at Lafaiete and Juiz de Fora, on Mineiro soil, at Vitória, and at Santa Cruz did not satisfy their objectives, which were (a) "to choose a location where raw materials would arrive at a reasonable price and from which finished goods destined for the major consumption markets would leave under the most favorable conditions," and (b) "to avoid large expenses over and beyond those of constructing the factory."[12] The projected National Steel Company or CSN (organized in January 1941) would construct and operate the plant; it would not finance major port or railroad construction, nor would it assume the higher costs and the risks of transportation breakdowns that were attendant upon sites far from the Rio and São Paulo markets.

Santa Cruz, near Rio, required outlays of 80,000 contos for port construction and dredging. Additional expenses included 6,000 contos for a waterline, 6,500 contos for improvement of a rail branch from Santa Cruz to Austin, on the Central, 8,000 contos for land acquisition, and 5 per cent interest on this capital. The total of 100,500 contos was considered prohibitive, especially when the expense of fortifying the site against naval bombardment and air attack was added.[13] Antonina, with its unproved ore fields nearby, was open to the same objections.

Vitória, also, was discounted on grounds of excessive expense and vulnerability to attack. The Commission estimated that 200,000 contos was needed to reconstruct the Vitória a Minas railway, to acquire rolling stock, to improve Vitória port, and to construct a twenty-kilometer branch line to the plant site.[14] Furthermore, the prices of finished products would be raised by having to transport them by rail to Vitória and so on through successive loading and unloading stages on the trips by ship and rail to Santos, Rio, and markets in the hinterland. In fact, the idea of exporting Itabira ore was given a lower priority than Volta Redonda even after the Brazilian government acquired the mining properties and the railroad concession from Farquhar in 1942. That the steel plant came first was a logical consequence of the recent decision to separate iron ore exports and the steel solution.

Santa Cruz, Antonina, and Vitória were rejected partly because these locations did not satisfy the economic criteria established by the Executive Commission. However, Macedo Soares's argument against incurring additional expenses was weakened by the fact that CSN spent about $10 million for a model industrial community. The construction of private houses, hotels, schools, sports clubs, and clinics was on a scale well beyond the requirements of a mere company town.[15] Now that Brazil was to have a modern steel industry, Volta Redonda was designed as the symbol of progress, with wide implications for Brazilian society. Life was to center around work in a disciplined hierarchy; almost everyone would live within sight of the plant, from managers housed on the hilltops, to technicians and foremen on the slopes, to workers clustered near the bottom. Up to date, and lavish by Brazilian standards, the planned community shows the range of requirements other than economic or military ones that were joined at this location.

The Executive Commission agreed with critics that for reasons of cheaper transportation alone the Santa Cruz site was superior. "But," it said, "taking into account the strong reasons of a *general economic* nature, of a *political, social,* and *military* order, we sought to remove the plant as far as possible from Rio, without *prejudicing* the essential *commercial* aspect of the plant."[16] Thus they were attracted to the Barra Mansa region in the moribund Paraíba Valley, a site midway between markets and raw materials. The public has never been certain about the criteria that determined this location, which is reason enough to explore them further.

C. Langdon White, the American geographer, lists several factors that influenced the selection of steel plant sites in the United States: markets, raw materials, inertia, transportation, labor, dispersal of the plant for military reasons, and capital.[17] To this list, culled from the geographic literature, White himself adds water; for the Brazilian case another factor would certainly be ownership and objectives of the plant.

Markets. Volta Redonda was favorably located to supply São Paulo and Rio with heavy steel products. These cities, lying less than 225 miles from the plant, accounted for over 75 per cent of the national steel consumption in 1940. Brazil's annual demand for steel was then estimated at 408,800 tons, of which 65 per cent was imported. As in the U.S. Steel report, the Commission decided not to overwhelm, but rather to coordinate its production with the existing steel industry. Charcoal-based production, it was reasoned, might be expanded to 300,000 tons. Together with Volta Redonda's capacity for 335,000 tons, these small plants ought to be able to supply a domestic market of about 600,000 tons by 1950.[18] But the economy expanded very rapidly. The actual demand in 1950 was 1,200,000 tons, which led Macedo Soares to activate his contingency plans for a larger plant much sooner than expected.*

Raw Materials. The plant was well located with respect to assembling raw materials; 75 per cent of them could be transported to Volta Redonda in one railroad car. Ample supplies of iron ores were already being mined by A. Thun at the Casa da Pedra mine in Minas Gerais. Nationalization of this modern, well-capitalized German operation had been proposed before, in 1938, by Paulo Denizot. It actually came into the government's possession in 1941 or 1942 with the German stipulation that no future production from these mines be exported. Thus the most important mining property in Mendonça Lima's defunct ore monopoly scheme became a key element in the Volta Redonda operation.

Coal was the major raw materials problem. The National Steel Company acquired extensive mining, washing, and loading facilities in Santa Catarina, and modernized the southern coal fields as a strategic national resource. The death of the coal baron Henrique Lage and the passing of his industrial empire, including coastal steamers (the Costeira Line), into government hands hurt the

---

* This was not difficult because extra foundations and gas lines had already been built on leveled areas alongside the original plant.

once-powerful coal lobby. This obstructionist group could no longer hold back modernization, although much remained to be accomplished with coal in later years.

For defense reasons it was decided to use both domestic and foreign coals. Once again, the U.S. Steel report pointed the way. In the event foreign coals were cut off, the plant could still function, though much less efficiently, by using 100 per cent national coal, which could be delivered over rickety, but still usable, railroads.[19] Even partial self-sufficiency was costly. In 1954, for example, the expense of transporting coal was responsible for almost 70 per cent of the entire cost of assembling raw materials. It has since been shown that Brazilian production costs can be lowered substantially by using all imported coal in combination with modern blast furnace techniques.[20]

The decision to use classic steelmaking methods undoubtedly limited the range of possible sites, especially in Minas Gerais. By ruling that coking operations had to be integrated with other units (blast and steel furnaces), the Commission would permit no alternative to an integrated plant. This the state of Minas Gerais discovered when it tried to persuade the Commission to locate the steelworks at João Ribeiro, near the mine, and to ship in coke on the Central do Brasil. The Mineiros' interest in electric steel furnaces and the Krupp direct reduction process had been discouraged before by Macedo Soares.

Inertia. At first glance, inertia was not an important locational factor. It was a major innovation to locate this large industrial plant in an old agricultural region, even though a ready supply of cheap land and labor, large open spaces, transportation, and nearness to Rio and São Paulo markets had been attracting light industry to the Paraíba Valley since 1930.[21] In 1937, two small iron and steel producers had located at Barra Mansa, and for many years the Valley had been discussed as a favorable location for steelmaking. Thus the momentum of industrialization was stepped up but was not initiated by Volta Redonda.

Since the Paraíba Valley lay within the industrial triangle defined by São Paulo, Belo Horizonte, and Rio, Volta Redonda posed no threat to the established centers of economic activity. Nonetheless, as expected, the location was controversial. São Paulo, with the largest steel consumption, Minas Gerais, with the iron ore mines, and Rio, with the existing ore- and coal-loading facilities, all claimed priority over Volta Redonda. Denied their long-held aspirations, some Mineiros called Volta Redonda a sure fiasco and complained that Vargas had deliberately arranged a "windfall" for the laboring classes whose savings would finance it.[22] However, the Paraíba Valley site had military backing, and Vargas's son-in-law, Ernani do Amaral Peixoto, controlled the Rio de Janeiro state government, in which Macedo Soares's brother, Hélio, served as Secretary of Transport. Given the Army's very great interest in an optimum solution, it seems logical to assume that these personal relations were helpful, but not determinant in the decision-making process. Furthermore, to deny regional claims was entirely consistent with tenets of Estado Nôvo centralism, as will be shown in the struggle over state oil refineries. In short, Macedo Soares avoided the established power centers to pioneer in a new region that could also be represented as a political and geographical compromise between the capital, São Paulo, and Minas Gerais.

Transportation. Freight costs and the Central's capacity to serve the projected steelworks (recently affirmed by Greenwood's group) were the major transportation factors. Sites in Minas Gerais at Lafaiete, near the mines, Juiz de Fora, and Entre Rios were rejected on the basis of prevailing freight rates. Furthermore, the Mineiros' alternative site (João Ribeiro) was considered uneconomical: trains that left the mining zone with 1,200-ton loads could not be expected to return up the steep mountain grades with more than 450 to 500 tons of return cargo.[23] With the exception of Santa Cruz, any location nearer to Rio or São Paulo than Volta Redonda would have necessitated higher freight charges. Thus the numerous advantages of Volta Redonda over Santa Cruz were considered worth the estimated 9,400 contos in additional yearly freight rates. However, a decade later the economic arguments in favor of a coastal plant were more compelling.[24] By 1950 Brazil had spectacularly outgrown its transportation system; the Central had failed to keep pace with postwar demand.

Labor. Prevailing wage rates and an unused supply of cheap

labor also favored the Paraíba Valley site. Though wages and sala-
ries were only a minor part of anticipated operating costs, the official minimum wage at Volta Redonda was 30 per cent lower than
in Rio de Janeiro. Free housing and lavish social services worked
against this advantage, however. Output and efficiency were expected to be better in the cooler Valley zone than in Rio's steamy
climate and less favorable working conditions. Although they
learned rapidly, most of the construction laborers and early factory
hands were Mineiro farm workers who had had no previous experience with machinery. Until the late 1940's, moreover, the industrial accident rate was discouragingly high; but soon on-the-job
training and technical schooling began to produce an efficient labor
force.

Dispersal of Plant for Military Reasons. Volta Redonda lay beyond the range of naval gunfire, in the strategic communications
corridor between Rio and São Paulo. Toluene, a coke by-product
used in the manufacture of TNT, was to be shipped to the large
government explosives plant at Piquête some miles to the west.
Thus the location was a particularly good redoubt for the World
War II period. Antiaircraft emplacements were the only fortifica-
tions required.

Capital. The Volta Redonda works cost the equivalent of $75
million before production began, after many delays, in the summer
of 1946. Rising costs (up 60 per cent by 1942) and a shortage of
equipment, caused by the war, plagued the planning and construction stages. But the venture was backed politically by the United
States, and financially—with credits of $45 million. This unusually
large assistance for these early days of foreign aid gave the project
financial continuity, but it did not noticeably encourage the skeptical Brazilian business community to invest. Volta Redonda, as an
untried government enterprise, remained less attractive to private
capital than the defunct U.S. Steel project.

In 1941 the Savings Banks and Pension Funds supplied over one-
half of the initial $25 million capitalization in Brazilian currency.
For this involuntary sacrifice of capital reserves, the funds were
given all the preferred stock. Guilherme Guinle (President of

CSN) put a brave face on the reluctance of private sources to purchase more than one-third of the common stock issue. Over 30,000 contos was pledged before construction began, he said, and this pledge was proof of the confidence of "businessmen, industrialists, and class associations."[25] However, strenuous efforts by the Brazilian Treasury netted only 83,000 contos in total private subscriptions, and this occurred despite the fact that principal banks, professional groups, large businesses, and the domestic steel industry were "urged" to participate.[26] The Treasury took the remaining common stock (167,000 contos). In 1944, the domestic capital was doubled, but private contributions again were low.

Volta Redonda, with its model town and interior location, was not the cheapest solution, but neither was it uneconomical. From the start of construction, CSN was protected as a key infant industry and its equipment was obtained at cost or near cost (though it was often delayed because of United States war priorities). Total expenditures for constructing the Volta Redonda complex were lower, in Macedo Soares's view, than costs for similar American plants constructed in wartime at Geneva, New York, and Fontana, California. As a modern, efficient operation, Volta Redonda was designed to be competitive with American steel products in Brazil after the war.[27]

Water. Unlimited supplies of fresh, soft water were immediately available from the Paraíba River, which ran past the steelworks. Macedo Soares estimated that in one 24-hour period the operation needed 200 million liters, or one and one-half times the daily water needs of Rio, and twice those of São Paulo.[28]

Ownership and Objectives of the Plant. For reasons of State policy, the CSN considered more political and social objectives than a private steel company might have. As an autonomous, mixed government corporation, however, the CSN was expected to be efficiently managed and competitive.* Existing State companies,

* Although federal or state governments usually own most of the share capital, Brazil's mixed companies are incorporated, publish annual reports like private corporations, and are exempt from the rigid rules governing federal employment. Some, like Volta Redonda, compete actively against private companies. They include private shareholders on their directorships, sup-

such as the Central do Brasil and the Lloyd Brasileiro shipping line, were notorious for being undercapitalized, mismanaged, and politics-ridden. This, Vargas and the military were determined to avoid. Volta Redonda was made independent of direct Treasury levies and the yearly federal budget; it would be run like a private industry. Finally, the mixed formula was an invitation to the Brazilian private sector to invest and lend moral support; Volta Redonda was no harbinger of socialism.

Initial operations were entrusted to Arthur G. McKee and Company, the United States engineering firm that designed and installed the plant. Soon the training of qualified personnel, and the healthy rivalry between Brazilian and American engineers to discover the best labor-training techniques produced results; in 1947 Brazilians assumed control. The top management positions were held by military engineers. In fact, since the beginning, tough-minded military leaders insulated the CSN from many political pressures and enabled Volta Redonda to fulfill its economic and other, related, objectives. But the plant was not run as a military operation, the workers were not placed under military discipline, and the objective was clearly industrial growth in general rather than arms production. In Volta Redonda the Brazilian Army carried out the technocratic role it had set for itself in the 1930's.

As a well-conceived industrial program, Volta Redonda had an almost immediate impact on the Brazilian economy. The coal and transportation industries were modernized, and new industries, such as canneries, and producers of cellulose and chemicals, commercial elevators, boilers, food concentrates, and explosives, were established in the Paraíba Valley. As planned, the steelworks stimulated rather than destroyed established steel producers.

But beyond the immediate achievement, Volta Redonda represented a new industrial era. Roberto Simonsen said as much in 1942 when he led 120 Paulista industrialists on a pilgrimage to the

posedly to inject a businesslike approach to management, but certainly also to retain close links with the private sector. Since mixed companies are also instruments of government economic policy, this function may conflict with strictly entrepreneurial goals. See Werner Baer, *Industrialization and Economic Development in Brazil* (Homewood, Ill., 1965), pp. 94–95.

plant. Shepherded by Simonsen and Macedo Soares, the industrialists were shown the impressive result of State planning for heavy industry. Their former, perhaps well-founded, prejudice against State industry softened. Under certain circumstances, Simonsen told them, the government ought to intervene with mixed companies. The report FIESP prepared enthusiastically endorsed all the economic, social, and political objectives that were fulfilled by Volta Redonda. "With triumphs like this," said one Paulista, "the country will experience tranquility, which is nothing less than the fruit of better living standards."[29] Brazil, in the words of Alberto Tôrres, did not know itself before, did not understand its own people. Now there was a vision of a new society before them.[30]

As for the model town, the National Steel Company's control of the social and economic power structure was paternalistic. This facilitated training programs, strict political controls, and efforts to adjust ex-farmhands, with their casual work habits and sex lives, to a new life ordered by regular work shifts. Paternalism was consistent with the government's labor goals and reflected the thinking of industrial leaders like Roberto Simonsen and Jorge Street, a pioneer for workers' housing, cafeterias, and day care centers. "There will be no class struggle at Volta Redonda," one industrialist remarked, for there "everyone will work for and with Brazil."[31] A new, socially conscious phase of capitalism had arrived, in which the causes of strife between management and labor were removed.[32] Labor would get a share, within a highly structured, controlled, and harmonious social system. This was nothing less than a vision of conservative modernization, which was the ideological touchstone of the Estado Nôvo era.

Volta Redonda was, finally, a major victory for Getúlio Vargas and the politics of conciliation. Men like Aranha and Major Macedo Soares had played important roles in bringing the steelworks to Brazil. Simonsen was developing his doctrine of complementarity between State and private enterprise; he had helped to bring the major interest groups around and to reconcile them with the military modernizers. Ultimately, however, the decision to conciliate as many interests as possible was made by Vargas. Luis

Simões Lopes, the former civil service chief, observed that Vargas was a nationalist who did not believe in State ownership for its own sake. In fact, the President would have preferred a private steel solution. Later, in 1953, when the Congress and the Army adopted a State monopoly over oil production and refining (Petrobrás), Vargas told Simões that he did not think Brazilians performed well under monopoly conditions. Personally, he preferred State ownership but not monopoly—his solution for the steel problem eleven years before.[33]

Volta Redonda was a success story. To analyze this achievement is to discover a mixture of economic, technical, political, and ideological factors. Economic nationalism was one of these elements, and because of this, Volta Redonda was very different in scope and purpose from the U.S. Steel plan that preceded it. In 1943, Vargas called the new works a symbol of economic emancipation and of Brazil's capacity to develop its own resources. Volta Redonda also symbolized a new and more broadly based economic nationalism, which Vargas astutely sensed would soon be the key to his own political future. This was the idea of a bigger Brazilian pie in which the workers would share. Broadening economic nationalism to encompass the masses became a constant theme of the old master as he turned increasingly to labor politics and populism. As for the military, the old nationalist arguments were resolved; and the plant was tangible proof of the Army's commitment to economic development.

To conclude, the government's approach to policy-making with regard to steel was flexible and contingent, in line with the usual style of the Estado Nôvo. After years of debate, Brazilians agreed on the need for a modern steelworks; they disagreed on the means. Whether or not to join iron ore exports with the steelworks, to follow regional solutions, or to permit foreign ownership and control —these were the outstanding issues until 1939–40. Several factions and interests maneuvered for the policy initiative until these questions were resolved, and the opportunities for securing foreign aid paid off. Distinguishing features in this account were the Army's role in pressing for the steel plant, and the extent to which economic nationalism was important for joining economic, political, and defense rationales together with a shortened time perspective. For these reasons, Brazil could wait no longer after 1937. Vargas's leadership was important. Realizing that the steel issue was ripe, Vargas committed his own and his government's prestige to finding a solution. Then he skillfully identified the plant with one of the goals of this authoritarian regime, namely economic progress without class conflict. Having conciliated the major interests, Vargas could represent Volta Redonda as a triumph for all Brazilians. Thus he contributed toward creating a climate of public acceptance for industrialization, and he popularized the idea that nobody would lose because of it.

True, Volta Redonda was a most visible monument, a status symbol of the kind developing nations have been eager to obtain; but it was more. Contemporaries knew that the plant was justified economically. Furthermore, the new works also marked a commitment by the State to oversee, promote, and perhaps to undertake directly the development of Brazil's vast natural resources. This was a giant step beyond the regulatory legislation of the early 1930's. Volta Redonda was thus a yardstick by which future governments would be measured.

PART III · PETROLEUM

7 · HORTA BARBOSA TAKES COMMAND

Vargas's plan for a State oil monopoly, Petrobrás, was sent to Congress in December 1951.* Almost two years later it emerged as the same State monopoly, but it had more stringent provisions than the original bill, which would have allowed some foreign investment. Following long, bitter, and factious debates, the Congress stipulated that only native Brazilians, on a minority basis, could hold capital in the new government company.

Vargas was unhappy with the final formula. As he signed Petrobrás into law in 1953, he could think of Volta Redonda and recall his earlier, clear-cut triumph over economic and political problems; but now, in his second presidency (1951–54), he was failing to master the politics of oil, and his position was weakening within the established and popular groups that supported him. The developing consensus on oil policy was not created by Vargas, but was inspired by popular nationalism, which channeled powerful, if conflicting demands to decision makers. What soon became Latin America's largest industrial corporation did not, therefore, have an easy birth.

The solution to the oil problem developed through three phases. The first phase began in the early 1920's and matured during the Estado Nôvo, when the National Petroleum Council (CNP) was founded by General Júlio Caetano Horta Barbosa. In the 1930's, development of the petroleum industry had a lower priority than

---

* The full name is Petróleo Brasileiro, S.A., or Brazilian Petroleum Corporation. Petrobrás was created by Law 2,004 (Oct. 3, 1953). Previously, the two most important statutes in petroleum legislation were Decree Laws 395 (April 29, 1938) and 538 (July 7, 1938), which established the National Petroleum Council and its powers.

steel manufacturing; moreover, opinion in the Army was divided over oil policy as it had not been over the steel problem. Shortly before the return to open, democratic politics in 1945, a second phase began. Oil became a major political issue as nationalists fought President Eurico Gaspar Dutra's plan to bring in foreign oil companies. Notable in the years 1944–49 was the extent to which the petroleum issue appealed to a newly participating public. In the third phase, 1950–53, the industry was given its present form. Vargas's political style and methods became outmoded, as the final battle over Petrobrás shows so well. Owing largely to the petroleum issue, the uses and appeals of nationalism changed in ways that he could no longer control.

This chapter is about phase one, when the petroleum issue first appeared.[1] Following a brief look at the situation between the wars, the focus sharpens on General Horta Barbosa's policy-making role from 1938 to 1943. After losing the policy initiative, Horta Barbosa resigned as director of the CNP in 1943, but he left a legacy of nationalist oil laws and policies that shaped the petroleum industry for years to come.

After 1930, many Latin American nations tightened their regulations regarding concessions and domestic oil markets, and Brazil was no exception. However, under Horta Barbosa, Brazil went further toward government control of production and refining than most nations of the hemisphere were prepared to go. In taking this path, the Brazilians were more consistent and determined than the Argentines, whose oil policies were Horta Barbosa's main inspiration. Mexico, by nationalizing distribution, went even further than Brazil, exerting government control over all phases of the business. But the famous Mexican oil expropriations in 1938 began with a labor dispute and had no direct influence on Brazilian policy. In fact, Brazil's course after 1937 was unique in at least three respects.

First, oil was not discovered in Brazil until 1939; and before Petrobrás began operating in the mid-1950's, both production and proved reserves were insignificant. Thus, for Brazil it was not a question of adjusting or restructuring relations with established foreign producers, as it was for Argentina, Bolivia, Mexico, Peru, Colombia, and Venezuela, but of creating an entirely new industry. The Brazilians were free to discuss the form of enterprise they wanted—private, mixed, or State—for exploiting and developing their unknown petroleum resources. The question was: which formula would best advance the nation's economic, political, and military interests?

Second, the most promising start for a nonproducer like Brazil was in refining. This approach was not exceptional, for France had pioneered it after World War I, and the Iberian nations soon followed. Uruguay, which had no domestic oil production, began refining in 1936. However, the usual Latin American pattern was to first find oil reserves and then move into refining, transportation, and marketing. The Brazilians bowed to necessity and tried to find in profitable refineries a substitute for the dynamic drive and excitement of a large oil strike.

Third, only in Brazil was the Army's role in developing a petroleum industry decisive in the 1930's. One recalls that after 1937 almost all State-sponsored industrialization in Brazil took place under auspices of the military. Hence the economic, financial, and technical requirements of this costly new industry were first seen as a paramilitary problem. Traces of the original tendency to view petroleum in this way still exist.

In brief, Brazilian policy by the end of phase one was distinguished by a vigorous discussion of options, a stress on refining, and the initiating force of General Horta Barbosa and the Army. Compared with Petrobrás today—a near-billion-dollar corporation—the concrete achievements of these early years are not impressive. But to emphasize that neither refineries nor producing oil fields existed before 1943 would be to miss the significance of this period, when the foundations of a national oil policy were layed. This achievement is all the more impressive in light of the very limited financial and physical resources the early oilmen had to work with and the political problems they confronted.

Geologically, Brazil was a vast unknown. Early surveys by foreigners such as Orville Derby, J. C. Branner, I. C. White, and

Chester Washbourne, and Gonzaga de Campos of the government's own Geological Service (SGM) had established that potentially oil-bearing sedimentary formations existed in one-third of the country. By 1938, the areas of greatest promise were thought to be the Amazon and Paraná basins, and a narrow coastal strip running north from Bahia. Without a major exploration program, however, no one could be certain that Brazil had oil. Only journalists and dreamers—*ufanistas*, for whom a nation so large had to have oil somewhere—were sure. As a dependency of the Ministry of Agriculture, the poorest ministry, the SGM had drilled only 56 test holes from 1918 to 1938. Moreover, the war delayed development of Bahian oil, which was found in 1939. When Vargas left office in 1945, crude production from the four small Bahian fields was still insignificant (about 25 barrels a day), and proved reserves were only ten million barrels.[2]

Exploration and development required a sizeable outlay of capital, which was scarce. Knowing the unproductive efforts of the SGM, São Paulo's state drilling program, and a few wildcat operations, Brazilian private investors shunned risky exploration in favor of profitable and more traditional investments in commerce and agriculture. Nor were the international oil companies much interested in Brazil. As first Mexico, between 1900 and 1910, Venezuela, in the 1930's, and then the fabulous Middle East began exporting oil, Brazil was not attractive to foreign oilmen. Of course the major oil companies (often called the majors) were in touch with Brazilian oil developments, and under certain circumstances they were prepared to risk some capital, as this chapter will show. But Brazil's isolation from large consumer markets, its growing but still modest domestic market (in 1935, only one quarter of Argentina's), and its poor internal transportation facilities were other sound reasons why for years the foreign petroleum companies made no serious proposals to find oil.[3]

In marketing, Brazil was tied to an oligopoly of five foreign companies led by Standard Oil of New Jersey and Anglo-Mexican, the Royal Dutch Shell affiliate.[4] Almost all the gasoline, fuel oil, diesel oil, and lubricants were imported from American and Brit-

ish refineries on the Gulf of Mexico or in the Dutch Antilles.*
These products, shipped in bulk, were unloaded at Belém, Recife,
Salvador, Rio, Santos, and Rio Grande do Sul for distribution to
affiliated dealers, most of whom were in São Paulo, the largest domestic market. Customers outside these port zones were subjected
to high taxes, heavy transportation costs, and unpredictable delays,
but those along the heavily populated littoral received good service. Jersey Standard's alligator trademark was familiar to kerosene users from all walks of life.

The economic logic of integrated operations applied nicely to
Brazil since the majors reaped profits from all phases of the business, from production to refining, shipping, and sales. After the
1929 crash, Brazil's market slumped briefly; but by 1933, gasoline
imports had recovered to near the 1929 record (2,496,000 barrels),
and from 1931 to 1940 the nation's overall petroleum needs grew
annually by an average of 6.4 per cent.[5] Foreign oil companies
complained about the fines and lawsuits brought against them
during the tenente period, about the retail price controls imposed
by state authorities, and above all about the uncertain exchange
control policies under which the orderly transfer of foreign payments often was delayed.[6] But since oil was a vital import, Brazil
saw to it that foreign oil companies were first to receive exchange
cover when it was available. All things considered, the profits must
have been substantial.[7]

The government itself had a vested interest in this trade. In
1939, duties on gasoline alone brought in $15 million to the Trea-
sury. Federal, state, and local governments relied heavily on oil
taxes: over half of retail gasoline prices at the pump was set aside
to cover some thirty-five different imposts. These revenues were

---

* Data for 1939 indicate that Standard annually sold Brazil about $10 million
in petroleum products, of which $2 million was in lubricants from the United
States, and the rest in fuel oil and gasoline from its refineries in Aruba, Dutch
West Indies, and Talare, Peru (operated by the International Petroleum Corporation). The Texas Company and Atlantic together sold about $10 million
to Brazil from continental United States refineries. Shell supplied about $5
million yearly from its refinery in the Dutch West Indies. Standard figures
cited in Memorandum, by Livesey (Economic Affairs), "Standard Oil Company of New Jersey Interests in Brazil," Feb. 17, 1939, DS, 832.6363/222.

reliable and growing. Furthermore, the authorities liked indirect taxation, which Brazilian consumers were used to paying, and which foreign subsidiaries bore the burden of collecting. All in all, Brazil's petroleum market rested on solid economic and fiscal foundations. The foreign companies, the United States and British governments, and Brazil's Finance Minister, Souza Costa, all wanted to maintain the status quo. Products from American refineries at home or in the Antilles were the largest dollar earners for the United States in the Brazilian trade. For his part, Souza Costa counted on oil duties to ease his budget problems. Before the war, Brazil could afford its oil imports, which were then growing moderately, and thus the capacity to pay was not yet a real issue. This traditional market was viable until wartime shortages and tanker sinkings slowed the vital oil flow.

Refining was the one sector of the industry that attracted Brazilian capital. With recovery in the mid-1930's, industrialists like Euvaldo Lodi began to appreciate the profit potential of refineries, as long as domestic products were taxed below similar foreign imports. In 1935 Lodi told the CFCE that a refining industry, using national or imported crude oil, would inevitably be built. France and Argentina had set the trend toward national refineries, which were vital for defense, he said. In addition to saving foreign exchange, the industry would stimulate demand for new products such as tinplate, wood crating, and steel drums, and for a larger merchant marine.[8]

Lodi was not exaggerating, and the foreign distributors, knowing their interests were at stake, were concerned. In 1936 they learned that a Brazilian entrepreneur (unnamed) was proposing to build a government plant in Rio, reasoning that a refinery producing a fourth of the nation's gasoline requirements would act as a restraint on the prices and profits of private domestic refineries.[9] Given the large disparity between duties on crude and refined products, domestic refining was increasingly attractive. Uruguayan and Argentine groups were operating two small topping plants in Rio Grande do Sul, and the Matarazzo interests, with Italian capital behind them, were founding another small plant in

São Paulo to supply their industrial empire.* By the late 1930's, the state governments of São Paulo, Bahia, and Rio de Janeiro each had a modern cracking plant on the drawing boards.

Different motives prompted Standard (in 1936), Texaco, Atlantic Refining Company, and Anglo-Mexican (all in 1938), to propose large refineries for Brazil. These steps were unusual, because the practice of these companies was to ship relatively little crude oil across the oceans and to refine it instead near the source, in very large plants. By shipping gasoline from the United States and the Antilles, for example, they ran no risk of having to crosshaul products that the small Brazilian market could not absorb. Protecting their market position in Brazil was the reason for these proposals. In effect, they wanted to establish legal rights prior to any new restrictive legislation, and to preempt refining from the government and domestic interests. In late 1937, Standard actually revamped a worn-out Canadian topping plant at Jaguaré, São Paulo. That the oil companies made these offers at all, and that Standard rushed through its dubious refinery point up the effects that noneconomic factors were having on the traditional oil market.

Having considered various features of the industry, including the growing domestic and foreign interest in refining, let us turn now to policy, tracing early trends in the politics of petroleum before 1938, when General Horta Barbosa took command.

Public interest in petroleum was aroused during World War I, when discussion centered on the economic and military consequences of wartime fuel shortages. Spurred to action, President Pessôa generously funded the SGM, but his successor, President Bernardes, abandoned the drilling program in order to pursue his own steel plans (mentioned in Chapter 4). Congress discussed means of accelerating exploration, but for all the talk in the 1920's about the need to find oil, the SGM after Pessôa was not given

* Ypiranga S.A., Cia. Brasileira de Petróleos Rio Grande (capacity of 44,000 tons per year); Uruguaiana, Distilharia Riograndense de Petróleo S.A. (12,000 tons per year); and Indústrias Reunidas F. Matarazzo S.A. [IME] at São Caetano, São Paulo (38,000 tons per year).

adequate funds for exploration and the large foreign companies were not very interested.

Such official neglect can only mean that the nationalist laws proposed by the SGM Director, Euzébio de Oliveira, and the Minister of Agriculture, Ildefonso Simões Lopes, in 1923 and after had little political weight. Seeking to shore up the long-faltering sugar industry, Pernambucan planters promoted alcohol as an additive fuel for gasoline. They joined with Army officers and deputies concerned about national defense in calling for restrictions on foreign investment. But the only result was a vaguely worded clause amending the Constitution to state that "mines and mineral deposits necessary for national defense . . . cannot be transferred to foreigners."[10] In fact, the proposed laws had little appeal because the demand for refined products was very low, there were few roads and almost no automobiles, and the railroads and ships used coal.

Propelled into influence by the 1930 revolution, the centralist-minded tenentes pushed through strong controls on mineral resources for the first time since the Empire. They feared the oil would be found, and lost to foreigners, before adequate safeguards were enacted. One of the first acts of Minister of Agriculture Juarez Távora was to cancel some blatantly corrupt state concessions by Amazonas and Pará. Other mining contracts were investigated, including Farquhar's Itabira Contract, before Távora went on to restrict foreign ownership and investment by the 1934 Mining Code. Furthermore, all mineral properties, prospecting permits, and mining concessions were transferred from the states' authority to a new federal agency, the Department of Mineral Production (DNPM), which replaced the inadequate SGM. On the negative side, Távora seemed totally preoccupied with administrative reforms. With little in the way of subsidies and incentives available, private domestic capital avoided mining. And with the small budgets that Souza Costa grudgingly allowed, the new DNPM was soon plunged into routine and resignation.

Meanwhile, the wildcatters were incensed at Távora's new regulations and controls. Their leader was José Bento Monteiro Lobato, the gifted Paulista publisher who dreamed of becoming the Brazilian Colonel Drake in a new Titusville oil rush.* Combative, boundlessly optimistic, but short of funds, Monteiro Lobato somehow had to find backers for his rickety drilling companies in Mato Grosso, Paraná, and São Paulo. Henrique Lage, another enthusiast, loaned a drilling rig, but the DNPM was not impressed with Monteiro Lobato or his drilling sites and ordered him to return borrowed government equipment. As a militant free-enterpriser, Monteiro Lobato thought DNPM "obstructionism" would frighten off investors. When a German equipment consortium (Piepmeyer & Co.) spurned his shoestring ventures, the would-be oilman accelerated his attacks on the DNPM in letters, in the press, and in his 1936 best seller, *The Petroleum Scandal.*

By the mid-1930's, Monteiro Lobato and his fellow speculators had made oil a cause célèbre. Taking the role of scandal monger, Monteiro Lobato luridly described how the demonic foreign trusts were grasping for Brazilian subsoil wealth, which, fearing competition, they did not want developed. The trusts, he claimed, therefore welcomed Távora's restrictive laws. Standard Oil agents had infiltrated the DNPM to make false and pessimistic reports on national oil companies like his own. Underlining his main point—"the government won't drill or let others drill"—were the themes of duplicity, treachery, and sellout.

Vargas went through the motions of a public inquiry, knowing all along that Monteiro Lobato's real purpose was to boom his stock. That the vehement Paulista deliberately misled the public about the real nature of his investments was later established beyond doubt by government investigators, but the role of injured patriot was convincing, even though Monteiro Lobato never did find oil.[11] His legacy was a new, more combative style, in which the defense of high stakes and the national interest justified license with the facts. Brushing aside the complex technical and financial aspects of the oil industry, he stressed conspiratorial politics, which was something the public could understand. A generation read

* Edwin L. Drake, who struck oil near Titusville, Pennsylvania, in 1859.

and believed his *Petroleum Scandal*, and echoes of it reverberate today.[12]

It bears repeating that the oil companies provided a vital economic function. Rich, powerful, and foreign, they were, however, an easy target, and because of their influence over politicians and the press through subsidies and advertising, the man in the street tended to inflate their role to demonic size. Monteiro Lobato supplied an effective vocabulary for articulating the public's fears. At the same time, considerable comment was devoted to the companies' reputed behind-the-scene role in the Chaco War and Italy's Ethiopian imbroglio. Politicians touched a popular nerve when they challenged "the monopolizing oil trust" in a series of well-publicized speeches and articles on tax and pricing disputes during the 1930's. Like far-off lightning, nationalism was charging the air. Though public confidence in the DNPM was shaken by Monteiro Lobato, there was no conspiracy. Rather, the persistent failure of the DNPM to find oil resulted from antiquated methods, rigid positions, and too little money.

When Juarez Távora received some samples of seepage oil from Lobato, Bahia, in 1932, he assumed they were fake. Oscar Cordeiro, the Bahian businessman who sent them, was a well-known talker and enthusiast, but Távora also listened to government geologists who said Lobato had no oil. The majors also avoided Cordeiro and discounted his claims. Unable to obtain a prospecting permit, Cordeiro launched a press campaign with Monteiro Lobato's aid, and Távora, irritated, refused to reconsider. Cordeiro persevered until 1939, when the DNPM did find oil at Lobato.

The first competent preliminary survey of Bahia was financed privately in 1936 by Guilherme Guinle, the prominent Rio banker. Convinced that Cordeiro's traces were real, chemist Sylvio Fróes Abreu, geologist Glycon de Paiva Texeira, and geophysicist Irnack Carvalho do Amaral, took leaves from their government posts and flew to Bahia at Guinle's expense.[13] Soon they were calling for an exploration program to discover whether oil existed at Lobato in commercial quantities. Vargas was encouraging. In 1938 Guinle and Murray-Simonsen, the Paulista bankers, founded a company to explore the Bahian Recôncavo, contracted J. E. Brantley of the Drilling and Exploration Company, and prepared to move ahead. The DNPM began to change under the prodding of de Paiva and Amaral. For one thing, they said, the government should replace its antiquated equipment and geologists who knew little of modern petroleum technology. Until engineers were trained, experienced foreign firms should carry out drilling and geophysical studies under contract. For another, the DNPM was wasting money on random test holes. It should contract drilling by the meter or offer to pay a percentage of production from developed fields. In April 1938 the Minister of Agriculture adopted these ideas, instructed Amaral to obtain proposals in New York from United States drilling firms, and asked de Paiva to draw up a three-year plan for petroleum development.[14] Nothing came of de Paiva's proposed new agency, which was to have been called the Petroleum Research Service. But the path to Bahian discoveries and the fields that are still Brazil's producing mainstays had been blazed first by Cordeiro, and then by Fróes, de Paiva, and Amaral. Their championing of modern methods was symptomatic of a new spirit sweeping through the government.

By early 1938, elements for a new national oil policy existed, prospects for domestic refineries were bright, and the foreign oil companies were reexamining their former limited role. Previously lacking was a catalyst, some fresh mixture of ideas, personalities, and institutions to dramatize petroleum and take charge. This the Army now supplied, having been spurred into action by nationalism, the gathering world crisis, and modernizing impulses. The policy initiative shifted from the Ministry of Agriculture to the Army, and in early 1939 the DNPM's Bahian operations passed under the newly organized CNP. J. E. Brantley's services were retained by the new Council, and Herbert Hoover, Jr., of the United Geophysical Company was hired to survey Bahia. The man who directed these dynamic forces was the military engineer General Júlio Caetano Horta Barbosa.

At 56, Horta Barbosa was a respected senior officer whose years of service stringing telegraph lines in the Far West under General Cândido Rondon, followed by hard duty on road and rail construction projects, had instilled in him a high regard for the Army's role in national integration and development. Having been wounded in the Canudos insurrection of 1897, and seasoned as a pathfinder, Horta Barbosa was deeply patriotic. His qualities of dedication, probity, and quiet competence, for which the old Brazilian Army was famous, were reinforced by austere personal habits (he was a vegetarian) and a belief in the tenets of orthodox positivism. His small feet and hands, which moved in an economy of gesture, reinforced an impression of precision. Góes Monteiro, the ebullient Chief of Staff, liked to say of his taciturn deputy: "I talk too much, but Horta talks too little." Here, in short, was a professional officer of the old school, an apolitical general who now staked his career and reputation on creating a petroleum industry.

Italy's invasion of Africa in 1936 spurred Horta to act. Writing as Chief of Military Engineers, he circulated an internal memorandum to Góes in which he interpreted Ethiopia as another example of the international scramble for oil reserves, and said that it showed the Italians had learned a major lesson from World War I: to defend (or expand) vital interests, modern nations and their armies needed oil. From this he concluded that Brazil, being totally dependent on foreign oil, was militarily weak, and all the while it was witnessing the "constant and uninterrupted penetration of Standard Oil, Anglo-Mexican, etc., into the furthest corners of our fatherland." For purposes of economic and military defense, these foreign labels had to be replaced with Brazilian names. And, with the DNPM having little success, "who better than the National Army could put life into this matter?"[15]

This theme of the nation in danger remained a constant in Horta's thought. To justify Army intervention, he recalled how Hubert Lyautey and other French officers had pressed for the economic development of Algeria. More important was the example of General Enrique Mosconi, the Argentine engineer who had built up his government's Yacimientos Petrolíferos Fiscales (YPF) to dominate Argentina's internal oil market. A prolific writer, Mosconi had also proselytized his ideas on national oil development throughout Latin America, and Horta Barbosa wanted to follow his lead.[16]

Soon Horta had his wish. Promoted to Deputy Chief of Staff in late 1937, he proposed in January 1938 to make petroleum a State monopoly within the existing "economic-nationalist reorganization plan" of the Estado Nôvo.[17] His point of departure was refining, which he feared the foreign companies would soon take over, and then integrate backward to production. Such an industry had obvious economic and financial selling points, the most important being that the high profits from refining could be used to finance exploration.

Horta openly preferred a statist solution, but he was nonetheless willing to consider a privately owned national industry operated under close supervision. He did not even rule out foreign capital, as long as Brazilians held the managerial positions, and the profits, after amortization and interest payments, remained in Brazil. For the time being, distribution would stay in foreign hands. Like many officers, however, Horta tolerated Brazilian industrialists but distrusted their motives. While serving on a commission to investigate Farquhar's Itabira, he had learned how the Brazilian steel trust operated to make high profits behind protective tariff walls. Now he was determined to forestall any domestic oil trust. Nor was he eager for Bahia, São Paulo, and Rio de Janeiro to carry out their state refinery plans. Restraining private gain at the public's expense, and preventing regional rivalries that might weaken the defense effort became his constant worries. Above all he wanted to prevent foreign interests from capturing the lead in refining.

Horta's ideas were based on studies by the General Staff, and they probably would have been proposed with or without the Estado Nôvo. But it is also true that the new regime gave the military great influence over economic policy, and to this extent Horta's views on development were typical of the early, more experimental phase of the Estado Nôvo. In fact, the Army's determination to move on with development was a major impetus of this regime and had lasting results. This January memorandum went to Góes, who initialled but did not read his trusted deputy's report, and on to the National Security Council, Vargas, and the CFCE for a detailed study behind closed doors.

Reporting secretly on Horta's memorandum, Domingos Fleury da Rocha, a geologist and Director of the DNPM, suggested guidelines modeled on those of Argentina.[18] Having drafted the Mining and Water Codes for Távora in 1934, Fleury was well prepared to translate Horta's ideas into legislative form. Like Horta, Fleury was deeply influenced by Mosconi. Thus, to make petroleum a public utility and to regulate it under a National Petroleum Council, as Horta proposed, was to follow the Argentine model for nationalizing the domestic oil economy. Argentine practice, however, had fallen short of Mosconi's ideal—their National Petroleum Council was never enacted—and after 1930 the Argentine general was isolated politically while his government dealt inconsistently with the established foreign interests. Horta urgently wanted to prepare his petroleum legislation before domestic and foreign pressures could dilute it, as had happened in Argentina, and before Brazil found oil. To this extent, he was moving beyond Mosconi.

Horta and his deputy Fleury first faced the fact that Brazil had no oil production. Mosconi had always said that price and market controls could not be fully effective until a substantial share of the market was locally supplied. For years, Brazil would lack the capital, transportation, and refineries to challenge foreign control. This left the nation open to pressuring and reprisals. Whereas a State monopoly was the ideal, it was only realistic for the government to cooperate with private domestic capital and to move cautiously. The first step, therefore, was to nationalize the industry and place it under the control of the CNP, which would have three main objectives.[19]

First, the CNP would encourage and also protect Brazilian private refineries against attempted take-overs by the trusts, while enjoining domestic capitalists from exploiting their consumers. Foreign capital would be allowed only in importing and distributing. In view of the reprisal threat, some foreign ownership of preferred stock and bonds would be permitted, but the management and common stock had to be held by native-born Brazilians.*

Second, this industry, which in other countries had been subject to concentrated ownership and monopolistic practices, was to develop under CNP planning, as a public utility. Production, quality control, plant size, location, ownership, transportation, imports of crude oil, and marketing—all would have to meet CNP specifications and approval.

Third, the new Council would impose uniform, nationwide prices on all oil products by lumping all internal taxes into one easy-to-collect federal tax, the *imposto único*. New roads, financed by this tax, and cheaper fuel would constitute strong incentives for developing the hinterland. As Mosconi had said, uniform pricing was one of the YPF's greatest achievements. The Brazilian interior was larger, less developed, and had a greater price differential from the coastal supply ports; but despite these formidable obstacles Horta believed the imposto único idea would become a major factor in national integration.

In sum, these were the policies that the CNP soon followed under Horta Barbosa, President, and Fleury da Rocha, Vice President. Though he was starting with almost no resources, Horta wanted to exclude foreigners altogether from production and refining, which was something that Argentina, for all its wealth and natural resources, was unable to achieve. In late March 1938, the CFCE's Chamber for Production, Consumption, and Transport secretly drew up a bill along these lines and sent it to the President.

If Vargas was skeptical, it was because he still shared the attitudes of his generation toward State industry. All along, he had been interested in Guinle's company, in de Paiva's reform plans, and in offers from the international oil companies with whom he was in contact. Getúlio was not then preoccupied with petroleum policy, however, so he followed Horta's lead. Yet he moved cautiously, hesitating to decree Fleury's bill until the full Foreign

* In later drafts, foreigners were barred from purchasing preferred stock because under Brazilian corporate law, preferred stock reverted automatically to common stock if after two years no dividends were paid. However, aliens could subscribe loans and bonds.

Trade Council, in lieu of the deposed Congress, shared political responsibility for approving it.*

Any legislation sponsored by the General Staff and presented as vital to national defense was sure to be approved—and it was, in a secret session held at Itamaraty Palace on April 29, although seeing this draft decree for the first time, some councillors had reservations about going it alone. A spokesman for the commercial associations said the government would have trouble explaining the law to foreign investors who were hearing unfavorable reports about Brazil. A few mouthed the "best customer" argument, according to which Brazil should never jeopardize United States exports for fear of reprisals. A domestic refining industry, they said, would surely cut into sales of American gasoline. Others were enthusiastic, feeling, as João Lourenço put it, that they were "laying the foundations of future greatness. Gentlemen of the CFCE," he concluded, "we have done our duty."[20]

Immediately a military aircraft was dispatched by General João Pinto, Chief of the Military Household, to Vargas, who within minutes was thumbing through the documents at São Lourenço spa in Minas Gerais. Still he hesitated, and sent for his Chief of Staff. Never having read the dossier, Góes Monteiro frantically called Horta for a briefing; then, having picked up the main points, flew to Vargas. "I'll sign gladly, if this is what you really want," the President told him. Góes gave a final defense, and so Decree Law 395 went to the *Diário Oficial*, where the presses were waiting, and appeared the morning of May 1 over all the ministers' signatures. Foreign Minister Aranha, knowing nothing of these events, was surprised to find the British and American Ambassadors waiting for him that Monday afternoon, on his return to Rio from weekending in Petrópolis. Jefferson Caffery of the United States asked him about the new restrictive laws, and Aranha replied that his government had no such policy. Then they showed him the decree.

The government had sprung its national oil legislation deliber-

* One recalls from Chapter 5 how the Army in 1939 again worked from within the CFCE to obtain civilian sanction for its steel plans. Vargas suggested this procedure.

ately before foreign and domestic pressure groups could mobilize. Law 395 had been passed secretly while Jersey Standard raced publicly to erect its rickety topping plant in São Paulo so as to claim prior legal rights to carry on refining. Soon this plant at Jaguaré was paralyzed. Yet in these tight-lipped Army maneuvers there was another, long-range objective, namely to facilitate Brazilian access to Bolivian oil.

Fleury, who had recently negotiated with the Bolivians, knew the situation well. On February 25, 1938, the two nations ratified notes drawn up in 1937 by which Brazil agreed to honor an old treaty obligation to link the Bolivian city of Santa Cruz de la Sierra to São Paulo by trunk railroad in return for concessionary rights to Bolivia's Oriente Province oilfields and crude oil payments. Bolivia, weakened by its defeat in the Chaco War, wanted its frontiers guaranteed and its oilfields developed. Brazil, after stalling the rail project for years, was now eager to secure nearby oil for defense, and to offset Argentine influence in Bolivia—especially in Oriente Province, a hotbed of separatist feeling.[21]

Having recently expropriated Standard's virtually inactive operations, the Bolivians were not being open-handed with their oil reserves except, perhaps, to the Argentines. Yacimientos Petrolíferos Fiscales Bolivianos (YPFB), their new oil autarchy, was not only modeled on Argentina's YPF but it was also run by two Orientales, Dionisio Foianini and Jorge Lavadenz who were closely linked to Argentine oilmen. Advised by Argentina not to ratify, the YPFB officials nonetheless badly wanted the new railroad to Santa Cruz, capital of their home province. To ease their dilemma, Foianini and Lavadenz decided to allow joint private Brazilian-Bolivian companies to explore if and when Brazil organized an official company to transport, process, and market Bolivian oil in Brazil. They insisted on not allowing any of their oil to be handled in Brazil by private companies through which Standard Oil might in some way maneuver to regain control of Bolivian fields. This formula was agreed to in the February treaty. Because they were disgruntled former officials of Standard of Bolivia, Foianini and Lavadenz wanted old scores with Standard to stay settled.

Thus two parallel events, the Bolivian treaty and the decision to organize a CNP, came together to give impetus to a State oil refinery. Part of Horta's reason for rushing through Decree Law 395 was to reassure the YPFB of Brazil's strong interest in the treaty formula. In authorizing the government to refine oil, the law also reflected direct Bolivian influence. For when the Oriente began to produce oil, Horta was determined to have a CNP plant in operation.[22]

To sum up: the 1938 oil laws charted long-range goals, such as self-sufficiency and economic independence, and to this extent they were a statement of moral commitment as well as law. They also were designed to facilitate such immediate aims as regulating the supply of petroleum, refining, and prospecting. Statism was the ideal, to be sure, but there was no rigid timetable. With big objectives and small resources, the government had to be flexible. Thus, the CNP was authorized to produce oil and refine "when judged convenient." As for distribution, it became a distant goal, as the system was already capitalized and foreign owned. In addition, Horta Barbosa knew that the refiner, not the distributor, controls prices. Clearly, he was determined to be flexible while feeling his way with the new CNP.

The Council was organized as a special organ of the Presidency, subject to military veto (never used). Cooperation with private enterprise was recognized formally by allowing two class representatives from industry and commerce to sit on the directorate. The ideal was to assure harmonious relations; the objective was to line up the Brazilian private sector in the fight against foreign penetration; the function of class members was advisory. These private sector members also wrote the reports on investigations, such as the one into Monteiro Lobato's questionable companies. Yet as Horta soon discovered, it was one thing to chart long-range goals and to take charge on the momentum of a military coup, and quite another to keep the policy initiative in a fluid system like the Estado Nôvo.

Through mid-1939 the Council moved rapidly to enforce its new regulatory powers, and its staff quietly drew up solutions to the twin problems of pricing and refining. All refining and drilling concessions were investigated to assure financial soundness and to verify Brazilian ownership and direction. Ypiranga, the largest refiner, was ordered to dispose of Argentine- and Uruguayan-held voting stock while Monteiro Lobato fought, failed, and was jailed. And when oil was finally found at Lobato, Bahia, in January 1939, Horta took over the DNPM operation, declared the Recôncavo area a national defense reserve, and thus terminated the unproductive wildcat era.

In July 1939, Horta sent Vargas two drafts of enabling legislation, one to set up a uniform national pricing system (the imposto único), and the other to establish a government refinery. I shall turn first to the imposto único, and then to the refinery decree, which was its complement (that is, the CNP refinery would process Bolivian oil and so reinforce domestic price controls by its production).

If few officials grasped the merits of a unified federal tax on petroleum products, in retrospect it was a landmark in Estado Nôvo legislation and one of Horta's main achievements. One recalls how poor transport and many local taxes pushed prices up outside ports of entry. Taking the average of 35 different oil taxes, Horta unified them into one tax rate, but kept the equivalent revenue value of the old taxes so as to maintain income levels. With this uniform tax, the CNP could set standard prices using the port cities as base points, thus nationalizing the market. For their part, the foreign distributing companies would be relieved of complex bookkeeping and irksome dealings with local officials. Interior consumers would pay less. Simple allocation and collection, moreover, opened the way for a highway finance plan, the first in Brazilian history. With their share (26 per cent) of fund income, states and local governments could draw on the Bank of Brazil to secure long-term highway bonds. Thus, disciplining prices and promoting national integration were two broad objectives of the imposto único. A third objective contemporaries found controversial, namely reducing tax relief for domestic producers.[28]

Originally, the CNP did not plan to monopolize refining. In fact Decree Law 4,071 (May 1939) granted the existing and prospective private plants de facto monopoly privileges and guaranteed market zones. The purpose was to protect them from dumping. But then Horta moved to curtail these handsome favors. In July, he asked Vargas to raise the existing federal tax rates under which domestic gasoline paid 100 reis per liter, as against 569 reis for imported gasoline, and crude oil entered almost duty free. The new imposto único rates were 629 and 825 reis, respectively. By scaling down the old tax relief bonanza to 25 per cent, the CNP sought to prevent profiteering and to force the three operating topping plants to modernize. To be sure, 25 per cent was still an ample profit margin, but there was more to Horta's argument. Stimulating private investment was not the general's main concern, as was shown by his plan to put ten-year limits on the refinery concessions, after which the assets reverted to public control. This tough provision could only mean that Horta was becoming less and less convinced that private industry was the answer. And Horta's pricing plan would not be complete until Brazil had its own large refining industry.

Mosconi always insisted on this. The old Argentine general, though confined to a wheelchair, held long, animated conversations with Horta in Buenos Aires in April 1939 and opened the YPF files to him as a case study in national independence. Again Mosconi drove home the point that government-owned refineries were the key to preventing foreign domination of the home market. In Uruguay, Horta learned how Carlos R. Veigh Garzón, the charming general manager of ANCAP, the Uruguayan fuel and cement autarchy, had bought an English-made and financed refinery, secured crude oil despite rumors of a boycott, trained a technical staff, and succeeded in supplying 90 per cent of his country's gasoline.[24] Mosconi and Garzón impressed the visiting Brazilian with their articulate brief for economic nationalism, and they requested Brazil to join with them in a policy of continental solidarity. After outlining his enthusiastic impression in reports to Vargas, Horta returned, convinced that he and his fellow South Americans had a special understanding, and that the policies of these neighbors coincided with the new Brazilian legislation and even reinforced it.[25] Plans for the CNP refinery reached Vargas's desk three months later.[26]

The CNP refinery became increasingly attractive to Horta as he saw plans, heard proposals, and caught rumors of new private and state government projects. After the world recession eased in mid-1938, there was a brief flurry of foreign interest in Brazilian industry in general, including refining. Several well-connected business figures were reportedly involved. Banker Corrêa e Castro, would-be PEMEX (Mexican oil) distributor, projected a 10,000 b/day refinery in Niteroi, and perhaps other cities; builder Raja Gabaglia, talked of a scheme to use German-made tankers bought on compensation; lawyer Santiago Dantas and the ubiquitous Lodi, with Murray-Simonsen behind them, were ready to finance the Rio de Janeiro state plant. Were some of these, as Horta believed, back door entrances for the foreign oil companies?[27]

Horta also reviewed proposals from three federal interventors, including Ernani do Amaral Peixoto of Rio de Janeiro, the President's son-in-law. Their challenge to centralism was clear, for profits might well be used to strengthen state political machines and regional economies at the nation's expense. Also, there was the possibility of direct negotiations between states and foreign companies. Doubtless Horta recalled São Paulo's 1937 concession of the Jaguaré site to Standard Oil. Outright opposition to the states was politically unwise. But he let it be known that with a 4,000 b/day government plant for Guanabara Bay now on CNP drawing boards, he wanted his own agency to become the nation's largest refiner.

Bahia's proposed refinery at Salvador was the first to fall, in mid-1939. The plant, which was sponsored by Interventor Landulpho Alves, would have funded a large political war chest, but Horta dissuaded Alves. Then a private plan was proposed by the Rio banker Drault Ernanny de Mello e Silva in conjunction with Bahia. But this too came to nothing. And though relations with the Bahian group had always been cordial, Horta was glad, nonetheless, when they backed out.[28]

Rio de Janeiro's 4,000 b/day installation was planned for São

Lourenço Cove across the bay from the CNP site in the Federal District. Warnings by CNP engineers that extensive dredging was required at São Lourenço failed to deter the state authorities. On September 21, 1938, they signed a preliminary contract with Foster-Wheeler, an American company which later agreed on a 1941 completion date at a dollar cost of $2.6 million. Major financing was arranged through the Murray-Simonsen group in São Paulo, who were correspondents to Lazard Brothers, bankers for Royal Dutch Shell. Upon completion of the plant, Murray-Simonsen planned to lease it back to the state, in exchange for a share of the profits. Since a Standard-Shell consortium was to supply the crude oil, Horta believed the majors were maneuvering behind the Rio project.

São Paulo's projected 6,000 b/day refinery and pipeline to Santos, also designed by Foster-Wheeler, was backed by the Bank of São Paulo and Roberto Simonsen. Together with Rio de Janeiro's, this plant would dominate the Center-South market and supply 70 per cent of the nation's gasoline, 22 per cent of its diesel and fuel oil, and 41 per cent of its kerosene. But the twin schemes died in late 1940, victims of the war and what their backers considered an insufficient profit margin under the new imposto único.[29]

Opposition from Rio de Janeiro, domestic producers, and the majors had failed to halt the imposto único tax bill, which was approved in September 1940.[30] Logic was on Horta's side, but few ministers grasped the dimensions of his consolidation plan. Among reports on the bill from Agriculture, Finance, Foreign Affairs, Justice, and Labor, only the last two were favorable. Finance Minister Souza Costa, a fiscal conservative and no innovator, raised the federal oil duties on his own authority while the CNP draft still was pending. Ultimately, however, he did not object to the imposto único, since current federal revenues were to be maintained. The most important supporting brief was written by Oliveira Vianna, the political sociologist, counselor at Labor, and follower of Alberto Tôrres, who quickly grasped the implications of a highway trust fund and unified taxation. To make certain that Vargas would read Oliveira Vianna's lucid report first, the CNP arranged for his private secretary, Luiz Vergara, to place a red flag on it. Being a connoisseur of good writing, Vargas soon found that the line of argument for national integration appealed to him, and he approved the draft legislation.[31]

Passage of the companion refinery bill was sought by Horta to make the CNP like the YPF, but without Argentina's foreign producers. This time the opposition was more formidable. Valentim Bouças, secretary of the Finance Ministry's Technical and Financial Council (CTEF), took strong exception to the idea of State-owned refineries. With ties to American interests through the import trade, he naturally advanced the "best customer" argument, a favorite of commercial groups well represented on the CTEF.[32] Bouças found an ally in Souza Costa, who on principle opposed costly State industrial ventures. Moreover, the Department of Public Service Administration (DASP), a sprawling civil service and budgetary agency, was challenging the CNP's independent status under the presidency. Souza Costa, in turn, backed up the DASP's attempt to tighten controls on the Petroleum Council. Not surprisingly, Vargas temporized and returned this bill for further study.

Difficulties over the refinery authorization, for which Horta had high hopes, revealed the limits of his power. Vargas protected the CNP from the DASP, but at a price. For though this showed the President's skills as master broker among ministerial interests, it also pointed to the limited bases of CNP support. The Council was held to a bare-bones budget that allowed only a token exploration effort in Bahia, and the DASP imposed rigid personnel policies that hindered Horta from building a technical staff. Overriding all these difficulties was the fact that by mid-1940, government energies were centering on steel, not oil refineries. Meanwhile, the war threatened to cause severe oil shortages, and the CNP had to shift its own priorities from building an industry to stockpiling, rationing, and distributing. General Horta Barbosa's period of greatest success had passed.

Still, Horta pressed on. He became increasingly impatient with private groups who attacked the imposto único while maneuvering to avoid the laws against direct foreign equity holdings. In

June 1941 he informed Vargas that private and state refineries were proving "detrimental to the collectivity." The former policy of collaborating with private industry was over, he declared. Now the CNP wanted to build refineries at Rio and at Salvador, near the newly discovered oil fields. There could be no effective development of the industry until the CNP monopolized refining and used the high profits not for private gain, as the entrepreneurs would, but for exploration.[33] In a nutshell, these were the arguments that were to become both doctrine and strategy for adherents to what might be called the Horta Barbosa school. The National Security Council approved his monopoly plan, but the DASP had many reservations, and here the matter stood as the war closed in.

Horta's hopes for implementing the government refineries soared briefly when in the March 1942 Washington Agreements the United States agreed to set aside $100 million for Brazilian industrial expansion. He requested financing for drilling rigs and a used American refinery in Houston, which Brantley had examined. Knowing that the oil companies had good Washington contacts, however, Horta was reluctant to permit William J. Kemnitzer, a petroleum geologist in government service, to examine the oilfields in Bahia. Aranha cleared the way by pointing out that Kemnitzer had authored a strong anti-monopoly study of the oil industry for the Anti-trust division of the United States Justice Department. Kemnitzer reported that four more rigs probably would increase Bahian production to 3,500 b/day, enough to operate a used 4,500 b/day refinery, which the Brazilians wanted badly. But Brazil's daily requirements for crude oil were approaching 32,000 barrels. With this in mind, Kemnitzer concluded that although Brazil did in fact have oil, the prospects for an early reduction in oil imports were not good.[34] Washington did not heed Horta's requests. Hardpressed militarily, and heavily committed to Volta Redonda, the Americans had little enthusiasm for refineries that would have no immediate defense role, and that were, moreover, in the usual investment sphere of American private companies.

In the meantime, Standard, the leading United States company, had made proposals in 1936, 1940, 1941, and 1942 to build a large refinery at Niteroi on Guanabara Bay. In return, it sought concessions in the Amazon and Paraná basins, coupled with changes in the exclusionist laws to assure "a sound and stable legal basis" of participation. It would welcome Brazilian capital as long as Standard of Brazil held majority control and had freedom to operate in all phases of the business. This was good news to Brazilian investors who were eager to attach their fortunes to Jersey Standard's. Vargas himself had been in contact with Howland Bancroft of Standard, through intermediaries. As with the steel issue, the evidence points to Vargas's preference for private Brazilian refineries or a cooperative venture between a United States company and the Brazilian government, with private management playing the key role.[35] Exploratory conversations along these lines were held with the majors. But after 1939, Standard moved toward a more conventional position, including requests for concessions; by mid-1941 the government was prepared to go along.

The Army reacted with vigor. As Horta wrote Vargas, to accept Standard's terms would be to abandon the entire nationalist policy, which now harmonized with that of other South American nations.[36] Furthermore, he believed that Standard's hints of a large-scale exploration program were misleading. In fact, the small amounts they were talking about ($10–$20 million at the most) were sufficient only to pinpoint Brazilian reserves. Rather than have foreign companies hold but not develop these areas, he preferred to carry on with the modest CNP Bahian drilling program and to postpone large-scale prospecting with State funds until after the war.

Twice Standard's proposals were all but approved, only to founder on Horta's rock-like opposition. In mid-1941, Napoleão Alencastro Guimarães, an aide to Mendonça Lima in the Ministry of Transport, brought Standard's offer to the National Security Council, which cleared it over the objections of War Minister Dutra, who opposed it for security reasons. Horta then sent Vargas a strong letter saying that as an officer he must obey, but that as Brazilian citizen he could not, and would resign. Vargas respected Horta's integrity. And now, as a dictator, he felt embarrassed, because the letter, if made public, would challenge him directly over an issue on which he did not feel strongly. Grasping his classic black cigar between the first two fingers and smiling, Vargas told Horta's aide (Captain Ibá Jobim Meirelles) that the letter was never written, that the National Security Council meeting was never held, and that petroleum, after all, was the Army's worry. One year later, in September 1942, Horta and Dutra blocked another offer sponsored by Souza Costa.

If in the short run these vetoes kept the American companies out, in the long run they became precedents that Horta's followers cited as dogma: a line once drawn must never be crossed. As for General Horta, he could take satisfaction in having veto powers, but he felt the loss of his initiative. He could secure neither the funds nor a clear government mandate for his CNP monopoly plan. The wartime fuel crisis, furthermore, having involved the CNP in unpopular rationing and priority decisions, focused attention on Horta's entire program. Was it the key to development or a roadblock to progress?

Opinions about oil policy were clearly polarizing. Simonsen's FIESP, commercial groups, the Finance Minister and others argued that Brazil lacked the capital and the technical and managerial skills to go it alone. They saw association with the international companies as an attractive alternative to State monopoly with its inefficiencies, high costs, and political involvements. Army officers, professional men, civil servants, and some journalists, however, disagreed. To them, constant vigilance against the oil companies was the price of economic independence. The rules for oil, they said, were different from those for any other industry. He who failed to understand this clearly was dangerously ignorant.

Proponents of both positions foresaw the extension of the military and economic alliance with the United States into large capital transfers, technical assistance, and an open world economic system in the postwar era. In this spirit, Roberto Simonsen called for a Latin American Marshall Plan in 1948, and Horta wanted United States public funds for the oil industry.[37] Horta's followers continued to stress economic and military defense, which showed that their world view had been set during the 1930's. They did not want technological isolationism, however. As Horta had always done, they would use the most advanced petroleum technology, and they would hire the best foreign talent, but Brazilians would be in control. The issue was not simply a clash between economic liberalism and nationalism; rather it was a question of the nature and degree of State regulation and control. Delegates led by Roberto Simonsen at the First Brazilian Economic Congress (1943) resolved that the government should revise its 1940 Mining Code and allow foreign capital "to collaborate in mining companies in a non-preponderant manner." This, they said, was the short, efficient path to petroleum exploration and development. But Rio's Union of Engineers demanded that Vargas hold the line against modifications in the oil laws. A foreign solution would be the fastest, they agreed, but it was reprehensible because any industrialization under the oil trust would lead to a diminishing of Brazilian sovereignty. As for relying on private domestic capital, it was unfair for the few to profit at public expense; thus a State solution was best.[38]

Horta's influence was waning and he knew it. He had opponents on all sides. Deeply committed to the oil laws and the CNP, Horta resigned rather than see the program of which he was the symbol and leader destroyed. When in mid-1943 he transferred to a field command, the anti-Horta forces were confident: "Fortunately, reason and common sense will prevail over suspicion and the nearly spent wave of xenophobia," wrote one prominent CTEF spokesman for foreign investment. Horta vigorously denied the accusations. Our nationalism, he wrote, was founded "only on the proposition, dictated by necessity, that mineral wealth should not escape the effective control and dominion of Brazil. Nothing more."[39] Phase one was over.

Brazilians in 1945 were tired of rationing, the black market in petroleum, and *gasogênios*, the smoking, piston-knocking substitutes for gasoline.[1] And now, the war over, they had large dollar reserves and wanted to consume. Owners of new automobiles and trucks wanted gasoline; industrialists wanted more fuel oil; commuters needed more and cheaper transportation; and domestic airlines planned to expand. Fuel requirements began to climb at 16 per cent a year and rapid mechanization brought the oil problem home to Brazilians from all walks of life. What began as pent-up demands for fuel became a political issue. This time, however, the decisions about oil were not made behind closed doors, but in front of Congress, reborn and responsive to the postwar euphoria over open, participatory politics. An opening to the oil companies was tried and abandoned. And though the petroleum problem remained unsolved in 1949, the nation at the end of the second phase had a new slogan, "o petróleo é nosso," which summed up the new politics of oil.

When World War II ended, the legal climate had already thawed considerably. Associational groups like those gathered at the Terezópolis Conference in 1945 were calling on Brazil to join the world trend away from "economic isolationism." Revisions in the restrictive 1940 Mining Code were being urged on the government by Simonsen's FIESP, whose own proposal for ownership—60 per cent national, 40 per cent foreign—was widely discussed.[2] The movement toward open access to Brazilian mineral resources was formally recognized in the liberal 1946 Constitution, and everyone expected that the general body of petroleum laws dating back to 1938 would soon be brought into line.

Colonel João Carlos Barreto wanted to reorient the CNP. Succeeding Horta in 1943, he brought to the presidency such contemporary assets as pro-American views and a close friendship with the Vargas family, but he had no previous experience with petroleum. In the days of wartime collaboration, it had become fashionable to question the "excessively nationalistic" oil laws. Barreto said as much, and more, because he believed strongly that Brazil had been getting nowhere under Horta. In his opinion, given the enormous task ahead, a State monopoly over exploration and refining could not be justified. When pressed he would say, "Well, isn't Standard Oil the best organized financially and technically to solve our problem?" Many high government officials agreed. As for the oil companies, they had been arguing all along that Brazil was far too big for any one company or for the government alone to explore and develop in a reasonable length of time.

In January 1945, Barreto urged the government to lift restrictions on foreign investment in oil stipulating only that Brazilian capital should have preference in any future development plans. Though he met opposition in the CNP Plenary, Barreto did not give up. At least, he wrote Vargas in May, no legal changes would be required to stimulate Brazilian private investment in refining, which was the quickest way to get plants in the major oil supply centers. If some of the profits were reinvested for exploration, so much the better.[3] To a large extent, therefore, Barreto's suggested guidelines meant turning the petroleum problem over to Brazilian private enterprise and, after statutory changes were made, to the oil companies.

News of Barreto's intentions, combined with the existence of hard currency reserves and heavy demands for fuel, was encouragement enough to private interests. In August, one Paulista group under Alberto Soares Sampaio, a railroad financier, and another led by Aristides de Almeida of Ypiranga Oil Company requested permission to build 10,000 b/day refineries in Rio and São Paulo, respectively. Vargas approved Barreto's refinery policy just before he was forced from office by a military coup, and in October bids for the refinery concessions were opened.[4]

The proposals had to be submitted within 30 days and would

only be accepted from groups that had an assured supply of crude oil and agreed to prospect. These conditions were ideal for Soares Sampaio, who had the Moreira Salles Bank behind him and, as Barreto knew, had obtained an agreement from Standard Oil to furnish equipment, 49 per cent of the finance, and a five-year crude supply. Ypiranga Oil Company was backed by Guilherme Guinle's Boavista Bank and by Pedro Luis Corrêa e Castro, through whom Gulf Oil's offer for financing and crude was secured. Apparently, the majors were maneuvering to keep tabs on the refinery situation while awaiting legal changes that would allow them to invest openly, in their own names.

Ostensibly, the competition was open, but in fact outsiders found it was almost impossible to secure crude oil contracts on such short notice. This was discovered by Drault Ernanny, a Rio banker and the force behind Bahia's prewar refinery plan, when all the majors refused to sell him crude. In part, it was because Drault was close to the old CNP leadership.[5] More importantly, since his project was totally supported by Brazilian capital, it did not fit the previous arrangements with the majors. Drault's bid survived, thanks to an eleventh-hour phone call from Ambassador Adolph A. Berle, Jr., to Standard Oil of California, which had never marketed in Brazil before. The ex–New Dealer's intercession in effect opened up the bidding. In addition, four minor plans were submitted, including the frankly speculative proposal by Raja Gabaglia, a well-connected contractor who had assurances for Mexican (PEMEX) crude oil.

Caught unawares by Drault and Gabaglia, Barreto announced another round of competitions on January 18, 1946. Rio and São Paulo were now authorized to have two refineries each, but Barreto made it no secret that he wanted the latecomers to withdraw. Drault and Soares Sampaio were competing for the 8,000 b/day concession in Rio; Ypiranga was fighting to get its 10,000 b/day proposal for São Paulo approved instead of Raja Gabaglia's 6,000 b/day plant. Hoping to narrow the field, Barreto gave each group 90 days to deposit cr$500 for each barrel of refining capacity, submit a signed, five-year crude contract, and agree to invest half

their profits in exploration. The terms were very hard. Raja Gabaglia dropped out in June, unable to raise the deposit, and his
rival withdrew when Gulf suddenly abandoned it. But the wheel-
ing and dealing was far from over.

Drault survived pressure from the CNP to relocate his Refinaria de Petróleos do Distrito Federal (later called Manguinhos)
in Salvador, Bahia, offers from Standard to buy him out, and a
financial crisis that resulted in the loss of majority control to Peixoto de Castro, a wealthy gambler-speculator. Throughout these
difficulties, his trump was a lease on two million square meters
of Manguinhos Cove flatlands, the best site on Guanabara Bay
(where Horta's CNP refinery would have gone), and one that his
rivals could not match. In late 1946, Soares Sampaio's Refinaria
e Exploração de Petróleo União (or União) lost ground as Standard withdrew its financing and equipment offers.[6] The CNP then
secured União's agreement to relocate at Capuava, São Paulo, in
return for doubling refinery capacity to 20,000 b/day, a so-called
onus that was really a handsome CNP bonus. Having finally secured their concessions, Manguinhos and União prepared to move
ahead, almost a year and a half after the first bids were let.

Their troubles were only about to begin. By 1947 it was too late
to take advantage of Brazil's dollar reserves, now vanished. Foreign
capital markets were tight, and Manguinhos's application for a
loan of ten million dollars from the Export-Import Bank no longer
interested official Washington. This financial situation, when
coupled with the maneuvering by which União and Manguinhos
had obtained their concessions, did not make Barreto's new policy
look very good. But nobody foresaw the series of financial and
political crises that were further to delay them until 1954.[7]

Trying to tap still more private capital, Barreto in mid-1946 set
up a mixed corporation, the Refinaria Nacional de Petróleo, to
refine crude oil from government-owned reserves in Bahia and to
accelerate exploration with diverted profits. There were wartime
precedents for this mixed-company option, notably in steel and
aluminum. Oil reserves were still very low—12 million barrels—
but the discovery of the new São João field promised to raise the

reserve / production ratio enough to justify a small 2,500 b/day government refinery at Mataripe, Bahia. The oil itself, being paraffin based, was suitable mainly for the production of lubricants. Mataripe was budgeted at cr$50 million, half in public capital and half from the Bank of Brazil, though open to public subscription.[8] But the mixed company, however attractive in theory, failed to attract private investors even though the stock issue was open for two years. Rising dollar costs and inflation at home helped to delay the project, and in 1948 Mataripe was projected upward to 5,000 b/day as a wholly government-owned subsidiary under CNP management. Three years later it became Brazil's first modern producing oil refinery.

Thus private capitalists did not step forward with a quick and relatively inexpensive alternative to government refineries. In fairness to Barreto, these refineries were ancillary to the main task he outlined to Vargas in May 1945: attracting hundreds of millions of foreign dollars to develop a continental-sized nation. In effect, this was tantamount to shifting the emphasis from national financing via refining profits, which Horta had favored, to a more conventional effort, beginning with exploration, in order to orchestrate the various sectors of the industry into a dynamic, integrated whole. To Barreto, the overriding problem was lack of money for exploration. With its totally inadequate funds of cr$300 million (about $10.5 million) the CNP from 1939 to 1945 had been unable to prospect more than 250 square kilometers. This situation was not Horta's fault, if only because he had been able to accomplish little in Bahia before the war closed in. But the contemporary view was that Horta's brand of nationalism was far too rigid to produce quick results.

The higher military officers in President Eurico Gaspar Dutra's new government (1946–51) accepted this view, which Juarez Távora, now holding down Horta's old job as Deputy Chief of Staff, advocated vigorously. Having been isolated politically from 1937 to 1945, Távora saw the old laws as out of date. His superiors agreed to liberalize the Estado Nôvo legislation in line with what they conceived was Brazil's need, as a capital-importing nation, for foreign investment in basic sectors of the economy. At the same time, they insisted on retaining State regulation of the industry and, for defense reasons, on assuring Brazilian control over the internal market. The problem, in short, was how to bring in the foreign oil companies without paying too high a price.

In February 1947, President Dutra appointed a blue ribbon commission under the CNP to prepare a new oil bill, and eight months later its draft of the Petroleum Statute was ready.[9] The Statute's guidelines were anchored on the concept of an indirect State monopoly. Development remained in principle a public utility, meaning that the CNP would continue to regulate the industry. The CNP exploration, production, and refining program would be financed with a new National Petroleum Fund, based on internal sources (CNP profits) and external government subsidies. To complement its own activities, however, the CNP could work with foreign companies on a concessionary basis. As the commission saw it, this program would accelerate the pace of exploration in order to achieve, in the shortest time possible, two interlocking goals: finding the oil and supplying Brazil's internal market.

Simple in its ends, the Statute's means were innovative, and unconventional. The commission bifurcated the national oil economy into internal and external markets. In the one, Brazilians would control refining and transportation through direct State action, and/or through mixed companies, using the FIESP 60–40 ownership formula. In the other, foreign companies could export their crude or refined products outright and set up the usual integrated operations under their control. But supplying the home market, including strategic reserves, took definite priority over exporting. In effect, the majors were being asked to become minority partners in Brazilian companies. Only when the home industry was built up could they recoup through exports their outlays for exploration and production, a highly capital-intensive sector. Clearly, the domestic chicken came before the foreign egg.

The reason for this strategy was partly financial: the commission wanted to tap foreign capital and experience in all phases of the industry. Tactically, it was thought that companies with assets in domestic facilities would have more incentives to bring their oilfields into production. The majors might otherwise hold Brazilian oil in reserve while exporting cheaper oil from the Middle East and Venezuela. Or they might not develop their fields as rapidly as the Brazilian authorities intended. Finally, the commission wanted a politically attractive solution. Build up the domestic industry first, the majors were told. This was the price for amending the nationalist oil laws.[10]

This, in brief summary, was the essence of Brazil's first comprehensive oil development plan. It must be said, however, that the Petroleum Statute of 1947 was weakened by some illusory thinking and by the accidents of timing. The Statute was not well received by the oil companies, and it was the commission's misfortune to release it just as the petroleum mobilization campaign began. In combination, these factors were fatal.

The oil companies' position was well known, both from the draft statutes that Shell and Standard submitted to the commission, and from the counsel of two well-known oilmen, Herbert Hoover, Jr., and Arthur A. Curtice. Laws similar to Venezuela's were apparently what the majors had in mind. They wanted the host government, in return for royalties and taxes on crude exports, to grant an "international concession," under which the companies would have the economic freedom to integrate operations under their own management, policies, and financial control. The least they were prepared to accept was 51 per cent control of the refining and transportation sectors, the right to dispose freely of their crude oil in international markets, and the authority to decide when and where to bring oilfields into production. Having years of experience in Latin America behind them, moreover, the companies doubtless saw in the Statute many possibilities for delays, arbitrary decisions, and favoritism.[11] In short, they thought they could get better terms, whereas the Brazilians wanted a kind of partnership along lines of their own choosing.

Hoover and Curtice said that the companies would not come in under the Statute. Brazil could not have it both ways. "A fundamental choice must be made," they informed the commission, "between a policy that will encourage private companies to undertake the development of Brazilian oil in preference to any other area of the continent, and a policy of continuing the present [restrictive] situation."[12] In 1949, Standard of Brazil's retiring President, Wingate Man Anderson, in effect confirmed that negotiations had been fruitless. "From what we know of this [Statute], we do not think our company or any other commercial enterprise could develop production successfully under its provisions. Obviously we could not favor its promulgation."[13] As for Barreto, he doubted whether Dutra's commission had offered enough incentives in refining and transportation to make the risks of exploration attractive to foreign capital.[14] He was right, but fundamentally the problem hinged on a basic, even naïve misjudgment—that it was possible to please everyone.

Another misjudgment was made in counting heavily on help from Washington. That the United States was concentrating on European recovery, and that refineries were being built in Europe on United States public funds while Manguinhos was rejected, were both facts well known in Rio. This did not discourage the Brazilians from believing that both the United States and Britain were following "New Deal" policies regarding oil, based on their wartime experiences with market controls and anti-trust laws.[15] But it did not follow logically that Brazil could take the same road with their approval and support. At hemispheric meetings in Chapultepec in 1945 and Bogotá in 1948, American delegates took a relatively traditional, liberal stand on economic issues, especially petroleum development. And although for strategic reasons the United States wanted Latin America's oil reserves developed, this did not mean that Rio could count on Washington's support in negotiations with the majors. Poignantly, the Statute was offered in a spirit of wartime collaboration; but now, with Brazil on the cold war periphery, the Brazilians discovered that their policy was not accepted in a similar spirit, and that they no longer had that kind of influence with the Americans.

By late 1947, the commission knew it faced a serious dilemma. The present bill could not attract foreign capital without changes in the provisions for national control that the military would not accept. Liberalizing the Statute would invite attacks, and perhaps defeat, at the hands of nationalists in Congress. Also, it was painfully clear that the partisans of both a State monopoly and the majors opposed this legislation.[16] The strategy of trying to steer a middle course between these two groups was not working. In fact, astute political observers knew that the Statute was in deep trouble even before Congress began debating it in February 1948. It is to the public background of these debates that we now turn.

To the extent that Brazilians thought about oil policy at all in 1945, it was as dissatisfied consumers rather than as aroused citizens. In their eagerness to dismantle their dictatorship, most politically aware Brazilians thought of nationalism as something to be played down, perhaps as vaguely illegitimate in the postwar liberal world. To them, the Estado Nôvo meant restrictive laws, arbitrary arrests, and censorship. (Knowledge that historians would later stress the regime's developmental aspects would have been met with disbelief.) Now they wanted to enjoy the new freedoms. Monteiro Lobato was out of prison, and his call for unfettered private initiative in oil was often quoted and his fraud forgotten.[17] During the Constituent Assembly debates (April–August 1946), the delegates voiced little specific interest in oil, but generally favored foreign capital participation in the development of their natural resources. Even the Communist Party (PCB) wanted to allow foreign capital in oil. A bill introduced by the Communists followed some offhand remarks by presidential hopeful Eduardo Gomes of the National Democratic Union (UDN; center-right liberals) to the effect that Brazil should look for capital everywhere, including the Soviet Union. Quite sincerely the Communists tried to arrange for Soviet aid.[18] Only in 1947 did the participating public begin to sense that petroleum was an issue. Why did oil become a public passion unequaled since the abolitionist campaign over 60 years before?

In part, it was in reaction to Brazil's marginal role in world affairs, the awareness of isolation that swept South America as the cold war intensified. In Brazil, as elsewhere, the reaction took the form of recrudescent economic and political nationalism. Vargas, in his famous speech to the Senate in 1946 upon returning from political exile, recalled how Brazil, under his leadership, had built up industry and expanded social justice through association with President Roosevelt in the war coalition. But the postwar mood of achievement, purpose, even greatness, that he evoked, was soon undercut by world events. American aid and interest shifted to other nations, leaving behind in Brazil a sense of relative deprivation. Vargas, ever the astute politician, sniffed the changing political winds, then vigorously raised the nationalist banner under which he returned to power. Similarly, UDN attacks on the old Estado Nôvo became irrelevant as new problems arose and nationalism gathered force.*

In part, the oil issue was popularized through the activity of intellectuals and politicians who regarded the USSR as a favorable example of State economic planning. The Integralists of the 1930's became the Marxists and center-left nationalists of the 1940's and 1950's. The growth of leftist sentiment was paced by PCB electoral gains in 1947, making the Communists Brazil's third largest party after the establishment Social Democrats (PSD) and the UDN. For some, the British Labour Party seemed to be a model for a humane solution to economic growth under socialism. This was the influence Vargas's Brazilian Labor Party (PTB) reflected with its vague but electorally appealing program of social justice, State planning, and recognition for the common man. Of all the political factors, the most important was the opportunity for open advocacy of all positions; the Brazilians' reaction to this new freedom was euphoric. Many who called themselves leftists and Communists were little interested in doctrine but had a strong desire for participation. For them, the oil issue was made to order.

---

* Vargas did not participate in the oil mobilization campaign, and only in 1949 did he begin to cash in on petroleum nationalism for the upcoming presidential campaign. His articulation of popular nationalism was symptomatic, but not causal in the late 1940's. As for the UDN liberals who came out against the Estado Nôvo in 1944, they were still trying to picture Vargas as a dictator long after large elements in the swelling postwar electorate had changed their opinion of Getúlio, or did not remember the dictatorship.

Again, in part, the popularity of the oil issue stemmed from frustration with the postwar energy crisis, in electricity as well as in oil. Most of Brazil's urban consumers were served by foreign power companies that either could not or would not invest in enough new facilities to keep pace with the burgeoning demand. In a nation still on the threshold of large-scale industrialization, the lawyers for Rio's Canadian-owned Light and Power Company were prominent and influential public men. Tales of the oil Companies' control over politicians and the press were based on as much fact as fiction. In short, the presence, prestige, and seeming permanence of these corporations was irritating, and in the eyes of some Brazilians unnecessary.[19]

The catalyst to the public debate was an open lecture series in April 1947 in the Military Club, where Generals Juarez Távora and Horta Barbosa aired their sharply contrasting views on the goals of national oil policy. Both men were by reputation officers of stubborn honesty and integrity, although Távora, the old tenente hero and now Deputy Chief of Staff, was better known outside the military. On April 24, Távora led off with a strong attack on the Estado Nôvo's legacy of "rigid nationalism," which he said would block any meaningful oil solution based on foreign help if it continued. In two follow-up talks he presented the middle-ground position of those who, like himself, had worked on the Petroleum Statute. Soon the press made him the national spokesman for the Statute and for an opening to the foreign oil companies. The established dailies, which had large advertising accounts with the majors, gave Távora's lectures full coverage, and the provincial papers ran reprints.

Horta, then in retirement, was shocked. He strongly believed that petroleum should not be publicly debated until fellow officers had discussed it fully and in private. As the founding father of the CNP, he resented Távora's failure to sound him out before the lectures. Furthermore, he believed Távora was dead wrong. "He doesn't know that he doesn't understand," Horta told close friends. Never the public man, Horta challenged Távora to a closed debate in the Military Club, but was refused. Horta then began giving public lectures of his own, which were better argued, better paced, and more dramatic than his opponent's.[20]

Horta's ideas were not new, but to the public, who had never known him or of the CNP during the rather austere and non-participatory Estado Nôva era, the lectures were a revelation. As before, Horta insisted that refinery profits were the key for unlocking oil reserves. To finance these government refineries he suggested using Savings Bank and Pension Plan funds (money that in fact Volta Redonda had already drained off). And like Távora, he unrealistically called for United States public loans in the name of continental defense.

What gave Horta's position force was not old arguments from the 1930's, but rather the general sense of confidence in national capacity that he radiated. Although Távora admitted that State ownership was the ideal, he added quickly that this was not yet attainable, given the present levels of Brazilian capital, technology, and administrative experience. Arguments like this played into foreign hands, Horta implied: the trusts wanted Brazilians to look upon themselves as inferior, whereas in truth they could pull it off. Although Távora stated that the oil companies were dangerous, he would still cooperate with them. Horta ticked off the results that could be expected: concessions leading inevitably to private armies (as in Mexico before 1938), foreign economic influence, control of local officials and, finally, to almost permanent foreign "cysts" in the interior. One general was for repealing the nationalist oil laws, the other said the laws were not anomalous but rather typified a growing world trend. And so it went, a magnificent, spirited, and above all democratic debate.

As both officers stumped the nation during that summer of 1947–48, almost everyone, from technocrat to concerned citizen, was discussing oil. To be sure, petroleum nationalism had been around for years. So had Monteiro Lobato's scandalous prose. What had changed was the economic urgency and the political setting. Credit for first promoting the oil issue as a nationalistic one belongs to the *Jornal de Debates*, a struggling Rio weekly that needed a new issue as its middle- and lower-middle-class readers lost interest in the usual fare of crime and corruption in the old Estado Nôvo. Circulation soared when it "discovered" oil.[21] Partisans of every political stripe were invited to write in its fiercely libertarian pages. Thus the *Jornal de Debates* and its many imitators began to write a new chapter in the history of Rio's popular press, now unshackled by censors. As a populist issue, the oil was theirs. Rumors that "Standards agents" (Hoover and Curtice) were behind the Petroleum Statute were circulated. Calls to action were raised. When the Petroleum Statute finally reached Congress in February 1948, public opinion was aroused and the populace of Rio was in an exalted mood. The stage was set for the first Brazilian mass movement of this century.

The Center for the Study and Defense of Petroleum (CEDP), or Centro, was founded in Rio in April 1948 as an action front to unite nationalist groups behind a government oil monopoly.[22] Like its adopted official organ, *Jornal de Debates*, the Centro was a magnet for heterogeneous radicals. Declaredly nonpartisan, the CEDP with its libertarian, grass-roots flavor appealed to those urban dwellers who in the early 1930's would have supported the tenentes, and later the Integralists or the Communists. In the early 1890's, their fathers had thrilled to the fiery nationalistic orations of Silva Jardim, who campaigned throughout the country in a colorful caravan of pageant wagons. To judge from its social bases, the Centro was the latest and certainly the most impressive manifestation of this recurrent strain of middle- and lower-middle-class radicalism in Rio.

In spirit the CEDP owed much to the National Union of Students (UNE). Before the Távora-Horta debates, this nationwide university student organization had accepted Monteiro Lobato's free-enterprise views. But for months now they had been battling right-wing toughs paid by the political police (DOPS) to rip down student wall posters on the oil issue. In March 1948 the UNE sponsored a Student Committee for the Defense of Petroleum. And when the parallel Centro was set up, the UNE lent prestige as an early convert to the idea of a government oil monopoly, provided student shock troops for street battles, and offered the services of a nationwide network of student committees already involved in popular agitation.

The action front was formally directed by two committees—one executive, the other consultative—on which served a medley of Positivists, democrats, Socialists, Communists, and ex-tenentes. Many in this inner core belonged to the Tijuca Anti-Fascist League, sponsors of the new Centro organization. From here the organization spread laterally across the city through a network of neighborhood political clubs like the League. The Director was Luis Hildebrando Horta Barbosa, the general's cousin and a Positivist who in mid-1947 had led respected old-line officers and engineers of the Positivist Club in calling for a National Petroleum Campaign. Providing respectability as Honorary Presidents were two nationalist leaders of past campaigns, ex-President Artur Bernardes and General Horta. The real power was vested in Secretary General Henrique Miranda, a professor of literature. With his close links to the PCB, Miranda knew how to discipline what might otherwise have beeen a short-lived movement. It was this union of grass-roots participation, respectability, and Communist organization that gave the Centro its great momentum and its capacity for growth.

Although the Communists were the best-organized group behind the Centro, the PCB itself was a latecomer to statism. Having been declared illegal by the Supreme Electoral Tribunal in May 1947, the party supported private capital in the hope of encouraging the so-called "national progressive bourgeoisie" to support its campaign for political survival. Just before the Távora-Horta debates it sponsored a mixed-capital oil plan, the National Petroleum Institute, based on 51 per cent government control.[23] But in October the Senate nonetheless voted to remove Communists from all elective offices, and the party's strategy accordingly shifted from cultivating established groups to winning popular support and strengthening its grass-roots electoral base in the municipalities. It was now argued that "Communists must know how to take leadership of the

masses and to direct their fights, for any one of these [popular] issues can be useful in the fight to regain legality."[24] For these purposes the oil controversy was made to order.

Furthermore, the PCB badly needed an issue to keep its own
members from straying. After the war, its Popular Committees
(cells) had grown rapidly, but now the rank and file was tiring of
endless discussions and literacy classes, the party's main activities
apart from running candidates in elections. Petroleum nationalism
gave the Committees a new lease on life just as the now illegal
party's star was waning.*

Fired by militancy, the Centro spread rapidly from Rio to the
states and municipalities. Congressmen and local officeholders
found that attacking the Petroleum Statute and *entreguistas* (sell-
outs) won votes. Very diverse people joined. Above all, the Centro
offered a way for the politically inexperienced to participate in a
national movement. Few realized or cared that the CEDP was
centrally controlled by the national headquarters, which sent its directives through the state secretaries to municipal branches, of
which there were scores. Its members themselves covered their expenses with dues, and their volunteer work required no elaborate
organization. In fact, the great majority joined not out of partisanship, but because they sincerely believed the nation was in danger.
Worried about inflation and vaguely leftist in outlook, they really
wanted to believe in Brazil's capacity to run its own affairs.
Charges of Communist domination they dismissed as smear tactics
or police harassment. Anyway, what if there were Communists in
the movement? Oil was bigger than any faction; hence everyone
was welcome.

In April, the CEDP and the UNE jointly sponsored a "Petroleum
Week" of speeches and demonstrations. Crowds gathered around
a symbolic oil derrick to hear Horta, Matos Pimenta of the *Jornal*

---

* Communists excepted, blue-collar workers were conspicuously absent from
Centro ranks. With its base in the government-controlled labor unions, the
PTB did not wish to antagonize the Dutra government as it moved into the
vacuum created by the outlawing of the PCB. This explains why Vargas and
other PTB figures avoided the Centro and were quick to sense the Communist
role in it.

de Debates, the Socialist Councilman Osório Borba, the Communist and ex-CNP engineer Fernando Luis Lobo Carneiro, and others proclaim the virtues of State ownership. Then followed petitions for Congress, public debates, and a final wreath-laying at the bust of Marshal Floriano Peixoto, the military-nationalist President of the early 1890's. In June, the first "Petroleum Month" was held throughout Brazil. During July and August, local meetings constantly attacked the Petroleum Statute, often referring to it as the *venezolano* in derisive comparison with Venezuela. In September, state conferences drew up theses. Enacting the Statute as law would be a "monstrous crime against the fatherland," Federal District conferees decided, since it was organized to serve the interests not of the nation but of "the great foreign oil monopolies, particularly the North American trust headed by Standard Oil, which had a direct influence in its formulation."[25] Their call for a State monopoly over all phases of the business was adopted by the National Convention that October. Finally, in December, the Centro's complete oil plan was presented to Congress on the steps near the stone bust of Tiradentes, the hero of Brazil's independence.

It was a genuinely national campaign, an open-ended mobilization almost unique in Brazilian history. Retrospectively, the popular aspect stands out as more important than the partisan core. There was even a "Queen of Brazilian Petroleum" contest, which Miss Petronilha Pimentel won with a striking photo. Arms outstretched, Bahian oil dripping from either hand, and shown to full advantage, the girl from Bahia won a cash prize and a trip to Argentina.[26]

Owing in part to the Centro's efforts, the Petroleum Statute never emerged from congressional committee, and by September 1948 the bill was politically dead. The Centro's capacity to mobilize people and concentrate them in Rio's narrow streets, especially around Congress and the federal offices, was an important factor. By molding public opinion, moreover, it created political restraints on legislators and the Executive. As for the public, it had gained a visceral feeling that the oil really did belong to Brazil.

Although the Centro took credit for defeating the Statute, at least equally influential was a small group of pro-Horta Army officers who, in mid-1948, in consultation with an advertising expert, made a massive direct effort to influence policy and opinion makers. Using a Military Club letterhead, they sent out 30,000 copies of Horta's lectures to a specially prepared list of recipients that included all members of the Military and Naval Clubs, all other officers on active duty, President Dutra, the members of his Cabinet, all executive officeholders, all Congressmen, Senators, state governors, mayors, and presidents of Municipal Councils throughout Brazil, the press, magazines, radio stations, public libraries, professional groups, the unions, and university and secondary school directors—in short, all those judged capable of influencing public opinion.

This saturation mailing brought results. Letters and telegrams poured back to Rio in support of Horta. Officers from a key Rio Grande regiment (Santa Maria) wired their support, and professors and students at the Military Engineering School took a collective stand against the Statute in defiance of War Minister Canrobert Pereira da Costa. Various other collective acts indicated the growing strength of anti-Statute feeling in the officer corps. Indeed, the very idea of a bulk mailing to opinion leaders, the first in Brazilian history, was predicated on the existence of a nationwide public opinion that could be reached.

The nationalist campaign revealed that Army officers, with their predominantly middle-class provincial origins, responded more vigorously than their naval counterparts, who were elitist and cosmopolitan. Jokes circulated about naïve naval officers who believed foreign allegations that Brazil would never be a low-cost producer; how could it, ran the argument, when a bottle of mineral water from the interior cost more than a liter of imported gasoline? Economies of scale were not, it seems, a well-known concept in the Navy. But despite the drift of Army sentiment—and by the end of 1948 the officer corps was overwhelming pro-Horta—not all officers joined the campaign. As will be shown in Chapter 9, several senior officers were concerned by what they saw as Communist infiltration under a façade of nationalism.

Thus another result of the oil campaign was to paint nationalism

with the Communist brush. This was a problem that earlier nationalists never had to face. On the one hand, nationalists were
asked explicitly to make a cold war choice between Russia and the
United States. On the other hand, the politics of oil had gone beyond the closed-door, administrative solutions to include a well-
demonstrated potential for mass mobilization. Both developments
made the Brazilian political elite uneasy. The Communists knew it,
and tried to manipulate the oil issue for their own purposes.

Many Centro delegates to the national convention stirred uneasily when Secretary General Henrique Miranda substituted strongly
worded attacks on the United States for mild, general references
to the international oil trusts. Left liberals and Socialists were ap-
palled by the violence that the Communist-led district branches in
Rio seemed to welcome during the Centro's frequent demonstrations. Not all could agree with the Communists when they invoked
the inevitable police incidents in an effort to discredit Dutra's "fascist" government. In early 1949, several moderates pulled out
publicly and Honorary Presidents Horta and Bernardes resigned
quietly.[27] Thereafter, the CEDP nestled close to Army backers in
the Military Club, with which it became intimately associated, and
confrontation tactics were abandoned.

Conservative Brazilians now found it easier to read "Communist" when they saw the word nationalist. For editor José Eduardo
de Macedo Soares, the mask was off, revealing the "true nature of
the 'oil is ours' movement. In large part, it is an audacious Musco-
vite activity with political, military, and economic aspects ... [It
is designed] to expand [Soviet] influence in the world."* As for
the DOPS, it was concerned about Communist penetration of the
interior through the Centro. The eagerness with which DOPS
agents broke up anti-Statute rallies was notable.

In Congress, meanwhile, the Petroleum Statute and its compan-

---

* José Eduardo Macedo Soares, "O petróleo é nosso," *Diário Carioca*, Sept.
28, 1948, p. 1. His was the classic conservative response to what stands, on
balance, as a genuinely popular, broad-based movement. The conclusion must
be that Communists and their sympathizers played a key role in the Centro,
and thereby gained prestige. Then, having identified itself with a popular
issue, the PCB strengthened its intellectual hold on the left, both civilian and
military, by defining nationalist issues and setting the style and content of
verbal combat.

ion bill to legalize 60–40 ownership could not have been more poorly timed. Abroad the Bogotá Conference was ending with massive street riots and anti-Americanism, while at home Congressmen soon had to debate the Export-Import Bank's $90 million loan to embattled foreign power companies in Brazil. And along with increased tensions, supporters of the Statute found that their own political costs were rising. Sustained opposition came from a loosely organized nationalist block of about seventy deputies. Old-line politicians like Artur Bernardes and Flôres da Cunha made a tactical alliance with Socialists, a handful of UDN and PTB party members, and the loyal PSD followers of ex–Labor Minister Agamemnon Magalhães and former Governor of Minas Gerais Benedicto Valadares.[28] On paper President Dutra had more than enough votes to defeat this heterogeneous opposition, and the Senate, being more conservative, was strongly for the bill. Yet Dutra never pressed his advantage. Rumors that he was interested in a less controversial solution were borne out in May, when the DASP's five-year plan went to Congress.

The DASP oil plan was part of an overall proposal to coordinate public expenditures for energy, transportation, and social overhead capital. Known popularly as SALTE,* the program was ready in March. Unifying the budget was well within the DASP's established authority; setting development priorities for other agencies, long an objective of the old Estado Nôvo agency, was another matter. But the Director General of the DASP, Mário Bittencourt Sampaio, wanted to be a strong minister, and he had Dutra's ear. One of Sampaio's main reasons for supporting SALTE was to strengthen his hand against the Finance Minister, Corrêa e Castro, who was trying to cut the DASP back and assume full budgetary powers.[29] On the oil issue, their antagonism was exaggerated by the fact that Corrêa e Castro held assets in Brazilian private refineries whereas Sampaio favored statism. The DASP's historic conflict with the CNP also came into play, since Sampaio's proposal to

---

* SALTE is an acronym from the Portuguese words *saude, alimentação, transportação,* and *energia*—health, food, transportation, and energy. The plan's petroleum section is in *Petróleo,* IV, 276–84.

allocate cr$2.5 billion for exploration, refining, and a tanker fleet was tantamount to countermanding the CNP's neo-liberal guidelines. In effect Barreto lost the policy initiative to Sampaio, who with President Dutra's blessing saw to it that his oil plan upstaged the Statute.

The SALTE oil plan was politically well-timed, simple, and financially attractive. It offered an immediate solution to Brazil's mounting fuel demands, a solution that did not depend on the oil companies. It confirmed the nationalist opinion of Brazil's capacity, and it preserved the Horta Barbosa oil laws. Its political costs to edgy deputies were accordingly minimal, as the Statute's would not have been. Financially, Sampaio promised to bypass the world dollar shortage by purchasing equipment from Europe, where Brazil had on hand an estimated six billion cruzeiros in blocked funds and compensation currencies. Once the planned fleet of fifteen tankers (from 10,000 to 20,000 dwt) came into service, over $14 million would be saved each year by putting transportation costs on a cruzeiro basis. Two new government refineries, one at Mataripe (5,000 b/day) and the other at an unspecified location (45,000 b/day), when combined with output from Manguinhos and União, would further ease the dollar drain. And when the production of Bahian crude oil was increased to match current consumption levels of 50,000 b/day, it was anticipated that dollar costs would once again decline.

In 1948, few if any experts realized the degree to which Sampaio's confident predictions were based on underestimates of future consumption and financial needs.[30] To Dutra the SALTE plan was attractive, and he decided to move ahead. He ordered the recently established joint Brazil–United States technical mission under John Abbink to work within Sampaio's guidelines, and he sent Sampaio off to Europe to negotiate while the SALTE plan was still in Congress. The Director General returned in June with French proposals to supply a large refinery and surplus railroad locomotives. Dutra then set up a purchasing commission, including Sampaio, Barreto, and the heads of the Ministry of Transport and the Bank of Brazil, giving them until August 31 to complete the negotiations.

Much to Sampaio's surprise, União announced at this juncture that it was signing a refinery contract with Cie. Five-Lille pour Constructions Mécaniques, a French consortium, and had asked the Finance Minister to release blocked francs. In turn, Manguinhos requested dollars to purchase its long-delayed plant from Foster-Wheeler. Having decided that the Petroleum Statute was dead, the two private groups were able to impress their official friends, and especially Corrêa e Castro, with their willingness to go ahead. When the Finance Minister smiled on their requests, the DASP Director accused them of profiteering with "the house silver" and pressed instead for direct government-to-government purchases. Dutra felt this pressure and wavered in his support for SALTE. In September, shortly after Corrêa e Castro had resigned, Sampaio submitted his own letter of resignation, claiming that the whole DASP program was compromised.[31]

Tensions rose until Dutra hit upon a conciliatory formula to pacify his warring ministers. On September 30, he asked Congress to approve a special appropriation for the 45,000 b/day State plant, the fifteen ships, the locomotives, and an oil pipeline, all of which had once been included in the SALTE plan. DASP functionaries were jubilant, for they considered the request to Congress a victory for their plan. The nationalists, then assembled at the Centro's noisy Rio Congress, responded with a new slogan: "The oil is ours, thanks to Dutra." Simultaneously, Dutra urged the Bank of Brazil to loan eight million dollars to Manguinhos, and convinced União to abandon France for Czechoslovakia, where it purchased the Gottwald Plant from Skoda. Their hard currency worries all but over, these private groups now claimed victory for their thesis that the government should experiment with three solutions—private, mixed-capital, and statist—while keeping foreigners out with the old oil laws. In sum, the "Dutra Solution" was neither statist nor free enterprise; it was erected on the bedrock of Horta's old laws. Congress responded to the President's vigorous prods, and in March 1949 his bill for SALTE credits passed.[32]

Once the bureaucratic thickets had been cleared, Dutra purchased the French refinery; in July Barreto signed a design, construction, and operation contract with the American firm of Hydrocarbon Research, Inc. Then the National Security Council selected a mountain-girded site at Cubatão, near Santos, for commercial and strategic reasons. In 1950, the $10.5 million project was enlarged by adding a fertilizer plant, and later, Brazil's first asphalt plant. The large plant size allowed engineers to take advantage of economies of scale in both construction (using Volta Redonda steel) and operation. The labor force was trained on the spot. Raw materials were no problem; it was domestic inflation, rather than the refusal of foreigners to sell oil, that dogged the project. In fact, Esso Export Corporation gave preference to Brazilian tankers in a five-year crude oil contract. However, significant dollar savings would not begin for two to three years after Cubatão began operating in 1955. In later years, several more State refineries were built in the effort to meet consumption.*

Critics rightly said that Dutra's was a partial solution, designed with immediate financial and commercial needs in mind. The CNP under Dutra and Barreto did scarcely any exploration. If estimated Bahian reserves had quadrupled to 44 million barrels by 1950, this was little more than a year's supply at current rates. Judging from one of the industry's main indicators, the ratio of production to reserves, the new refineries would have to use imported crude oil for years to come. In fairness to Barreto it must be said that he had

---

* Other Dutra projects were the $33 million order placed in Europe and Japan for a 225,000-ton tanker fleet of coasters and ocean-going vessels, and the new Santos–São Paulo pipeline, which was paid for out of CNP funds earmarked, but not yet spent, for exploration. For the Cubatão refinery see Brazil, CNP, *Relatório*, 1949, pp. 63–68. Originally, Belém was considered. A refinery at the mouth of the Amazon would be convenient, because close to Venezuelan crude supplies, until Amazon oil was discovered, and it would also fit into the Amazon Development Plan. Then the interest in regional development gave way before commercial and strategic interests. Cubatão (later called Presidente Bernardes) produced aviation gasoline for the Air Force and Brazil's burgeoning civilian airlines, ordinary 76-octane gasoline, fuel oil for Paulista industry, diesel oil, kerosene, propane gas, and by-products. The asphalt plant greatly accelerated paving and road construction, its production of 116,000 tons being both cheaper and larger than the previous high of 81,000 tons imported in costly steel drums. The crude oil contract ESSO (Jersey Standard) made with Cubatão was consistent with company policy: try to prevent or to control a Brazilian industry but, failing that, sell petroleum, equipment, and technical assistance to the new customer.

counted on foreign capital to finance exploration, and the Statute
failed. In turn, Sampaio's SALTE plan was no real answer to exploration because the funds were not only inadequate, but also
were subject to yearly budget cutting and delays.[33] Only a long-
term, autonomous investment policy would suffice, and that was
the problem Getúlio Vargas faced as President in 1951.

Dutra's compromise was politically vulnerable to attacks from
those nationalists who would accept nothing less than a statist solution. To be sure, professional groups like the Engineering Club
found the mixed bag of State and private refineries attractive; but
the political lustre was wearing off. In late October 1948 a bill to
expropriate Manguinhos and União appeared in Congress. Matos
Pimenta thundered against Manguinhos in articles that were sur-
passed for hyperbole only by some of Bernardes's accounts of the
Standard Oil conspiracy. It was true that the Brazilian companies
had failed to raise all their capital as stipulated in the concessions.
This gave an opening to the Centro and like-thinking politicians,
who called for direct State control of the entire industry. Charges
of deals and favors were not easy to refute, especially when a deputy like Hermes Lima, the Socialist and self-styled public con-
science on petroleum, rose to speak in March 1949.

In the Senate, Drault Ernanny defended Manguinhos ably, with
the government's support. He explained how the tight exchange
situation had forced the private companies to seek readjustment of
the original terms. Since 1946, he added, his group had carried
heavy, and so far unproductive investments. Furthermore, 50 per
cent of all their future profits were committed to exploration, and
the concession was perfectly legitimate under the existing oil laws.
The companies survived, but with diminished prestige. Even busi-
ness-oriented papers such as *O Globo* and *Correio da Manhã*
joined those who said the government had gone too far in bailing
out the private groups. "Without doubting the President's good
faith," *Correio* said, "we think this refinery matter still has aspects
as dark as the color of petroleum itself."[34]

Statism was again in vogue by 1949. Having ebbed after 1943,
Horta's pro-monopoly thesis was reaching high tide. In petroleum,

at least, the arguments for mixed companies and partnership, which went back to Roberto Simonsen, had lost political appeal. Everyone knew that the days when a private solution could command strong public favor were over. The only safe and sure way was through the State, Oswaldo Aranha affirmed, as he staged a political comeback in postwar domestic politics. His mentor, Getúlio, implied the same while traveling the last miles of his presidential campaign back from exile to Catete Palace. Vargas stood on his old record, including the strengthening of controls over natural resources and the founding of the CNP. Certainly, he said in Bahia, a State monopoly such as Uruguay's "ought to be carefully examined before any final solution is adopted." Pledging his government to further the petroleum industry, he warned against letting foreigners into oil reserves and affirmed his faith in national capability. These phrases from the Horta legacy were what his responsive audiences wanted to hear. And Vargas, winning by 48.7 per cent of the total vote, a near absolute majority, became President in 1951 in the new image of a progressive nationalist.[35]

Vargas's plan for Petrobrás was flexible, contingent, and conciliatory. The bill he sent to the Chamber in December 1951 was
undeniably tailored to fit the current political climate, which was
favorable to State control. It was not a partisan plan; it was an
industrial project that, after the expected quick approval by Congress, would be turned over to economists and technocrats. To
Vargas, who wanted a soundly financed, workable solution, this
aspect of the plan was fundamental. Occasionally he had seemed
to lose sight of it, notably during the recent presidential campaign.
But if he expected political gains from Petrobrás, the "new Vargas"
hoped to reap them by solving the oil crisis, not by exploiting the
politics of oil. Yet by May 1952 the Chamber had transformed
Petrobrás, politicizing it in a way that Vargas and his staff never
anticipated or intended.[1]

Vargas said his bill was a nationalist solution, and it was; however, he still hoped to keep open the options within a structure of
State control. To this end, private capital and regional interests
were given a role in the projected mixed company, and foreign
groups were allowed to participate contractually in Petrobrás subsidiaries, and directly in allied industries such as petrochemicals
and equipment fabrication. Broadly straddling the ideological center, Getúlio had expected to win the support of all but the most
intransigent free traders and extreme nationalists. This formula
failed. And in June the embattled President cried out during a
speech in Bahia: "I have flown that nationalist banner all my public life, and nobody can snatch it from me!"[2]

But Vargas was vulnerable, as his opponents knew. Supple rather
than consistent, relishing ambiguity over dogma, Vargas did not

make a credible petroleum nationalist. Once he had been ready to strike the colors and accept a foreign solution. Memories of his 1941 talks with Standard still rankled among Horta Barbosa's followers. Often he had unfurled the nationalist flag to catch the breezes of opportunity. This the radical nationalists could not forgive. Certainly that nationalist flag always seemed to be placed on ground of the President's own choosing. To outflank him, all 81 UDN deputies proposed a total State monopoly oil plan. In short, the political opposition to Petrobrás was as determined as it was diverse, and Vargas failed to withstand it. Why did Getúlio suffer what must be called a political reverse over his oil project?

His strategy for development, a dual approach using foreign and State capital, was basically outlined during 1951. Plans to modernize the railroads and to initiate shipbuilding were drawn up by Finance Minister Horacio Láfer in conjunction with American advisers. These plans were based on massive foreign capital inputs, and some on direct foreign investment (as were the feasibility studies for automotive and heavy electrical equipment industries that the President's Industrial Development Commission carried out later). Responsibility for energy, however, was assumed by the State after the President's Economic Advisory Staff under Rômulo de Almeida decided that foreign groups either could not or would not invest enough in oil exploration and in electrical energy to meet national needs. Almeida, a former Simonsen aid, was prepared to follow his dead mentor's dictum: the State must step in when private enterprise cannot overcome basic obstacles to industrial development. Vargas had reached this position himself in the steel crisis. Almeida's Advisory Staff drew up the plans for Petrobrás and Electrobrás (the State power company), and the National Coal Plan, knowing all along, however, that these projects were only one part of the administration's program. In fact, the dual strategy was well adapted to Vargas's own views on developmental nationalism.*

These plans appealed to Vargas's technocratic bent, and also to

---

* President Juscelino Kubitschek (1956–61) later employed the same dual approach, expanded on Vargas's plans, and popularized the slogan "fifty years

his very strong desire for a reputation as a great builder. True, many who had endured the Estado Nôvo continued to see him as the master manipulator, but his brilliant triumph at the polls in October 1950 proved that voters by the millions believed in a new Vargas. And by a superb effort of imagination, the aging President did identify himself with a new generation of young economists, technocrats, and lawyers. He gave his excellent young staff heavy responsibilities and in return won their loyalty and admiration. The sense that Brazilians were planning their own development excited them. Vargas set them to work in the privacy of Catete Palace while he ran political interference outside. If in public he sometimes implied that he favored statism, in private he always insisted on the best available technical and economic solutions. The young staffers, like their President, were pragmatic nationalists, as the decisions behind Petrobrás bear out well.

That Brazil faced a fuel crisis had been clear since 1949, Dutra's last year in office. In addition, the demand for airplanes, trucks, and cars was far from satisfied. In 1951, over a hundred thousand motor vehicles were imported—nearly 20 per cent of the existing fleet. Basic products such as cement, which used large quantities of fuel oil in the manufacturing process, were in short supply. Furthermore, Vargas planned to reequip the railroads with several hundred diesel locomotives. With fuel imports rising 20 per cent a year (as they had since 1949), petroleum products that cost $200 million to import in 1951 (at 120,000 b/day) were expected to drain off $500 million in scarce foreign currency by 1955 (at 250,-000 b/day). That these estimates were highly exaggerated (see below) does not alter the fact that in 1951 a crisis was perceived, and the government felt it had to act.[3]

The nation's balance of payments did improve briefly, from

---

of progress in five." For a good analysis of Vargas's programs and the economic situation, see Thomas E. Skidmore, *Politics in Brazil, 1930–1954* (New York, 1967), Ch. 3. Though I have leaned heavily on Skidmore's treatment of Vargas's second presidency, I have reinterpreted the Petrobrás episode to show how Vargas, far from leading the politics of oil, was hard pressed on this issue by the petroleum nationalists, who did not trust him, and by the conservatives.

1949 to 1951, but then the effects of rising heavy industrial imports, coupled with increased fuel charges and the stockpiling of raw materials due to the Korean War, reversed this favorable trend. By late 1951 an exchange crisis loomed. Economists from the United Nations Economic Commission for Latin America proved what Vargas's staff had already realized, namely that Brazil's capacity to import was severely limited. The oil crisis had to be solved in the next few years or Brazil would face a difficult choice: impose rationing or sacrifice part of the economic program. This forecast was clear enough.

The international situation, by contrast, was ambiguous. War in Korea and the Abadan dispute between Iran and British oil interests combined to drive up shipping and fuel prices. Brazil's vulnerability to disruptions in the world oil market was once again brought home. Advantages were seen in Washington's eagerness to develop Western Hemisphere reserves for defense and in the foreign oil companies' reviving interest in Brazil, with its rapidly growing internal market. Perhaps the majors were now prepared to explore and produce on terms that the Brazilians could accept.

Vargas entered the presidency with no firm ideas on oil policy beyond his commitment to solving the energy crisis and to assuring government control of any new oil industry. Within these flexible guidelines, he probed various possible deals with the oil companies during the early months of his new government. Important ministers like Láfer and João Neves de Fontoura at Itamaraty urged him to accept something like the 50-50 profit-sharing terms that the majors had worked out with Venezuela in late 1948 and that were becoming standard in the industry.[4]

The British wanted to invest, and in fact oil was the only sector of Brazil's economy that interested them, a FIESP economic mission learned. London financial circles reportedly thought Vargas would be more sympathetic than Dutra. Assis Chateaubriand's O Jornal quoted American oilmen as saying that Standard was ready to develop oil on a 50-50 share basis.[5] However groundless these rumors may have been, in fact the majors were interested and the conversations continued. And though the companies probably insisted on controlling any oil they might find, the idea of profit sharing was something new. Typical of these press reports inspired by special interests was *O Diário de São Paulo*'s account in July on the majors' new-found willingness to work within Brazilian oil laws on a partnership basis, similar to the Amapá manganese project in which Bethlehem Steel shared control (49 per cent) with a Brazilian group. *O Diário* also suggested that this "New Deal" in oil could channel foreign capital into private refineries, such as União's Capuava plant and a new version of the old Niteroi plan.[6] However exaggerated, these reports showed that private groups and the major companies were holding conversations of their own.

The private Niteroi plant had been proposed in early 1950, while Dutra was still President. Two financial groups, Max Leitão da Cunha of Rio and Cia. Paulista de Investimentos of São Paulo, had revived the old Rio de Janeiro plan with the blessing of Ernani do Amaral Peixoto, now the elected state Governor. Socony-Vacuum agreed to design, operate, and supply the 30,000 b/day operation with crude oil. Capital requirements were set at cr$120 million in common stock held by native Brazilians, and cr$480 million, the lion's share, in bonds to be subscribed mostly by American insurance companies.[7] Everything had fallen neatly into place, foreign finance, token backing by native Brazilians, and the support of Amaral Peixoto, the main advocate of a concessionary oil policy within Vargas's inner circle. It was all legel under existing laws, and General João Barreto at the CNP sponsored the plan. However, the National Security Council sent it back to the CNP to study further until the new President announced his policy toward private refineries and the role of massive foreign finance.

Undoubtedly, the foreign options were carefully considered in the absence of United States public loan funds. Given what we know of the steel story, it seems likely that Vargas was prepared to consider an association with the foreign oil companies. Certainly, he did not close any doors or dash many hopes in those early months. Smilingly, he listened to all comers and waited. Former Vice President João Café Filho recalls how Vargas, "even after seeing his [specific] plan rejected by Congress, still believed he could devise some means to attract foreign capital."[8] His respect for private management practices, his desire for sound finance and technical control, his lack of interest in statism per se are as apparent here as in the case of steel. Only when he had explored all the options did Vargas in mid-1951 turn to a State solution.

At that time, Vargas and his technical adviser Almeida became convinced that their objective, a crash program to solve the oil crisis, was not shared by the majors, who had more modest exploration goals.[9] Glutted with crude oil, the companies did not see their interest in prospecting vigorously; they wanted reserves at little cost, or so Almeida and Vargas believed. Significantly, this confirmed one of Horta Barbosa's main tenets. With no guarantee of an immediate, large-scale effort in exploration and production, the political risks of a foreign capital solution were simply too great for a President who in recent speeches had given every indication that the exclusionist oil laws would stand. Continuous soundings among political leaders convinced him that petroleum nationalism ran deep in public opinion. Possibly his decision to work for a State monopoly was strengthened by his alarm over the high rate of foreign profit remittances that had been encouraged by the then overvalued exchange rate.[10] Thus the three factors of inadequate foreign offers, domestic political realities, and exchange worries came together in late 1951 to finally foreclose the trouble-laden foreign option.

Having once decided on a State exploration program, it was logical to integrate refining with the official State company and not to permit it to expand in private hands. From this perspective, the foreign proposals to private groups such as Max Leitão only made the situation more confused. Furthermore, Vargas's conversations with the majors had upset many nationalists, who did not trust him. Alarmed, the CEDP began to look for support outside the Military Club, and in June 1951, despite police harassment, held its second national convention to expose Niteroi as a front for Standard and to again proclaim State monopoly as the only answer. Having re-

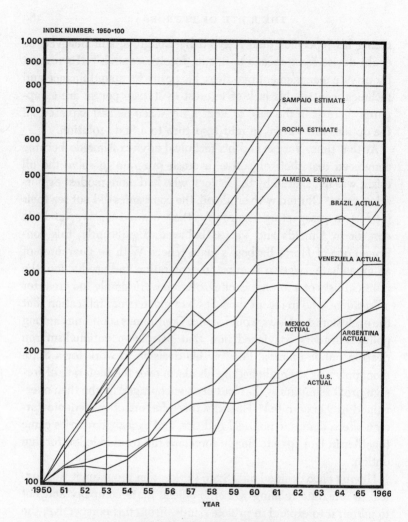

INDEX NUMBER: 1950=100

SAMPAIO ESTIMATE
ROCHA ESTIMATE
ALMEIDA ESTIMATE
BRAZIL ACTUAL
VENEZUELA ACTUAL
MEXICO ACTUAL
ARGENTINA ACTUAL
U.S. ACTUAL

YEAR

*Fig. 1. Index for Increase in Annual Demand
For Major Refined Products*

SOURCE: Contemporary estimates for the rates of increase in Brazilian demand are computed from figures in Rômulo de Almeida, *Os fundamentos da "Petrobrás,"* (Rio, 1952), p. 9. The actual rates of increase, for Brazil and other countries, are based on United States Bureau of Mines statistics.

cently played populist politics himself, Vargas was vulnerable to these attacks. Again, the risk was too high for any expected returns, and the Niteroi plans of his son-in-law and others were allowed to gather dust.[11]

Petrobrás was drawn up secretly by Almeida and several CNP experts, including Jesus Soares Pereira, João Neiva de Figueiredo, Irnack C. do Amaral, Plínio Catanhede, General Arthur Levy, and Hélio Beltrão. Vargas took the political soundings, while channeling interested persons through his office. Among them was General Horta, who declined Vargas's invitation to reenter public life as director of the new company but urged his former chief not to modify the basic oil laws. To achieve eventual self-sufficiency in oil, Almeida's group wanted Petrobrás to move ahead in all sectors of the industry except distribution. The result of their urgent deliberations was the President's proposal for a large, integrated government corporation, organized flexibly as a holding company and (unlike SALTE) based on capital sources independent of the yearly budget. Then in December the plan was announced and the public debates began. Before these and the congressional debates can be analyzed, however, we must examine Almeida's original bill in some detail.[12]

Economically, Petrobrás was keyed to Almeida's estimates of future fuel demands (see Fig. 1), which he expected to level off after 1954 owing to payments difficulties, but still to increase at 14 per cent each year. Drawing up a projection that he considered conservative, Almeida set crude oil needs at 250,000 b/day by 1956, and 480,000 by 1961. To achieve full self-sufficiency in crude oil, Brazil would have to invest on the order of $625 million and $1,200 million for 1956 and 1961 respectively, based arbitrarily on standard United States cost estimates of $2,500 for each b/day. By adding the necessary new refineries, tankers, and other installations, his estimates for complete autonomy were doubled to a grand total of $1.24 billion (cr$25 billion) for 1956 and $2.4 billion (cr$48 billion) for 1961. This projection of demand gave Almeida a yardstick for measuring the capital requirements. But it had to be

an educated guess, not fact, and therefore it was controversial.*
On the basis of this projection, Almeida's team reached two basic
conclusions.

First, Brazil did not have the financial resources to initiate an
all-out effort to attain self-sufficiency. It would be necessary to
start with a more modest program, something like half a billion
dollars, or cr$10 billion. Even when spread over five years, from
1952 to 1956, the capital requirement was heavy. Half would be
spent on exploration and producing more crude; the goal was
100,000 b/day by 1956. One-tenth would be absorbed by the fleet
for adding new ships to a capacity of 500,000 tons, or enough tanker
capacity for 100,000 b/day, 45 per cent of the estimated 1956 demand. Refining, budgeted at more than two billion cruzeiros,
should rise to 180,000 b/day of derivatives by 1956. An experimental bituminous schist plant was also included at one billion
cruzeiros. In line with Horta's old decision, distribution was not
included in these plans. If all went well, the company should expand rapidly after this initial start.

Second, there were limits to self-financing. Given the rapidly
rising demand, all profits from internal operations like refining
would have to be reinvested in several new plants and tankers.
Probably nothing would be left to finance exploration, the most
capital-intensive sector. This contradicted one of Horta's main
theses, the old CNP strategy of self-financing, now enshrined by
many nationalists as conventional wisdom.

Vargas wanted Petrobrás to be financially independent of the
yearly Federal budget and Treasury levies, as the CNP and
SALTE were not, and this meant new taxes. Resources on a scale

---

* In 1951, Brazilian experts did not foresee that the demand for fuel, which
had been so great after the war, would slacken to an average yearly increase
of 7.4 per cent, around half Almeida's estimate, between 1956 and 1961.
This lower actual demand, together with decreasing world crude prices, rising
domestic production, and expanding domestic refining operations, resulted in
the holding of dollar costs for imported crude and refined products below
$300 million per year after 1956. The effect of this was to modify Petrobrás's
capital requirements in the late 1950's. However, the 1951 estimates were
those with which contemporary actors had to deal; the battle over Petrobrás
in the Chamber of Deputies took shape accordingly.

adequate to meet the company's objectives had to be raised somehow without bearing disproportionately on industrial and commercial users of petroleum or offending the powerful import lobby. Kerosene, a mass consumption product, was another item on the fuel list that Vargas, as PTB leader, was not eager to tax. Knowing that Brazilians disliked direct taxation, he decided to tap the *imposto único*, which supported the Federal Highway Fund. He had, however, just vetoed a bill to raise the 1940 imposto único rates across the board, partly because of pressure from cement manufacturers and the truckers. Almeida got around this difficulty by tying Petrobrás and the Highway Fund together; 25 per cent of the proposed new imposto único rates, which weighed most heavily on gasoline users, were earmarked for Petrobrás. Split 40–60 between the Federal government and state and local governments, this 25 per cent came to cr$4.8 billion in new capital for Petrobrás by 1956. Stock issued on these receipts would be held by states and municipalities throughout Brazil. This stock diffusion must have appealed to a former dictator who was now eager to show his allegiance to federalism. Thus Horta's great legacy, the imposto único on petroleum derivatives, was used once more to further national objectives.

The remaining capital needs were supplied from various sources. At first, Vargas toyed with the idea of a workers stock subscription to give Petrobrás a popular base, but then rejected this as impractical. (One recalls the steel parallel, when the General Staff suggested parceling out Volta Redonda stock among Army officers and civil servants.) The less politically attractive alternative was to tap private automobile owners in the middle and upper classes, as well as commercial land, sea, and air carriers, for a five-year, compulsory stock issue worth cr$2.1 billion. Additional taxes of cr$1.88 billion were to come from sales of new cars, parts, and accessories. A luxury tax on soap, beer, and other consumer goods was included. Total revenue from all these taxes came to nearly nine billion cruzeiros over a five-year period. When the estimated value of existing CNP properties was added, some cr$2.5 billion, Petrobrás would have more than enough original capital to achieve the "sound and unimpeachable finance" (i.e., ten billion cruzeiros over five years) that Vargas demanded.

Initially, the Federal government was to own all common stock —twenty million shares, worth four billion cruzeiros—but later it would need to hold no more than 51 per cent to assure control over the parent holding company and subsidiaries. Widespread ownership and flexibility were the guidelines; there was no monopoly language to frighten private investors away. State and local governments and vehicle owners would soon be heavy investors in the new company. Private capital was invited on terms that opened up 100,000 shares of voting stock to each private refinery with native investors, and twenty thousand shares to each individual native and naturalized Brazilian, and to companies organized under Brazilian law. Total private holdings in the parent company were limited, however, to 15 per cent maximum of all voting stock.

In theory, foreigners could thus hold up to one-tenth of one per cent of the voting stock in the parent company. Allowing this minute crack in the exclusionist laws was a classic Getulian maneuver intended to conciliate his congressional opposition, notably the UDN, which had backed the Petroleum Statute in 1948 and was now expected to come out strongly for a free-enterprise solution. Moreover, he must have thought that this would satisfy the nationalists without discouraging potential private investors, foreign and domestic, in equipment manufacturing and petrochemicals. As for the subsidiaries, the door was open to private domestic capital, subject to majority control by Petrobrás and, where appropriate, to the old 1938 oil laws assuring Brazilian stock ownership in exploration, transportation, and refining. Petrobrás was also given the authority to issue bonds, decide on the proportion of preferred stock, and contract foreign loans.

Petrobrás was organized as a mixed commercial society. Like Volta Redonda, it was subject to the laws over private corporations rather than the regulations governing State autarchies. Financially, this allowed Petrobrás to attract private capital, first from vehicle owners on a compulsory basis, and then from other sources voluntarily. From the managerial standpoint, Almeida and his associates thought the existing State autarchies were far too rigid. Personnel policies were another consideration. The CNP had always been restricted by federal employment regulations, and in the autarchies, government employees had civil service rights and perpetual tenure after ten years; hence featherbedding (*empreguismo*) was common. Above all, they wanted Petrobrás to be more like a private industry than a State company; the State-run Central do Brasil Railroad was particularly notorious for inefficient operations. To this end, private investors could elect up to two of the nine Administrative Council members, and could serve by appointment on the four-man Executive Directorate, whose members had to be native Brazilians. Overall policy decisions would remain with the CNP, however, subject to presidential veto.

As regards the specific managerial structure, the Almeida group had no set ideas except that Petrobrás should be a holding company, like the major oil companies, with flexible policies depending on the operation. For example, Petrobrás might want to run Cubatão and a future government plant near Rio as one operation or, if feasible, to join the Mataripe Refinery with producing oil fields in Bahia. Association with foreign groups, in petrochemicals especially, looked attractive. Operational experience would suggest the specific structure; for the present, Almeida and Helio Beltrão (who worked on organization) did not want to make any decisions prematurely. Here was another advantage of the mixed company, the formula Simonsen had favored if the government was to pioneer in new industries.

Politically, Petrobrás fit into the moderate stream of Brazilian nationalism. No harbinger of State socialism was intended; rather, Petrobrás would dominate the industry, thus becoming a virtual State monopoly. Concessions of the Venezuelan type were out; contractual agreements and equipment loans were welcome and anticipated. The existing private refinery concessions were retained.

Vargas, in his message sending Petrobrás to Congress, expressed his confidence in national capacity and pride in this internal solution to an old problem. And though it bears repeating that Petrobrás was first and foremost a technocratic solution to financial, economic, and technical problems, it is obvious that Vargas would not have sent the bill if he thought it was politically weak. In fact, the bill was drafted 12 times before Vargas felt it met political realities and took sufficient account of the suggestions of some two dozen prominent public figures and insiders.[13] Finally, the bill was tailored to conciliate the Congress, and Vargas may have wanted Petrobrás to be the first fruits of his proffered coalition with the UDN.

In summary, Vargas, Almeida, and the staff of experts working on the bill saw Petrobrás as a broadly based, independently financed holding company. This amounted to a de facto State monopoly with a flexible, mixed organization in which private capital might play a large role in the subsidiaries and associated ventures. Major financing was tied to the imposto único (25 per cent of proposed new rates), a compulsory stock subscription by vehicle owners, a luxury tax, an auto parts tax, and a Treasury advance, the whole coming to over eight billion cruzeiros. With existing CNP assets this totaled ten billion cruzeiros. This five-year finance plan was expected to get under way in late 1952 after a brief pro forma journey through the Congress.

The reaction from the major dailies, which were usually hostile to Vargas, was mixed. The *Correio da Manhã* called the bill "moderate statism." Other established papers followed suit, or reserved comment for further study. The *Diário de Notícias* was wary, having reported fully on the 1948 oil debates. What is the government's intention, the paper asked. If it wants foreign capital, Vargas should admit this openly. Or if it intends a nationalist solution, it must establish airtight controls at the directorship level and over the capital stock. In effect, what the press told Vargas was that after his campaign rhetoric some explaining was in order.[14]

Explanations were all the more pressing now that Petrobrás had emerged from technocratic councils into the Congress, with its nineteenth-century humanistic and oratorical traditions. There a straw poll of federal employees hinted at a deep split. The Senate *porteiro* (doorman) Sr. Luis Gomez Carvalho pronounced: "Unfortunately, Brazilian resources, including petroleum, cannot be developed without foreign financial aid." He must have been influenced by the entreguista Senators, *Jornal de Debates* commented. Over at the Chamber of Deputies, however, all the functionaries interviewed came out strongly for State monopoly.[15]

The petroleum nationalists in the Chamber were a highly diversified group led by Bernardes. Already suspicious of Vargas, they were miffed because the President had not been over-solicitous in sounding them out.[16] They were not prepared to accept anything less than complete State monopoly over all phases of the industry. Other deputies held their fire, with the prominent exception of Aliomar Baleeiro, the UDN's hatchet man, who branded Petrobrás as inflationary, and said (erroneously) that foreigners holding the preferred stock would receive dividends before Brazilians. Since Baleeiro had led the recent UDN fight to block Vargas's legal accession to the Presidency, his views were taken to be highly partisan.

Nationalists in the Military Club thought Petrobrás had been submitted to Congress prematurely, before their objections were met, although General Horta, the Club's Vice-President since 1950, accepted Vargas's assurance that the bill was nationalist. "Brazilians have a special sympathy for mixed companies," he said, "a factor the government has astutely played upon. Once tightened up by Congress, that is, once private capital was barred from the Directorate and the states and localities were assured of participation in future subsidiaries, the project, Horta believed, would be "the most certain path for us to obtain what the majority of Brazilians want: State monopoly."[17] Other officers were even more emphatic. They demanded broad changes in Petrobrás to assure an explicit State monopoly. Specifically, they pointed out how the subsidiaries could be open to pressure and control by foreigners operating through domestic *testas de ferro*, or front men.[18] Alarmed, this group organized itself in a Military Club Commission around a nucleus of Centro members, in order to "study" Petrobrás.[19] Centro President General Felicíssimo Cardoso issued a statement condemning Petrobrás altogether. By late December 1951 like-thinking deputies and journalists were echoing Cardoso's view that the mixed-company formula permitted an intolerable breach that Standard Oil and other companies would take advantage of in their quest for Brazilian resources. And soon nationalists like deputy Lobo Carneiro were calling the bill "entreguista."[20]

The government was not worried yet. In a vigorous New Year's address in 1952, Vargas criticized foreign companies for excessive profit remittances and promoted his Petrobrás as "the nationalist solution," thus covering his political left flank. Vargas had the votes, and he let Majority Leader Gustavo Capanema shepherd Petrobrás through the Chamber while Almeida answered critics in the press.* He turned to other business, confident of passage through both houses within six months. As it happened, Capanema could not hold the Chamber and Almeida's spirited assurances—"the real aim of a nationalist petroleum policy is to produce oil, not slogans"—did not offset the legitimate doubts and sheer opportunism of those deputies now organizing to combat Petrobrás.

The first trouble arose in January 1952 from the ranks of Vargas's own PTB. Petrobrás had just reached the committees when Euzébio Rocha (PTB–São Paulo) released his substitute draft on the floor. As a prominent leader on the PTB left wing and a Centro member, Rocha was considered something of a petroleum expert in Congress. The deputies now had to consider two bills back-to-back.[21]

Unlike the government's bill, Rocha's draft outlined a rigid monopoly based on much simpler financing. Almeida's mixed formula and cr$10 billion capital were retained, but little else. Rocha assigned all exploration and production explicitly to the State, ruled out private refineries, and eliminated private capital in all sectors except for holdings by native Brazilians in State marketing outlets. No longer organized as a holding company with subsidiaries, his Petrobrás would act directly. The Directors must not have had any

---

* On paper, the government's Majority included 112 PSD deputies, 51 PTB deputies, and 24 PSP deputies, including some members of the eight small parties. The Minority formed around 81 UDN deputies and some party dissidents. Having canvassed party leaders and key deputies in late 1951, Vargas was convinced that Petrobrás would pass.

connection with private oil companies for a decade prior to serving. The stock, all publicly owned with majority Federal control, was to be issued against a gasoline excise tax increase of 40 centavos per liter. All of Almeida's other taxes were eliminated, including the compulsory draft on vehicle owners. Rocha concluded that there would be more than enough capital when this gasoline revenue was added to the value of CNP properties, the expected profits from refineries and the fleet, and the probable Brazilian government loans for exploration.

Backed by the nationalists, Rocha maneuvered skillfully among his fellow deputies. Some PTB men went along in the hope of pressuring Vargas, whom they accused of neglecting his own party while courting the UDN. Vargas's indifference to his own party's fortunes had prompted Labor Minister Danton Coelho to resign in September 1951, and this falling-out still rankled in the PTB. Thus Vargas talked with Rocha, in part to please PTB dissidents but also to find out how strong the nationalists were in Congress. Furthermore, Rocha had a sizable following in Rio and São Paulo that Vargas could not ignore. For his part, Rocha relished telling the Chamber how Getúlio had expressed surprise to learn that he, Rocha, had not been consulted in the drafting of Petrobrás. Once he knew Rocha wanted changes, Vargas supposedly replied: "The more nationalist this bill can be, the more it will protect State interests, defend against profiteering by the few, and satisfy my own desires." As for himself, Rocha concluded, all he wanted was to adapt Petrobrás to that "genuinely Brazilian company" Vargas mentioned in his December message sending Petrobrás to Congress.[22]

Tactically, Vargas erred: seeing Rocha lent prestige to Rocha's own bill. Some deputies began to wonder what Vargas really wanted. Stories made the rounds of how Getúlio had been poorly served by his advisers. "Why the great contradiction between the message, which is nationalist, and the bill which is entreguista?," Bernardes asked rhetorically. "From what I know of the trusts, this is their bill, having been passed from one of their front men to an economist who advised the President."[23] Bernardes then recounted how twice before he had foiled conspiracies by foreigners, first Itabira and then UNESCO's Hileian Amazon Project. The grand old man of Brazilian nationalism was making his last great fight. This made good press copy. Vargas's credibility, and more, his integrity, were being questioned by the petroleum nationalists.

Equally telling for the fate of Petrobrás were the doubts Rocha and his fellow nationalists cast on Almeida's financial estimates. In speeches and interviews, the PTB deputy hammered home the old Horta theme of self-financing from petroleum refining and transportation profits. Furthermore, he said the government finance plan was not only excessive for the objectives of Petrobrás, but also inflationary and therefore harmful to the masses. The same goals could be accomplished by taxing the car-owning rich. Few deputies had the expertise to challenge this argument, which had the added virtue of simplicity. And the press, hard put to follow all the facts and figures, was often less than accurate in reporting these events.

Bernardes's Committee on National Security then reported out the Rocha substitute bill in early March after drastically reducing his total capital outlays to three billion cruzeiros over a seven-year period. Bernardes, deeply suspicious, really believed that the government's "fantastically high" capital base of eight billion cruzeiros was destined to wreck the project, since such a sum, in his opinion, could never be collected without causing inflation and mass suffering. Then he added a final bizarre twist. He assigned the main role in exploration to foreign companies under contract, thus justifying his much-lightened capital load for Petrobrás.[24] Foreigners, he thought, would take the oil on almost any terms.

Almeida was now thoroughly alarmed. Bernardes, as the leader of the nationalists, had authority and prestige. Even so, the fact that Bernardes was indulging his well-known weakness for ambitious, under-financed State industrial projects was not, by itself, so important. What made the danger real was the backing Bernardes received from Mário Bittencourt Sampaio, Dutra's former DASP Director, whose SALTE plan had been repudiated by Vargas and Almeida. Eager to vindicate himself, Sampaio produced figures to show how Almeida's Petrobrás would bring in over six billion cruzeiros in excess funds. All Petrobrás really needed was a 30 centavo per liter increase in the gasoline tax. Given this tax, plus Treasury outlays and operational profits, Petrobrás could finance enough refineries to meet the demand while eliminating the private refiners, with whom Sampaio had crossed swords in 1948. In short, Petrobrás ought to be able to accomplish more for less money.

In response, Almeida issued *The Fundamentals of Petrobrás*, a pamphlet giving the government's official answer to congressional critics. Almeida showed how Sampaio had overvalued CNP properties and expected profits, and he cited Sampaio's own projection —20 per cent a year to 1961—as typical of Sampaio's inflated estimates.[25] Hindsight reveals that Almeida's projection was more accurate (although still far too high; see Fig. 1), but at the time it was Sampaio, a well-known civil servant and Dutra ally, who cast doubts on the younger man's economic and financial rationale. The Chamber, which was overwhelmingly composed of lawyers and other non-technocrats, had little insight on the issue. It was all the more confusing when Rocha revised his projection (to 18 per cent per year) to lie between Almeida's and Sampaio's. Moreover, the nationalists found Sampaio an articulate political ally, and the PSD's so-called dutrista bloc was sympathetic to his views.[26]

By late April, 1952, the government bill still had not emerged for amendment by the plenary body, although all the committees save Bernardes's had approved it. Deputies were becoming restive and Majority Leader Capanema, not being a technical man, had difficulty explaining things to his supporters. Since the nationalist group was trying to show they were more nationalistic than Vargas, modifying the bill became a patriotic duty. Catching the club-like spirit that came from bargaining with the Executive, many deputies felt that this was the Chamber's finest hour. Idealism mixed with political calculation eroded support for the government's bill. In mid-March, a study committee of the Progressive Social party (PSP) under Carlos Castilho Cabral issued a well-reasoned, qualified endorsement of the bill that hinged mainly on tightening control of the subsidiaries.[27] Even the majority PSD, an amorphous, center-hugging amalgam of establishment politicians, called vaguely for some amendments that would assure full State control while holding tax increases to the minimum.[28]

Tension mounted. Meanwhile the War Minister, Newton Estillac Leal, had resigned in March, and two bitterly opposed slates of candidates prepared to contest the biennial Military Club elections in May. The incumbent Nationalists led by Estillac and Horta were under attack by the Democratic Crusade under Alcid Etchegoyen and Nelson de Mello. Hard-liners among the out's accused their rivals of tolerating Communists in the Officer Corps and of allowing pro-Soviet propaganda in the Club's magazine, notably an anonymous apology for North Korea. For their part, the Nationalists campaigned as if they were running a plebiscite on petrolem. In Estillac's words, "That vote in 1950 and especially the one coming up has a significance—the oil question." Nobody was surprised when the Military Club's Petroleum Study Commission released its report in April calling Vargas's Petrobrás "profoundly entreguista."[29]

Outsiders watched this election to see how the Army stood on a range of controversial issues that had been raised in the absence of firm leadership from Estillac Leal. A Centro General (Artur Carnaúba) was the Club's interim President until August 1951, when Estillac resumed direct command. But by then polarization had begun. The opposition formed up on anti-Communist ground to snipe at him while Estillac's faction tried to shift the battle to their own best position, petroleum.[30] Those officers in the Nationalist camp who were disturbed at the deepening military ties with the United States (as a result of the Korean War a military aid pact had just been signed on March 15) in turn antagonized cold warriors among the "democratic crusaders" who worried about Communists infiltrating the Army. The sides split further apart when Estillac resigned as War Minister, to be replaced by a relatively junior officer without great prestige, Brigadier Espírito Santo Cardoso. And in late April, the strength of the Etchegoyen slate was bolstered by the adherence of prominent UDN officers, notably

Eduardo Gomes (whom Vargas defeated in 1951) and Juarez Távora.

These disputes all touched on questions of leadership and of corporate behavior. How much should officers speak out on political issues? Was the Club an opinion leader, or a social and benefit society within the Army corporation? The lines had never been clear since the late Empire, and indeed opponents in the Club were often enjoined not to speak out on politics in order to silence them. Under Estillac's unusually loose leadership this old corporate issue arose again to heat up the May election.

Centro President Felicíssimo Cardoso followed the tradition of Benjamin Constant, the activist officer from the nineteenth century with whom his father had been close, and the spirit of *tenentismo*, which he had espoused in the 1930's. As Second Vice-President of the Military Club, Cardoso saw no conflict in roles when he campaigned to save natural resources. Neither did many other officers. But the opposition argued that defense problems such as oil should be discussed and decided quietly, in the National Security Council and other specialized organs. To them, the fires of what Etchegoyen called "this generic petroleum theme" had to be banked. Communists were exploiting the oil issue. The Army's professional image, they felt, was not enhanced by rhetorical nationalism, which furthermore reminded them of the Estado Nôvo and Italy under Mussolini. When it came to officers speaking out on public issues, their example was MacArthur, whom President Truman had just fired.

Ironically, petroleum was not a real issue, for both groups were in fact nationalist. Since 1949 the great majority of Army officers wanted a State monopoly and the Horta Barbosa thesis was triumphant. Certainly Etchegoyen did not campaign for a concessionary policy. And even Juarez Távora felt called upon to state that the "democratic ticket will continue to defend State petroleum monopoly—by the State or a mixed company—but using honest arguments."[31] What concerned him and also many moderates who were in neither camp was the use to which a few radicals were putting petroleum nationalism.

Estillac Leal was embarrassed by some of his more partisan supporters. Known for hasty, off-the-cuff remarks, he had changed his nationalist views little from the tenentismo of his youth. Quite sincerely, he wanted to unify the Club around "a sound nationalism, not a sterile Jacobinism"; but, like Vargas, he was finding out that postwar nationalism, with its cold war and populist aspects, was difficult to control. As the campaign reached its climax, several Nationalist officers, including Cardoso's son, were arrested by the Military Police on grounds of subversion and crypto-Communism, while the Democratic Crusade was tarred with what amounted to treason charges in the equally abusive language of the petroleum nationalists. This stopped when Etchegoyen won by a two-thirds majority, and he enjoined officers from speaking out on controversial public issues.[32] Verbal fallout from these barrages had already hit the Chamber of Deputies, however, and the public was highly excited as well.

On April 28, shortly before the Military Club elections, the UDN dropped its own bombshell by coming out for a State oil monopoly at the same time that it gave full moral backing to the Democratic Crusade. This was no way to court the military, unless nationalism ran deep in the Officer Corps, as it did. A few days later, still before the elections, its bill for a National Petroleum Company (ENAPE) was submitted by the reporter Olavo Bilac Pinto, the Deputy Minority Leader Luis Garcia, and the combative Bahian Aliomar Baleeiro.[33] Capitalized at cr$10 billion over five years like Petrobrás, ENAPE's funds would come from the imposto único (the 25 per cent for petroleum in the Highway Fund), CNP properties and profits, and special credits and public loans. All private refineries were to be absorbed within a year, as ENAPE, a wholly public company, moved to monopolize all sectors, including distribution if desired. To protect the people's interests, company accounts would have to be submitted once a year for approval by the Tribunal das Contas (government auditors) and by Congress. ENAPE even had a profit-sharing plan for its employees. Why did the UDN, champion of free enterprise, take a position that nationalists applauded and conservatives called "demagogic opportunism"?

Largely it was the pressure of opportunity. Having fought for the Petroleum Statute in 1948, the party now undermined Petrobrás in mid-1952. Public opinion against Petrobrás was rising, and with Vargas's brand of nationalism now suspect, the UDN gained popularity by outflanking him. Playing the politics of oil also gave it a partisan issue that unified its members and thus held off Getúlio's call for a broad, center coalition. Perhaps, as Almeida believed, the UDN leadership wanted to cripple *any* State oil plan by adding rigid, unworkable features; when it failed, they could substitute a private solution. Perhaps Bilac Pinto, the prominent UDN leader from Minas, reflected the Belo Horizonte business community's hostility to foreign participation in natural resources development, which went back to the days of Farquhar.[34] One thing is certain: the UDN hit on a brilliant partisan move to embarrass Vargas. And the nationalists welcomed their new allies.

The cumulative effect of all this politicking was to cause Petrobrás to founder in May. Capanema's government forces outvoted the UDN 132 to 78 on a resolution to limit plenary debates (which the UDN wanted to prolong) on the various committee reports. But to ram through Petrobrás would be to confront the growing concensus in Congress that controls on private capital, both foreign and domestic, should be tightened. Furthermore, the companion tax bill, which raised the imposto único rates, needed the votes of deputies who would resent a power play over Petrobrás. One recalls how Rocha and Bittencourt Sampaio had already cast doubt on Almeida's entire financial base. Now the UDN had its own ENAPE finance plan. Vargas thus faced a difficult situation. He used all his skills to prevent the UDN from lining up support from other parties while he and his staff decided what to salvage from Petrobrás and what to bargain away for votes.[35]

The bargaining over Petrobrás took place from late May to late July 1952 in a highly charged atmosphere. Dutra came out for State monopoly, while recounting for the public how in 1942 as War Minister he had stopped Standard Oil. Lobo Carneiro announced that the Centro would hold its next convention in July. "In our First we defeated the Petroleum Statute; in our Third we'll surely defeat Petrobrás, the *entreguista* bill." Hostile critics questioned

Vargas's motives. "On the oil question, as on everything else, the former dictator's opinions are changeable and uncertain," said *O Estado de São Paulo*. Another critical paper, *Correio da Manhã*, was much fairer: "In defense of Vargas, it can be said that the government tried to avoid ideological and political controversies with this bill by stressing the economic aspects." Yet to think it "could avoid the ideological aspects was illusory."[36] For his part, Vargas first talked tough at Candeias on June 23, in the famous flag speech, during which he also attacked Dutra for sponsoring the old Petroleum Statute; then at Cubatão on July 12 he tacked by praising Dutra and offering to select Petrobrás's first president from the UDN.

Behind the scenes, meanwhile, Vargas was insistent on maintaining the financial integrity of Petrobrás, meaning Almeida's tax and capital provisions. He accepted the exclusion of foreign capital, minimal in the original bill, but insisted on domestic private capital participation. The mixed formula was not negotiable, although now the monopoly was defined explicitly and more rigidly as the exclusive activity of a mixed company directed by the government.[37] Furthermore, Capanema insisted that political responsibility for any compromise bill would have to be shared equally among all party leaders; should any *bancada* (delegation) fail to accept this compromise, Capanema threatened to ram through the original bill.[38] The final vote would thus be tantamount to a sense-of-Congress resolution, thereby protecting Petrobrás and the President from further partisan maneuvers. These positions held, but at the cost of less flexibility in ownership and management. Thus the former technocratic project became politicized.

Vargas's own PTB wheeled into line once foreigners were excluded from the stock subscription.[39] The Progressive Social party of São Paulo's populist Governor Adhemar de Barros worked closely with Vargas after having backed off from the original bill in April. Bernardes, dean of the nationalists, was satisfied when monopoly provisions were made explicit, and provisions for subsidiaries, which he had called "another Panama," were tightened up to prevent direct financial ties with foreign companies. As the political risks diminished, so the huge PSD bloc became easier to manage, and by late July, Vargas had enough firm votes. But still the UDN held out.

When Vargas offered Bilac Pinto a choice between compromise and his intransigent opposition, the UDN backed down. Negotiations continued, with Vargas giving in to congressional watchdogging—the UDN's yearly audit to him meant influence peddling—in return for the UDN's withdrawal of its ENAPE plan. But on the controversial private refineries, the UDN stood firm. A compromise was finally reached when further expansion of existing concessions after 1953 was specifically prohibited but CNP construction deadlines for the long-delayed Manguinhos and União ventures were extended by two years. With this final roadblock to an inter-party agreement cleared, the Chamber began voting in September.

Amended thus, Petrobrás was now no longer Vargas's own—waspishly the press referred to this new bill as the "nationalist plan"—but he had salvaged the essentials while achieving a measure of consensus in the Chamber. Bernardes, satisfied, retired from the Chamber, thus closing a 50-year political career. Only the Centro held out for a total State monopoly, indicating its decision not to play within the established political rules. Hopes for a UDN-government center coalition continued, as old friends Aranha and Flôres da Cunha made political soundings for the President. Vargas urgently wanted Petrobrás enacted into law so that Congress might enact the rest of his economic program, including Electrobrás. Regionalism, however, was hardly less difficult to subdue than the fires of partisanship.

This new dimension to decision-making now embroiled the Chamber in sectional debates. Bahia lobbied effectively to give the oil-producing regions, i.e. Bahia, a stock royalty and the right to invest preferentially in Petrobrás refineries that used their crude oil. But the point of contention was Aliomar Baleeiro's amendment to increase Highway Trust Fund benefits for poorer states and crude oil producers.

Under the 1948 law (302), Baleeiro argued, the large consumer

TABLE 5

Criteria for Distribution of Imposto Único

Program	Percentage based on			
	Consumption	Population	Area	Production
1948 Law 302	60%	20%	20%	—
1952 Baleeiro's plan				
imported	33⅓	33⅓	33⅓	—
domestic	25	25	25	25%
1953 Pasqualini's plan				
imported	40	40	20	—
domestic	36	36	18	10

SOURCE: Adapted from Alberto Pasqualini, Senate Finance Committee Report, Tables II and III, April 8, 1953, *Petróleo*, XI, 221–22.

states received the lion's share of imposto único revenues for their own road plans (see Table 5). In weighting the state quotas toward consumption rather than area and population, the wealth and highways were concentrated in São Paulo, Rio, and the South, prejudicing the poor Northern and Western regions, which all needed roads. Furthermore, most of the Federal quota—that is, 40 per cent of all imposto único receipts—was being spent on the Rio–São Paulo highway, thus further benefitting the large consumer markets. Baleeiro's new state quotas, one set for imported products, another for refined products from Brazilian crude, shifted more than 12 per cent of total revenues to the less favored regions (see Table 6). São Paulo, the largest consumer, stood to lose almost 27 per cent of its old quota, whereas Amazonas, a huge state with minimal consumption, would receive a 60 per cent increase, and Bahia, at current rates of consumption and production, would receive an increase of almost 35 per cent.

São Paulo officials fought Baleeiro all the way, having just begun a four-year road-building program based on monies from the present tax system.[40] But the South lost, and Baleeiro's new quotas were written into Petrobrás, thereby assuring its passage in late September.[41] The companion bill to increase imposto único rates, including Almeida's 25 per cent for Petrobrás, cleared the Chamber in November 1952. Rapid progress through the Senate was expected now that the major revisions were completed.

TABLE 6

State Quotas in the Imposto Único
(*Percentages based on 1952 receipts*)

State	Basis of quotas			Distribution of quotas (per cent of impost)		
	Per cent of national consumption	Per cent of population of Brazil	Per cent of area of Brazil	1948 Law 302	1952 Ba-leeiro's plan	1953 Pasqua-lini's plan
Developed South						
Rio Grande do Sul	9.48%	8.04%	3.64%	8.03%	7.03%	7.73%
Santa Catarina	2.63	3.01	1.22	2.43	2.28	2.50
Paraná	7.19	4.10	2.60	5.65	4.61	5.03
São Paulo	37.47	17.63	3.19	26.63	19.34	22.63
Federal District	12.77	4.60	.02	8.57	5.77	6.94
Rio de Janeiro	6.15	4.44	.55	4.69	3.69	4.34
Minas Gerais	7.94	14.95	7.50	9.26	10.08	10.63
Total	83.63%	65.77%	18.72%	65.26%	52.80%	59.80%
Underdeveloped North and West						
Amazonas	.34%	1.01%	20.53%	4.51%	7.26%	4.63%
Pará	1.00	2.18	15.67	4.17	6.26	4.40
Maranhão	.33	3.05	4.32	1.67	2.56	2.21
Piauí	.26	2.03	3.21	1.20	1.83	1.55
Ceará	1.55	5.22	1.98	2.37	2.89	3.10
Rio Grande no Norte	.83	1.88	.68	1.01	1.13	1.22
Paraíba	1.43	3.30	.73	1.66	1.81	2.03
Pernambuco	4.36	6.54	1.25	4.17	4.03	4.60
Alagoas	.56	2.11	.37	.84	1.00	1.14
Sergipe	.34	1.24	.27	.50	.62	.69
Bahia	3.14	9.35	7.27	5.20	7.00	6.61
Espírito Santo	.91	1.66	.53	.98	1.02	1.13
Mato Grosso	.48	1.01	16.28	3.76	5.89	3.85
Goiás	.84	2.35	8.02	2.59	3.73	2.88
Total	16.37%	42.93%	81.11%	34.63%	47.03%	40.04%
Grand total (incl. disputed area)	100.00%	100.00%	100.00%	100.00%	100.00%	100.00%

SOURCE: Adapted from Alberto Pasqualini, Senate Finance Committee Report, Tables II and III, April 8, 1953, *Petróleo*, XI, 221–22.

But six months later Petrobrás was still in the Senate. Clearly Vargas had again misjudged the disruptive politics of oil. In brief, Senate leaders refused to honor the Chamber's party understanding to support Petrobrás, and many Senators wanted exposure or simply wanted to speak out. The attack on Petrobrás was led by Assis Chateaubriand (the publishing baron), Plínio Pompeu, and

Othon Mäder, all three affiliated with the UDN. Chateaubriand, having begun his career as Farquhar's lawyer, came out openly for a concessionary policy. Napoleão Alencastro Guimarães, a long-time advocate of foreign participation, the sponsor of Standard's bid in 1941, and now in the PTB, embarrassed Vargas by giving the impression in press interviews that his chief intended to carry out a flexible policy toward foreigners. Again, doubts about Vargas's "real" views were raised, although he was in fact strongly in favor of the Chamber's bill. On the other side, Landulfo Alves, ex-Governor of Bahia and friend of Drault Ernanny, defended the State monopoly but saw no reason to limit the private refiners. Kerginaldo Cavalcanti (PSD–Pernambuco) and Domingos Velasco (UDN–Goiás), an ex-tenente, led the fight for a complete State monopoly.

And so the Senate debates continued into June 1953, opening every wound, raising every doubt, causing division and thus eroding the Chamber's compromise over Petrobrás. The private-capital forces, being well entrenched in the Senate and having the support of industrial and trade associations like FIESP, tried to amend the Chamber's exclusionist clauses. But Alberto Pasqualini (PTB–Rio Grande) turned the tide with a highly competent pro-government report for the Senate Finance Committee.[42]

The Senators offered several amendments to the bill, the most important of which was to let Petrobrás contract out prospecting, drilling, and producing services, with payment in money or oil, and to allow participation in the use of any oil so found. This was a compromise measure to tone down some of the Chamber's monopoly provisions. Pasqualini, acting on government instructions, offered an amendment which struck down Baleeiro's quota scheme with the strong backing of Center-South politicians and associational groups.[43] As Table 6 indicates, the underdeveloped states won reduced concessions, and benefits to producing regions were lowered to 10 per cent in order to prevent logrolling for exploration rights. In August, the Chamber sustained this amendment 121 to 66. However, by a vote of 145 to 49 the Chamber refused the Senate's recommendation to allow private refineries to expand,

and by 134 to 45 it barred foreigners from disposing of crude oil in payment for services under contract.* Thus on the whole the Senate debates and changes were futile, given the lower house's views and the drift of public opinion. The Chamber struck down almost all the Senate's amendments and Petrobrás was voted for the last time in September. It then passed into law on October 3, 1953.

Vargas, by then, was in deep political trouble. The long debates had raised speculations and conflicting technical arguments while eroding his prestige. His centrist brand of nationalism was no longer attractive, and his hopes for a workable center coalition with the UDN were dashed. Anti-Petrobrás sentiment among conservatives, whose support Vargas could ill afford to lose, had surfaced during the Senate debates. Groups like FIESP and the Federation of Commercial Associations condemned the principle of State ownership which, with the impetus given by the oil campaign, they feared might lead to collectivism. North-South tensions had surfaced. As for the extreme left, it claimed Petrobrás was incomplete, and continued to use petroleum nationalism as a means to politicize the masses and to challenge the established order.

True, Vargas had saved the essentials of Petrobrás, but the birth of this new company showed that his style of consensus politics was outmoded. Pilloried by the opposition press, and beset with scandals involving Euvaldo Lodi and other old cronies, Vargas did not reap any quick political benefits from Petrobrás. During June and July 1953 the cabinet was drastically reshuffled to bolster his sagging government. Vargas brought in his old friends from the 1930 revolution, Oswaldo Aranha (to Finance) and José Américo de Almeida (Transport); the appointment of his protégé João Goulart (to Labor) was intended to show his interest in rebuild-

---

* These key roll call votes indicate that about one quarter of the Chamber considered the final bill too rigid. See *Petróleo*, XII, 325–54. On the refineries, 21 UDN and 19 PSD deputies voted to allow expansion, and on contracts with foreign firms, 19 UDN and 17 PSD votes went for the more liberal Senate formula. These dissenting deputies numbered among their ranks such prominent public men as Herbert Levy (UDN leader in São Paulo), Edmundo de Macedo Soares e Silva (founder of Volta Redonda, PSD–Rio de Janeiro), Carlos Luz (PSD-Minas) and Daniel de Carvalho (an old Farquhar supporter, PR-Minas).

ing labor support and regaining the left. Thus the scene for his last year in office was set: respectability and financial retrenchment with Aranha (of the UDN), and a partisan opening to the left and populist elements under Goulart (of the PTB).

As for Petrobrás, could it be financed in the current balance-of-payments crisis and under worsening inflation? Almeida's original cr$10 billion financial base might be no longer adequate since the company was two years behind schedule. Alarmed, the Bank of Brazil President, Marcos de Souza Dantas, another important figure from the 1930's, urged Vargas and Aranha to cover equipment purchases with gold reserves in New York. It happened that the vehicle owners compulsory stock subscription brought in enough to sustain Petrobrás, but Aranha and many leading financiers were worried.[44]

Vargas rarely mentioned Petrobrás in his last months as President. Disappointed, he surely felt he had hatched a politicized project with reduced chances for success. That Brazilians married to foreigners could not hold stock became something of a derisive joke among middle-class Brazilians. As anti-Vargas sentiment spread in 1954, many felt that the new company, headed by the UDN's Colonel Juracy Magalhães, would be dismembered for a formula closer to a concessionary regime.[45] But Vargas had the final word on August 24. He took his own life, leaving a note that charged domestic and foreign groups with undermining his whole economic program, especially Petrobrás. Angry crowds surged outside the palace in a kind of plebiscite for the fallen President. Thus in death he took back the banner of nationalism, overwhelming his critics on the right and the left who threatened Petrobrás as well as his historical reputation.

In 1968, the balance sheet for Petrobrás was favorable. The 15 years after Vargas signed Law 2,004 cannot be analyzed here; but it can be said that the existence of Petrobrás and the fact that it was one of the world's largest enterprises were reasons enough to call it a success story. Certainly it was not the financial disaster early critics said it would become; it was one of the great spurs to growth under President Juscelino Kubitschek, who pumped millions of dollars and cruzeiros into the domestic economy through Petrobrás. After the 1964 revolution it again became a mainstay in the capital-accumulating process of rapid industrialization. No one could measure another benefit, which was nonetheless real: the pride Brazilians felt in solving a Brazilian problem with their own resources.[46]

Efforts to attain self-sufficiency were much more successful in refined products by 1966 (93 per cent of consumption) than in production, which at 116,000 b/day still trailed behind the total crude demand of 354,000 b/day. The failure to find enough oil stemmed not from a lack of effort or from technological isolationism, but rather from a chance roll of the geophysical dice. The $300 million Petrobrás spent on exploration from 1954 to 1960 may be something of a world's record for yielding minimal results, and Petrobrás, unlike the international major companies, had no spread of operations elsewhere to offset its bad luck.[47] In 1968 offshore drilling on the Sergipe coast seemed promising and domestic production had now reached 51 per cent of crude oil consumption, but nobody thought of Brazil as a major oil producer. In fact, the main favorable trend was the declining price of imported crude— from $2.85 per barrel in 1958 to $1.96 in 1966—which contributed greatly toward success in refining. Also in 1968 two 100,000-ton super tankers were ordered; these would modernize Brazil's aging fleet and cut transportation costs substantially.

Financially, Petrobrás had, by 1968, capital and reserves totaling Ncr$2,269,043,000, making it Latin America's largest industrial concern.[48] Though troubled by inflation and foreign exchange problems during most of its 15-year life, Petrobrás did not have to supplant Almeida's basic finance plan with other devices. However, it is probably safe to say that because Petrobrás hired the best available talent, including Arthur Link, a former Standard Oil vice president who was chief of exploration from 1954 to 1959, foreign suppliers and their governments were more willing to make large equipment loans. Aside from its imposto único quota, the company was supposed to be self-financing in 1968, but whether or not it was would be hard to establish on the basis of publicly available information. Certainly the profitability of Petrobrás improved dramatically after April 1964. The ending of exchange subsidies for imported derivatives, on which Petrobrás's low domestic prices had been pegged, was the decisive factor in revitalizing the company. And after years of inactivity, the corporation's stock began to move briskly on the Rio and São Paulo exchanges.

In management, the record was open to debate. Petrobrás continued to be overcentralized and subject to gigantism, twin weaknesses that were built into the revised bill in 1952. The company did not really act as a holding operation, for it would not allow decisional autonomy to subsidiaries. Efforts since 1955 to decentralize had failed, in part because the policy-setting organ for Petrobrás, which was the CNP, fell into decline, and in part because in contrast to Volta Redonda there was an unusually high turnover in top management (nine presidents and dozens of directors by 1964) until the military revamped Petrobrás. Only then did the corporation appear willing and politically able to differentiate between investments in mandatory sectors—exploration, transportation and refining—and sectors outside the statutory monopoly, such as petrochemicals and distribution. Seemingly the trend to gigantism had been corrected. In late 1968 Petrobrás announced that it would associate its new subsidiary, Petroquisa, with private French and domestic capitalists to construct Petroquimica União. Following investments of $475 million in the next six years, this associated company hoped to become Latin America's largest petrochemical complex.[49]

Until recently, Petrobrás was virtually a free agent in the councils of government. Having two votes, the company President needed only one ally on the four-man Directorate to become a czar over oil whom no civilian chief executive could touch. In fact, Petrobrás took on traits associated with the majors: it advertised extensively in the press, it had a large publication and information department, and it was a strong political power. One President said he could elect a hundred deputies. Subsidies to the student movement (UNE), an old ally, helped to assure a supply of shock troops. Petrobrás became a sacred cow. Attempts to modify its structure or redefine its priorities, let alone to destroy its monopoly (as some Senators attempted to do in 1955), were repulsed by Petrobrás and its allies with charges of entreguismo.[50] Over 15 years, nationalism had become an ever more unifying force. For one thing, it gave a psychic income no economist could measure. For another, it was a mantle broad enough to accommodate a great variety of Brazilians. Vargas's experience was tragic. But with luck and timing, even an authoritarian regime could master the politics of oil, as happened when President Humberto Castelo Branco (1964–67) won approval of his reforms of Petrobrás from the left. To be sure, there had been opportunism. Under President Kubitschek, production was increased substantially to show how the government was "solving" the oil problem; the price was an undercutting of reserves, and costly, not to mention wasteful, production techniques. Before his fall, President João Goulart (1961–64) expropriated the private refineries at a mass rally, knowing there was no economic reason for it. Held to strict quotas, the refiners for years had turned their extra capacity over to Petrobrás. They were reinstated in July 1965 by Decree Law 56,570. Radical nationalists, backed by Communists, helped to undermine the Higher Studies Institute, a brilliant heterodox group that formed under Kubitschek's administration to work out a Brazilian ideology of development. Oil was the principal issue over which moderates were forced to leave the Institute.[51] In sum, nationalism had been an important element in the creation of Petrobrás, although only a firm hand could control it. And it was certain that, as a national issue, the politics of oil was a significant political experience for a whole generation of Brazilians.

Reflecting on the years 1938–53, one recalls three distinct policy phases: the Horta era, the anti-Statute mobilization, and the Petrobrás debates. Clearly, the final 1953 solution followed many years of sustained discussion by government officials, private interests, the military, politicians, and that part of the public which was politically aware. Vargas himself saw Petrobrás as one of several technocratically inspired projects, little anticipating that petroleum would become the dominant issue of his second presidency.

Together with his excellent staff, the President gauged the politics of oil wrongly, and his brand of conciliatory politics failed him. As for Petrobrás, it was, as planned, a powerful engine for development.

But the significance of petroleum policy-making under Vargas cannot be summed up in isolation. The next chapter assesses the three cases and relates them to propositions that were raised at the outset of this book.

CONCLUSION

The Vargas era saw a marked increase in the authority and capacity of the national government. Brazilian policy makers developed a future orientation and a confidence in national purpose that in the broadest sense can be called developmental nationalism. And although they often differed on the means, the goal, industrialization, became widely accepted among technocrats and the politically active public alike. This created a precious legacy for present-day Brazilians who are attempting to lead their nation's great ascent. This study has traced three of the early milestones along their way.

In retrospect, the trade, steel, and petroleum cases reveal not some special capacity of Vargas's to set comprehensive policies, but rather the continuous redefinition of means and ends. For example, Volta Redonda did not result from a clearly defined master solution. Instead, it followed from a long series of decisions that were influenced by circumstances, political and social groups, and personalities. Similarly, nobody "created" Petrobrás. The government's oil monopoly was the culmination of a drawn-out debate about various options.

Trade policy was remarkably diffuse, owing to the number of people involved in policy-making, the conflicting domestic influences, and the chaotic conditions of the international trade and monetary systems. Thus Vargas's Foreign Trade Council (CFCE) was unable to fulfill its intended role as master coordinator of trade and economic policy. Rather, the CFCE provided a useful sounding board for interest groups and the bureaucracy, and was a means of exchanging information. Vargas himself used it to strengthen his authority and to legitimize his actions. But with key ministers acting outside the Council, there were important independent voices in policy-making. Furthermore, the extent to which policy was influenced and even determined abroad, in Washington and Berlin, diminished the CFCE's effectiveness; this was highlighted by the activities of Brazil's semiofficial intermediaries, Valentim Bouças and Olavo Egydio de Souza Aranha. Since no single institution or group determined trade policy, it was practically impossible to set a coherent trade strategy that went beyond maintaining and expanding markets. The related question of what kind of trade a developing nation should have was in large part left unanswered.

By contrast, steel policy was made in a more orderly fashion. Thanks to the Brazilian Army, Vargas and his ministers were under heavy and continuous pressure to produce results. Within the government, moreover, there was widespread agreement that an integrated, modern steelworks was necessary and desirable. Several factors came together after 1937 to clarify the decision-making process. For one thing, Percival Farquhar's "king solution" to coal, capital, transportation, and ore exporting lost ground, chiefly because he lacked financial backing. For another, the centralized Estado Nôvo dictatorship shifted the balance of power from regional and private domestic interests to the national government. The circumstances under which foreign financial and technical assistance was offered also affected the policy process. The solution chosen was one on which influential Brazilians could agree. Brazilians were to control the steel plant, which was designed for self-sufficiency in wartime, a primary consideration of the Army. But the entire existing industry was not regulated as a public utility, as the military's Special Commission had recommended in the CFCE in 1939. The emergence of a role for the State in heavy industry was therefore acceptable to private Brazilian industrialists. For Vargas, this happy outcome harmonized with the Estado Nôvo's ideology of conservative modernization.

Unlike steel policy, where a flexible, conciliatory formula was adopted, petroleum policy took the direction of outright State control over all phases of the business except distribution. The thrust of Horta Barbosa's early policy initiatives was vastly reinforced by the oil mobilization campaign of 1948. Alternative solutions based on mixed, or foreign-financed companies were defeated by two main factors: Horta's moral legacy and the financial and political weaknesses of these alternatives. Disagreements within the military over petroleum policy were largely resolved by 1949. Henceforth they concerned style and tactics, rather than the generally agreed upon goal of government ownership and control. Private groups, however, were unhappy with what they regarded as a turn toward statism. When Vargas and his technocrats almost lost control of Congress it was clear that policy-making had become more complex because of popular participation in an open, democratic system. The politicized monopoly that emerged was divisive at the time. However, Vargas's suicide, the passing of time, and the corporation's undeniable vitality healed many wounds.

Viewed comparatively, the three cases reveal progress toward the internal control of policy-making. Trade decisions in the 1930's were highly dependent upon events and policies emanating from foreign capitals. In part, this was because trade policy by definition was concerned with the international arena. But in part, I would suggest, it was because Brazilian officials tended to be followers in trade matters, whereas with regard to steel, they had a much clearer idea of what they wanted and what they could accept. German-American rivalry resulted in making available to Brazil a great deal of money for the steelworks, and the final decision to separate ore exports from steelmaking stemmed from the U.S. Steel report in 1939. But the result, Volta Redonda, was primarily a Brazilian solution. In 1951, the industrial policies of Vargas's second presidency reflected the impact of developmental nationalism. Exogenous elements were reduced in petroleum policy because the government, reinforced by public opinion, opted for an independent solution. Clearly, however, the unwillingness of foreigners to invest heavily in Brazilian petroleum exploration was a key element in that decision.

Interest groups have been touched upon insofar as they influenced the policy-making process. Although it cannot be said that these groups controlled policy-making, it is clear that foreign and domestic interests had access to the corridors of power. Perhaps the principal check on their influence was their own inability to command sufficient resources independently of the government. Thus they approached the State not as powerful initiators, but as suppliants with hat in hand. This was borne out in the steel episode: domestic projects from Siciliano Junior's to Henrique Lage's all depended on large government subsidies. And it was demonstrated in petroleum: domestic refiners, whether acting independently or in league with the major companies, could not raise enough capital after General Barreto had sanctioned their plans in 1945. Furthermore, formal interest groups were less ubiquitous in policy-making after 1951 partly because Roberto Simonsen was dead and Euvaldo Lodi had lost prestige, and partly because the open postwar political system was more complex than the semicorporatist, bureaucratic Estado Nôvo. Furthermore, interests now had to work through an active Congress that was responsive to public opinion, as well as directly through the ministries and the President. Twice, in 1948 and in 1952–53, petroleum solutions acceptable to private interests were defeated in open debate. Vargas heard these interests out when Petrobrás was being drafted in 1951, but they did not make policy.

Foreign interest groups were represented by their embassy personnel, and by Brazilian advocates and go-betweens. The major oil companies had ties with advertising agencies, the press, and certain politicians. But they were not omnipotent. It cannot be said that the oil companies "prevented" Brazil's progress in petroleum development, as Monteiro Lobato claimed for his own reasons. On the contrary, foreign groups became seriously interested in Brazil's steel and petroleum potential only in the mid-1930's. For Vargas, it was not a question of containing demonic foreign trusts, but of deciding what elements of the foreign options were viable and desirable. The evidence is clear in the case of U.S. Steel (1939–40), and in the President's later discussions with the oil companies prior to the establishment of Petrobrás.

The Brazilian Army was an important initiating group, but it was not monolithic in its thinking on development. General Macedo Soares e Silva, the Army steel expert, did not share Horta Barbosa's views toward the foreign oil companies. General Juarez Távora emerged as the principal Army advocate of an opening to the majors. The fact that both Horta and Távora were well-known spokesmen for the nationalist viewpoint indicates that there was no single attitude toward economic nationalism within the military. Moreover, the rather simple and direct views of the early tenentes, and the military nationalism of the Estado Nôvo, which followed, were buffeted by cold war issues and the emergence of popular nationalism. Postwar Brazil became a more complex society, and the Army, Brazil's preeminent national institution, reflected the change.

All three of these cases were touched by Brazil's relations with the outside world. A web of influence, power, and initiative reached beyond the purely juridical fact of national sovereignty to affect the policy process. Brazilians were highly aware of this foreign presence during the Vargas years, but various groups and personalities interpreted its significance differently. Many responded to the appeals of nationalism, which was a means of defining their own position in relation to foreign options and influence. But not all Brazilians who were comfortable with economic nationalism looked on nationalism in its postwar political aspects with equanimity.

In tracing the growth of economic nationalism, this account has analyzed the emergence of a developmental ideology that identified Brazil's future with industrialization. In this, the Army took the lead during the 1930's when military officers examined the nation's military and economic defense requirements. The Army's views were expressed forcefully, and later, under the civilian technocrats in Vargas's second presidency, a more sophisticated view of planning and direct governmental action was developed as a result.

The international environment stabilized under the hegemony of the United States after 1942, assuring the return to liberal economic practices and an open monetary system. This militated against nationalism, but as Brazil's international influence dwindled during the cold war, an inward perspective developed within the government that was favorable to developmental nationalism. Now, of course, Brazil was no longer an important pawn of two rival systems. But German-American rivalry, even at its height, had never opened up the possibility for foreign aid in petroleum, as it had in heavy industry. After the war, Brazil's options remained the same: develop the industry with the major international companies or with domestic resources. Nationalism, as we have seen, was a key factor in the decision.

Various groups used economic nationalism to advance their own interests. Monteiro Lobato's campaign was only one example. Industrialists in Brazil's domestic steel industry sought government protection and subsidies in the name of nationalism. Not to be forgotten, also, was the strain of anti-foreign sentiment that Artur Bernardes personified so well in his campaigns against foreign control of natural resources. On balance, however, the most important contribution of nationalism under Vargas was toward setting and then popularizing the goals of development.

Economic nationalism was used to identify priorities, and to invest the State with authority to initiate action. It reflected an urgent desire to achieve results, as when Major Macedo Soares wrote Mendonça Lima in 1939 that it was, above all, time to build the steelworks. It was a positive perspective on balance-of-payments crises, which brushed aside long-term economic and monetary limitations with demands for immediate action. During the Vargas years, economic nationalism was broadened in scope from protecting natural resources to supporting policies that called for the utilization of these resources. That industrialization would hasten national well-being and enhance the dignity of the nation were concepts that Vargas skillfully identified with his own political personality.

At the same time, Vargas's limited use of nationalism for political mobilization indicates the basically conservative cast of his political system. He and his party, the PTB, avoided the 1948 oil mobilization campaign, which they saw as opening new possibilities for leftist, radical, mass politics. Consensus, not conflict, was the essence of Vargas's style. It was Volta Redonda, with its model city and message of technological and social change from above, that typified his brand of nationalism. Later, Vargas did not control the emergent new consensus over petroleum, because he shied away from taking a forthright stand on such a divisive issue. Others, like the UDN and the radical nationalists, welcomed petroleum nationalism, and made use of its conflictual aspects to attack the President and his economic program.

The Petrobrás crisis showed also that Vargas's highly personal, ad hoc, and contingent style of leadership was becoming out of date. He had drawn on patrimonial traditions to reinforce the presidency; corporatist councils, notably the CFCE, had strengthened his hand in the 1930's, and a brilliant technical staff became his policy-making arm in the 1950's. Why, then, were his programs pilloried in the press and delayed in Congress? Never the party man, Vargas searched in vain for an old-fashioned conciliation with the UDN when what he needed was vigorous leadership to shore up his PTB and to hold the amorphous PSD. Congress and the press were powerful institutions which he had bypassed or controlled during the Estado Nôvo, but which he could not dominate in the open, postwar system. Vargas, who understood the uses of power very well, was unable to master the growing demands of the public to participate in the political process.

His decision-making load increased simultaneously with a more complex political system. Vargas had to play many roles: populist labor leader, ally of the politicians in power, friend of business and of foreign investment in sectors outside petroleum, initiator of technocratic development projects, and protector of the nation's financial health in an inflationary situation. Certainly the exercise of presidential power was more complex, and for Vargas these were an embattled final four years.

Finally, it is clear that the three cases involved issues in which rather sharp policy alternatives were posed. At the same time, they dramatized Brazil's international involvement, thus maximizing the potential for a nationalist reaction. Therefore, the cases throw into sharp relief the issues of regionalism, interest group objectives, presidential power, and inter-ministerial rivalries and conflicts. Not all the policies of the Vargas years showed these same highlights, or contrasts, or modes of action. The problems of social welfare legislation, patronage, and State-sponsored labor unionism, for example, were not influenced by such a broad range of interests. Those issues primarily concerned domestic urban groups. Nor did the debates over the allocation of revenues among federal, state, and local governments exhibit the same characteristics as the three case studies. Agriculture and education—two pressing issues in the late 1960's—did not receive enough attention from Vargas and his contemporaries, yet these problems, also, took their own forms. However, the trade, steel, and petroleum issues were much discussed by contemporaries, which makes them typical problems of the times. They reveal the inner workings of the Vargas system, showing the interplay of influence, personality, and ideology. I would make no claim that these case studies point out paths to future policy. If relevant features of the recent Brazilian past have been brought to light, however, the historian's task is fulfilled.

NOTES

NOTES

Complete authors' names, titles, and publication data for works cited in the Notes are given in the Bibliography, pp. 260–70. All microfilms cited are in the United States National Archives, Washington, D.C. The following list includes abbreviations used in the text and in the Notes:

AA   Aranha Archive

AN   National Archive (Arquivo Nacional)

AM   Meirelles Archive

AS   Simonsen Archive

AV   Vargas Archive

BN   National Library (Biblioteca Nacional)

CEDP   Center for the Study and Defense of Petroleum (Centro de Estudos e Defesa do Petróleo)

CEDPEN   Center for the Study and Defense of Petroleum and the National Economy (Centro de Estudos e Defesa do Petróleo e da Economia Nacional)

CFCE   Foreign Trade Council (Conselho Federal de Comércio Exterior)

CNI   National Industrial Federation (Confederação Nacional de Indústria)

CNP   National Petroleum Council (Conselho Nacional do Petróleo)

CSN   National Steel Company (Companhia Siderúrgica Nacional)

CTEF   Technical Economic and Financial Council (Conselho Técnico de Economia e Finanças)

DASP   Department of Public Service Administration (Departamento Administrativo do Serviço Público)

DNPM   Department of Mineral Production (Departamento Nacional da Produção Mineral)

DOPS   National Security Police (Departamento de Ordem Política e Social)

DS   United States Department of State

EFCB   Central do Brasil Railroad (Estrada de Ferro Central do Brasil)
FIESP São Paulo Industrial Federation (Federação das Indústrias do Estado de São Paulo)
FR   *Foreign Relations of the United States*
MRE   Ministry of Foreign Affairs (Ministério das Relações Exteriores)
MVOP   Ministry of Transport and Public Works (Ministério da Viação e Obras Públicas)
PCB   Brazilian Communist Party (Partido Comunista Brasileiro)
PSD   Social Democratic Party (Partido Social Democrático)
PSP   Progressive Social Party (Partido Social Progressista)
PTB   Brazilian Labor Party (Partido Trabalhista Brasileiro)
SGM   Geological Service (Serviço Geológico e Mineralógico)
UDN   National Democratic Union (União Democrática Nacional)
UNE   National Student Union (União Nacional de Estudantes)

INTRODUCTION

1. Vargas, *A nova política*, X, 53ff.

2. Vargas, Mensagem No. 469, de 1951, in Brazil, Congresso, Câmara dos Deputados, *Petróleo*, V, 16.

3. Thomas E. Skidmore has written the first competent book-length study. In his *Politics in Brazil*, he provides a clear general chronology and cogent political analysis with considerable attention to economic issues. This trailblazing book points up the need for special studies based on extensive documentary research before new syntheses of the Vargas years can be attempted.

4. Leff takes the structural approach in his analysis of economic policy-making in the postwar period. The section on patronage is persuasive. Insightful, suggestive, and valuable as his study undeniably is, however, it cannot be used to explain the formation of Brazil's steel and petroleum industries. In part, this is because of insufficient documentary evidence (Leff relied heavily on interviews) to support the analysis. In part, it stems from an overrigid application of the structural approach to specific cases. For example, Leff's contention (pp. 102–3) that postwar economic decision-making was singularly free of political pressures and conflict is supported by a very brief and misleading reference to steel policy (footnote 28). I found that regional politics and group pressures pervaded the making of steel policy.

5. Conclusion based on Peláez, pp. 32ff.

6. The argument follows Leff, p. 106.

7. The lack of current studies on patrimonialism is notable. See the suggestive leads in Veliz, Gordon (pp. 22–33), and Dix. For Brazilian corporatist theory consult Oliveira Vianna, Azevedo Amaral, and the key European influence, Manoilescu, *O século do corporativismo.*

8. Donald Keesing suggested this approach, on which I have elaborated.

9. Of the anti-imperialist intellectuals writing before 1914, Alberto Tôrres was the most explicit. Brazil would be partitioned or dominated by the great trusts, he warned, unless a strong, centralized state was organized to protect natural resources and to consolidate Brazil's diffuse, regionalistic society. Consult his *O problema nacional brasileiro,* the classic of Brazilian nationalism. Others besides Tôrres were Euclydes da Cunha, Sílvio Romero, and Salvador de Mendonça. For interesting leads see Assis Barbosa, I, 229.

10. At present there is no history of the modern Brazilian Army. Regional forces were crushed in the 1932 São Paulo state revolt and in the 1937 triumph over militia forces in Rio Grande do Sul led by Interventor (governor) Flôres da Cunha. The mission of the 1930's, which was to prepare for a possible confrontation with Argentina, was changed in 1942 when Brazil mobilized and sent an Expeditionary Force to fight with Allied troops in Italy. This wartime association with the United States Army was later extended into hemispheric defense planning during the cold war period. In 1951, the decision not to send troops to Korea (as the Americans wanted) indicated that the Brazilian Army looked to the Atlantic basin as its sphere of strategic concern.

11. Maciel Filho, "Conclusão e continuidade," *O Imparcial,* July 17, 1940.

12. For example, General Góes Monteiro's *Exposição* to President Vargas, Jan. 1934 [mimeo.], p. 10, AA: "In a new country like Brazil, a *well-organized* Army is the most powerful instrument the government has for educating its people, consolidating national spirit, and neutralizing the divisive tendencies introduced by immigrants." The tenentes' political role as authoritarian nationalists is examined in my "Tenentismo in the Brazilian Revolution of 1930."

13. Draft of letter, Aranha to Antônio Borges de Medeiros, Rio, [May?] 1932, AA.

14. Peláez's analysis of these events is persuasive. It revises Furtado's thesis on the transfer of domestic capital out of foreign trade and into domestic industry during the 1930's. See Furtado, Ch. 32.

15. This interpretation follows Peláez.

16. Furtado, p. 220.

17. Macedo Soares e Silva, "Conferência," in FIESP, p. 63.

CHAPTER 1

1. For a concise analysis of German policy see United States Tariff Commission, *Foreign-Trade and Exchange Controls in Germany*. United States policy is discussed in Sayre, Beckett, and Diebold. See also the recent, short summary by McCann.

2. Simonsen, *Níveis de vida*, p. 22.

3. Francisco V. Oliveira Vianna, Brazil's first political sociologist, developed the rationale for associating interest groups directly with the political elite in decision-making. Citing postwar French, Italian, and German practices, he stressed the advantages the government would gain from information exchange and coordination with the economic power holders, and he emphasized communality, not conflict. *Problemas de política objectiva*, Part IV "O problema do governo," pp. 151ff. The tenentes also advocated technical councils. See Clube 3 de Outubro, especially pp. 40–41.

4. For the years 1929–32, coffee was 72 per cent of Brazilian total export value, and cotton 2 per cent (1929 only); the percentages for 1936–38 were 42–46 for coffee and 18–19 for cotton. United States Tariff Commission, *Foreign Trade of Latin America*, pp. 84–85.

5. The United States supplied 79 per cent of Germany's cotton in 1932, Brazil only .1 per cent; for 1934 the figures were 59 per cent and 2.6 per cent; for 1935, 24.2 per cent and 26.6 per cent. By 1939 the United States' share was only 19.1 per cent, and Brazil supplied 27 per cent. German statistics cited in Diebold, p. 28.

6. United States Tariff Commission, *Foreign Trade of Latin America*, p. 79.

7. *Ibid.*, Table 7, p. 88.

8. Snyder, pp. 787–802.

9. Great Britain, Department of Overseas Trade, *Report* for 1931, pp. 18–20. The Brazilian government sold this wheat in the domestic market, and with the proceeds bought up excess coffee stocks as part of the coffee price support program.

10. Bouças, *Exposição e voto*, Sept. 30, 1935, in CFCE, Processo 257, "Preço da gasolina na praça do Rio de Janeiro," AN. Iuyamtorg, the Soviet trade organization based in Uruguay, had sounded out the Brazilians in 1931 on a possible coffee-gasoline exchange following the abrogation of a similar barter contract with Argentina in 1930. Russia's later disinterest in Brazil stemmed from a combination of high coffee prices and the inward turn of Soviet economic policy under Stalin. For

Brazil see Monteiro Lobato, pp. 234–39; for Argentina consult Frondizi, p. 254.

11. Memorandum by W. R. Manning of the Division of Latin American Affairs, Washington, May 20, 1933, *FR, 1933*, V, 45–46.

12. Telegram 66, the chargé in Brazil (Thurston) to Acting Secretary of State, Rio, July 18, 1933, summarizing United Press despatch from Washington, *ibid.*, p. 14.

13. Memorandum by Wilson, Washington, Aug. 11, 1933, *ibid.*, p. 16.

14. Bouças, CFCE, Processo 257, AN. Bouças was replying to the Rio de Janeiro Chauffeurs' Union and other groups who protested the oil companies' decision in May 1935 to meet inflation with increased prices. Also fighting the price hike was Pedro Ernesto Baptista, the populist governor of Rio's Federal District whom Vargas deposed in late 1935. Complete documentation may be found in the CFCE Processo.

15. Barbosa Lima Sobrinho, *Alcool-motor*, pp. 12–19. By 1937, all gasoline sold in Brazil was 10 per cent alcohol.

16. Despatch EC/1, the Acting Minister of Foreign Affairs (Cavalcanti de Lacerda) to Ambassador Lima e Silva, Rio, Jan. 4, 1934, MRE.

17. Letter, Bouças to Aranha, New York, March 7, 1934, AA.

18. Letter, Cyro de Freitas-Valle to Souza Dantas, Director of the Exchange Control Board of the Bank of Brazil, Washington, June 26, 1934, Annexed to Ofício 298, Freitas-Valle to Cavalcanti de Lacerda, Washington [June 1934], MRE. Among other things, these bankers were influenced by the Foreign Bondholders Protective Association, a pressure group that attempted (unsuccessfully) to involve the United States government in measures to force the Brazilians to resume full payment on the foreign debt, that is, beyond the Aranha debt consolidation plan.

19. Ofício 324, Freitas-Valle to Cavalcanti de Lacerda, Washington, July 19, 1934, MRE.

20. Ofício 328, Freitas-Valle to Cavalcanti de Lacerda, Washington, July 23, 1934, MRE.

21. Telegram EC/138, Freitas-Valle to MRE, Washington, Aug. 10, 1934, MRE.

22. Telegram EC/130-21300, MRE to Freitas-Valle, Rio, Aug. 11, 1934, MRE.

23. Telegram EC/186, Freitas-Valle to MRE, Washington, Sept. 12, 1934, MRE.

24. Telegram EC/130-21300, MRE to Freitas-Valle, Aug. 11, 1934, MRE.

25. Telegram EC/133-41720, MRE to Freitas-Valle, Aug. 15, 1934, MRE.

26. Letter, Souza Dantas to CFCE, Aug. 13, 1934, in Processo 1, "O problema dos congelados," AN.

27. *Correio da Manhã*, Sept. 27, 1934, p. 2. However, the paper did not imply a connection between clearing and debt resumption.

28. Telegram, Freitas-Valle to General Flôres da Cunha, Alegrete, Rio Grande do Sul, July 20, 1934, in CFCE, Processo 3, "Accordo comercial Brasil-Alemanha," AN.

29. On coffee see *Correio da Manhã*, Aug. 25, 1934, p. 2, and Oct. 2, 1934, p. 8. Proposal, Herm Stoltz & Co. of Rio to Minister of Transport, offering to exchange coffee for renovation of the Lloyd Nacional (deficit government shipping line) and for coal, made in letters of April 1933, Dec. 1933, and Aug. 1934; the letters from the German firms are in CFCE, Processo 29, "Proposta de troca de mercadorias," AN.

30. Letter, Otto Behr & Co. to the Commercial Attaché in the Brazilian Legation, Berlin, Sept. 3, 1934, in CFCE, Processo 10, "Convênio Comercial Brasil-Alemanha," and letter of Sept. 29, 1934, in CFCE, Processo 29, "Proposta de troca de mercadorias," AN.

31. Records of the German Foreign Office (Economic Department), in United States National Archives, K226287–325, roll 4465, microcopy T-120. The principal document is reprinted with commentary in my "A German View."

32. Letter, Souza Dantas to CFCE, Rio, Aug. 31, 1934, Processo 4, "Convênio comercial com a Alemanha," AN.

33. Letter, Kiep to the German Foreign Office, Rio, Nov. 7, 1934, K224920–26, roll 4463, microcopy T-120.

34. Souza Dantas, "História verdadeira dos 'marcos de compensação,'" long article in *Correio da Manhã*, July 1, 1937, p. 8.

35. Letter, Kiep to the German Foreign Office, Rio, Nov. 7, 1934, K224920–26, roll 4463, microcopy T-120.

36. Conversation between Souza Dantas and Freitas-Valle, reported in a Memorandum for the Ambassador [Aranha] by Freitas-Valle, Washington, Nov. 13, 1934, annexed to Ofício 517, Aranha to Foreign Minister José Carlos de Macedo Soares, Washington, Nov. 16, 1934, MRE.

37. Report by J. M. de Lacerda, August 1934, CFCE, Processo 4, "Convênio comercial com a Alemanha," AN.

38. Letter, Bouças to Aranha, Rio, Oct. 5, 1934, AA.

39. Great Britain, Department of Overseas Trade, *Report* for 1934, pp. 21–22; also Telegram EC/67-71700, Souza Costa to Aranha, Rio, Sept. 15, 1934, MRE. Souza Costa estimated that commercial arrears then totaling about £15 million would all be covered by the Bank of Brazil.

40. Telegram EC/172-61245, Souza Costa to Aranha, Rio, Sept. 20, 1934, MRE.

41. Telegram EC/211, Aranha to MRE, Washington, Oct. 2, 1934, MRE.

42. Letter, Vargas to Aranha, Rio, Oct. 16, 1934, AA.

43. Telegram EC/210, Aranha to MRE, Washington, Oct. 4, 1934, MRE. (This cable was lost in transmission for several days. Macedo Soares had asked in Telegram EC/187-52020 of the same date if Washington would condemn compensation with countries whose trade was balanced or unfavorable to Brazil, e.g., Germany.)

44. Telegram EC/218, Aranha to MRE, Washington, Oct. 6, 1934, MRE.

45. *Ibid.*

46. Telegram EC/189-71520, MRE to Aranha, Rio, Oct. 6, 1934, MRE.

47. Telegram EC/219, Aranha to MRE, Washington, Oct. 7, 1934, MRE.

48. Telegram, Schmidt-Elskop to the German Foreign Office, Rio, Oct. 11, 1934, K224809, roll 4463, microcopy T-120.

49. Memorandum, Souza Dantas to the German Trade Delegation, Rio, Oct. 13, 1934, K224866–68, roll 4463, microcopy T-120.

50. Telegram EC/199-71600, MRE to Aranha, Rio, Oct. 12, 1934, MRE.

51. Telegram EC/247, Aranha to MRE, Washington, Oct. 27, 1934, MRE.

52. Letter, Vargas to Aranha, Rio, Oct. 30, 1934, AA.

CHAPTER 2

1. Telegram EC/354, Aranha to MRE, Washington, Nov. 1, 1934, MRE; Letter, Aranha to Vargas, Washington, Nov. 13, 1934, AA.

2. Telegram EC/215-51930, MRE to Aranha, Rio, Oct. 25, 1934, MRE; Letter, Kiep to German Foreign Office, Rio, Nov. 7, 1934, frames K224920–26, roll 4463, microcopy T-120; Letter, Kiep to German Foreign Ministry, Montevideo, Nov. 13, 1934, K224929–31; Memorandum, Sampaio and Souza Dantas to Kiep, Rio, Nov. 8, 1934, K224963–64.

3. Memorandum, Kiep to MRE, Nov. [8], 1934, K224932–34; for the Portuguese text of this agreement, see K224935–37. The date was left open until the Brazilians signed.

4. Telegram EC/225, Souza Costa to Aranha, Rio, Nov. 1, 1934, MRE.

5. Notes between Paul Hechler, Reichsbank Director, and the Bank of Brazil, Rio, [Nov. 1934], in Portuguese, K224941–49.

6. Telegram EC/215-51930, MRE to Aranha, Rio, Oct. 25, 1934, MRE.

7. *Correio da Manhã*, Dec. 1, 1934: "São Paulo could place all of this year's crop in Germany alone." Telegram EC/248-71730, MRE to Aranha, Rio, Dec. 1, 1934, MRE.

8. Telegram EC/300, Aranha to MRE, Washington, Dec. 7, 1934, MRE.

9. Hull, I, 373. Eight hundred thousand bales of cotton was the precise amount.

10. Telegram EC/308, Aranha to MRE, Washington, Dec. 15, 1934, MRE.

11. Telegram EC/271-21530, MRE to Aranha, Rio, Dec. 24, 1934, MRE.

12. Letter, Aranha to Vargas, Washington, Jan. 8, 1935, AA. Also Telegram EC/316, Aranha to MRE, Washington, Dec. 31, 1934, MRE.

13. Summary article in *A Noite*, Dec. 8, 1934.

14. Letter, Kiep to German Foreign Office, Rio, Nov. 7, 1934, K224920–26, roll 4463, microcopy T-120.

15. Memorandum by Souza Dantas, Nov. 26, 1934, in CFCE, Processo 29, "Propostas de troca de mercadarias," AN.

16. Consult the records of the German Foreign Office (Economic Department) in the United States National Archives, K226287–325, roll 4465, microcopy T-120, and Wirth "A German View." German interests looked into the 1933 steel plan by a Paulista industrialist, Alexandre Siciliano Junior, discussed in Chapter 4. In late 1934, Fritz Thyssen's Vereinigte Stahlwerke (United Steel) may have offered to construct a steel plant in exchange for Brazilian iron ore and raw materials. Two years later Ambassador José Moniz de Aragão reported from Berlin that the Germans saw "vast possibilities" in collaborating in Brazil's industrial development. Capital goods "will become more important," he added optimistically, "because the trend of German exports is toward furnishing machinery for installing new national [i.e. Brazilian] industries, for example in textiles, paper products, and steel." Ofício 170, "A indústria alemã e o Brasil," Moniz to Pimentel Brandão, Berlin, April 24, 1937, MRE. German industry, however, turned inward after 1937, concentrating on war preparations; as before, consumer goods and industrial raw materials, rather than industrial machinery, led the list of German exports to Brazil. Germany, having pioneered in the field of industrial aid from 1934 to 1938, now reduced its offers of capital goods, whereas the United States, in late 1937, with Export-Import Bank finance, began to make important proposals (see Chapter 5).

17. Brazil, Congresso, Câmara dos Deputados. *Annaes*. Sessão 9 de setembro, XVI, 132.

18. "Comércio exterior do Brasil," *Observador*, Ano 1, No. 4, p. 17. Also, Great Britain, Department of Overseas Trade, *Report* for 1935,

pp. 28–29. Since January 1935, Germany had purchased more than half of the total Brazilian cotton crop at prices 10 to 15 per cent above Liverpool quotations.

19. Letter, J. A. Kulenkampff to Kiep in Berlin, Rio, May 14, 1935, K225143ff, roll 4465, microcopy T-120; Telegram, Schmidt-Elskop to Foreign Office, Rio, May 15, 1935, K225153.

20. Telegram, Schmidt-Elskop to Foreign Office, Rio, June 13, 1935, K225171. For a discussion of the 1935 issues and strategies see the long letter by J. A. Kulenkampff to the Foreign Office, Rio, Nov. 20, 1935, K226340–49, roll 4465, microcopy T-120.

21. See the full debates in Brazil, Congresso, Câmara dos Deputados, Annaes, Vols. 15–16.

22. Telegram 151, the chargé (Gordon) to Cordell Hull, Rio, June 6, 1935, FR, 1935, IV, 301.

23. Manoilescu, Theoria do proteccionismo, pp. 200ff. According to this doctrine, all nations would get richer in an expanding international market if there were a more equal division between the production and consumption of industrial goods. Therefore, the rich industrial nations should, out of self-interest, help the poor nations to industrialize.

24. Simonsen, Aspects, p. 7.

25. Letters, Bouças to Aranha, Rio, June 28 and Aug. 16, 1935, AA.

26. Telegram 200, Ambassador Gibson to Hull, Rio, Aug. 27, 1935, FR, 1935, IV, 312–13.

27. Sessão 11 de setembro, Brazil, Congresso, Câmara dos Deputados, Annaes, p. 209.

28. Simonsen, Aspects, pp. 20–24 and p. 62.

29. Letter, Bento A. Sampaio Vidal, President of the Sociedade Rural Brasileira to CFCE, quoting text of telegram sent to Chamber of Deputies, Rio, Oct. 30, 1935; Letter, Sampaio Vidal to CFCE, Nov. 14, 1935; Letter, Sociedade Mineira de Agricultura to CFCE, Belo Horizonte, Jan. 8, 1936; Letter, Câmara de Propaganda e Expansão Comercial de Curitiba, Dec. 12, 1935; Report by João Maria de Lacerda for CFCE, Nov. 28, 1935, all in CFCE, Processo 300, "Instituto Nacional de Exportação," AN.

30. Report by Valentim Bouças, reporter, dated Jan. 6, 1936, in ibid.

CHAPTER 3

1. Memorandum from Secretaria de Estado das Relações Exteriores, Rio, Sept. 5, 1935, PR 6260, in Presidência Archive, 1935, AN; for German motives see Telegram NP/40, Quartin to MRE, Berlin, Oct. 10, 1935, MRE.

2. Ofício 39, Moniz to Macedo Soares, Berlin, Jan. 29, 1936, MRE.

3. Bastos, p. 181, and Letter, Humberto Arruda to CFCE, Rio, [July? 1939], in CFCE, Processo 961, "Exportacão de algodão sob a regimen de marcos compensados," AN. Mário Simonsen and Harold Fehrmann were the managing directors of SOINC in Rio; Wilhelm Beutner, a Prussian lawyer, was Souza Aranha's contact with German officials in Berlin.

4. SOINC memorandum, n.d., attached to Ofício 13, Moniz to Macedo Soares, Berlin, Jan. 10, 1936, MRE.

5. Ofício 13, above.

6. Memorandum of Agreement with the Brazilian Representatives, Washington, Jan. 30, 1935, *FR, 1935,* IV, 339.

7. Ofício 59, Moniz to Macedo Soares, Berlin, Feb. 12, 1936, MRE.

8. Ofício 88, Moniz to Macedo Soares, Berlin, March 2, 1936, MRE. These were sterling accounts that the Bank of Brazil owed to various foreign banks in German territory, and commercial arrears in free currencies.

9. Inferred from Letter, Souza Aranha to Aranha, Rio, June 11, 1936, AA.

10. Welles made the point. Memorandum for the Ambassador [Aranha] from Freitas-Valle, Nov. 13, 1934, annexed to Ofício 517, Aranha to Macedo Soares, Washington, Nov. 16, 1934. MRE.

11. Unlike the Paulistas, Northeastern cotton growers were not exempted from the 35 per cent official exchange rate requirement in time to ship the 1935–36 crop. *O Imparcial,* Feb. 29, 1936. For the telegrams, in order, see Governor Argemiro Figueiredo of Paraíba to Vargas, June 21, 1937; Associação Comercial de João Pessoa to Vargas, same date; Associação Comercial do Amazonas to CFCE, Feb. 12, 1938; and Sr. Overbeck, representative of export commerce on the Bahian Commercial Propaganda Commission to Vargas, Aug. 5, 1937, all in CFCE, Processo 575, "Ajuste comercial Brasil-Alemanha," AN.

12. Letter, Souza Aranha to Aranha, Rio, June 11, 1936, AA.

13. Telegram 17, MRE to Sampaio (in Paris), Rio, March 4, 1936, containing Vargas's instructions, in PR 16358, Presidência Archive, 1936, AN. CFCE, Processo 333, "Sistematização dos entendimentos comerciais do Brasil com as nações estrangeiras," AN.

14. Telegram EC/44, Moniz to MRE, Berlin, May 7, 1936, MRE.

15. Letter, Souza Aranha to Beutner, Rio, April 8, 1936, K226377, roll 4465, microcopy T-120.

16. German Foreign Office memorandum on a telegram from Souza Aranha to Beutner, detailing conversations in Rio between Souza Aranha, Vargas, and Souza Costa, April 1, 1936, K226362–63. CFCE policy statement, Rio, April 16, 1936, K226392.

17. Telegram EC/51230, MRE to Moniz, Rio, April 30, 1936, MRE.

18. Telegram EC/44, Moniz to MRE, Berlin, May 7, 1936, MRE, and Ofício 163, Moniz to Macedo Soares, Berlin, May 11, 1936, MRE.

19. The views and actions of the United States are succinctly presented in FR, 1936, V, 247–81. To Welles, political (i.e., security) considerations were paramount. One year later, when the German accord was renegotiated, Aranha was informed that "the material aspect does not disturb his [Welles's] government because Brazil imports fewer American goods than Argentina, which sells almost nothing to the United States; the political and moral aspect was more important, since the Brazilian position would hurt American international prestige." Letter, Aranha to Vargas, Washington, June 4, 1937, AA.

20. Telegram EC/56-62300, MRE to Moniz, Rio, June 5, 1936, MRE.

21. Macedo Soares's explanation to the Comissão de Diplomacia e Tratados da Câmara dos Deputados on July 1, 1936, included in José Carlos de Macedo Soares, pp. 147–64.

22. Great Britain, Department of Overseas Trade, Report for 1936, pp. 45–46.

23. "Comércio exterior do Brasil," Observador, Ano 1, No. 7, p. 17.

24. Maciel Filho, O Imparcial, May 26, 1936.

25. Letter, Aranha to Bouças, Washington, July 1, 1936, AA.

26. Telegram EC/98, Moniz to MRE, Berlin, June 16, 1936, MRE.

27. Remarks of Senator Eloy de Souza from Rio Grande do Norte, in Correio da Manhã, June 11, 1936, p. 2.

28. "O acordo comercial teuto-brasileiro," Correio da Manhã, June 19, 1936, p. 5.

29. Letter, Bouças to Aranha, containing verbatim extracts of the CFCE session, Rio, June 25, 1936, AA.

30. Ibid.

31. Despatch CJ/91, Mario de Pimentel Brandão for Macedo Soares to Aranha, Rio, July 25, 1935, MRE.

32. Letter, Farquhar, to Alexander Malozemoff, Rio, March 3, 1939, Malozemoff File, BN.

33. Letter, Aranha to Vargas, Washington, June 18, 1935, AA.

34. Arthur Schmidt-Elskop, the German Ambassador, advised his government that Vargas's "remaining in power would be advantageous for German-Brazilian trade relations because he always defends and furthers them in spite of many difficulties with other governments." Political Report to the German Foreign Office, Rio, March 4, 1937, 6939H/E518306, roll 3155, microcopy T-120.

35. Interview with Herbert Feis, The Orchard, Maine, July 9, 1966. Among those interested in promoting Brazilian development were Economic Adviser Feis, Export-Import Bank President Warren Lee Pierson,

American Affairs chief Laurence Duggan, and Secretary Welles for political affairs. Federal Loan Administrator Jesse J. Jones and Assistant
Secretary Will Clayton held more traditional views toward Brazil.

36. Telegram, Vargas to Aranha, Rio, Nov. 17, 1937, AA.

37. Shortly after the Estado Nôvo coup, Brazilian authorities moved
to ban Nazi party political and cultural activities among German-Bra-
zilians in Southern Brazil. After having been kept waiting for two hours
to see Vargas, the German ambassador (Karl Ritter) told the President
that if the ban were not lifted, trade relations could be interrupted. Vargas replied, as Ritter had expected, that he did not want to treat these
two questions together. "Such little questions," Vargas added in his
slow, precise French, should not jeopardize more important questions,
as for example placing large orders in Germany for the Brazilian Army.
"I [Ritter] interrupted him and said that if the question of the Party is
a little question for him then he should give in. For Germany the treatment of the N.S.D.A.P. is not a little but a fundamental question. Besides, the development of business, even on a large scale, is not of any
importance to us." (Vargas appeared to accept this line of argument,
but knowing Germany needed Brazilian raw materials, he allowed the
ban to continue in force.) Memorandum of interview with Vargas, Ritter to the German Foreign Office, Rio, Feb. 25, 1938. 6939H/E518439–
43, roll 3155, microcopy T-120.

38. Telegram 653, the Ambassador in Rio (Curt Max Prüfer) to the
Foreign Office, Rio, July 2, 1940, in United States, Department of State
Documents, p. 101.

39. Interview with Admiral Augusto do Amaral Peixoto, brother-in-
law of Alzira Vargas do Amaral Peixoto, the President's daughter, Rio,
Jan. 4, 1965.

40. Maciel Filho, *O Imparcial*, June 15, 1940.

41. Bastos, pp. 182–83 and p. 232. Because the steel credits had
already been pledged in principle (May 1940), this interpretation,
while plausible, cannot be the main reason for Vargas's enigmatic remarks.

CHAPTER 4

1. Edmundo de Macedo Soares e Silva, "Conferência," in FIESP,
p. 54.

2. Siciliano Junior, *Memorial, O plano siderúrgico*, for President
Vargas, Dec. 25, 1934, in CFCE, Processo 118, AN.

3. For an economic study of the industry, consult Baer's "Development of the Brazilian Steel Industry."

4. Macedo Soares, "Linhas gerais da carta enviada ao Sr. Wolf,

Presidente da United States Steel Products Co.," attached to letter to João Mendonça Lima, New York, May 10, 1939, AV, no. 70, v. 31 (Jan.–June 1939).

5. For historical studies see Bastos, Rogers, and Macedo Soares e Silva, "O ferro e o carvão."

6. For Farquhar's many plans and enterprises see Gauld.

7. Courtesy of Hilgard O'Reilly Sternberg.

8. Gauld, p. 427.

9. In 1936, Farquhar estimated that final operating earnings would be $7,920,000 on four million tons f.o.b. Santa Cruz, $10 million for five million tons, $13.9 million for seven million tons, and $20 million for the full ten million tons of ore exports. After interest on the first mortgage bonds and debentures totaling $56 million, the profits left for reservations, amortization, and common stock dividends were large: $4,145,000 for four million tons, and $6.2 million, $10 million, and $16 million for the other tonnages. "Itabira Operating Earnings Work Sheet, Ore and Railroad," New York, Feb. 23, 1936, I-8, 28, 1, BN.

10. Hexner, p. 218 and p. 244.

11. "Confidential Memorandum of Conferences of Mr. Percival Farquhar re 'Itabira,' March 8 to 24 [1936] in Great Britain and Germany," I-8, 35, 3, BN. Farquhar talked with British steelmakers, shippers, and financiers in London, and with Vereinigte Stahlwerke executives and Reichsbank officials in Berlin.

12. Letter, Farquhar to Andrew J. Mellon, Rio, Aug. 16, 1937, I-8, 20, 11, BN; letter, George Farquhar to Percival Farquhar, New York, Dec. 4, 1937, I-8, 20, 42, BN.

13. Letter, Farquhar to Alexander Malozemoff, his New York partner, Rio, March 24, 1939, Malozemoff File, BN; letter, Farquhar to Bouças, Rio, July 18, I-8, 21, 29, BN.

14. In accordance with its exchange policies, the Reichsbank wanted German boats to do the carrying, and insisted on tying purchases of Brazilian ore to sales of German goods, such as coal or mining equipment. Thyssen proposed that this equipment be paid for by issuing Itabira debentures in Germany, secured by the ore contract. Letter, Thyssen to Farquhar, Hamburg, Jan. 20, 1936, I-8, 21, 17, BN; also "Confidential Memorandum," cited in note 11, and Gauld, pp. 309–10.

15. Aranha bluntly told Farquhar that "we would find ourselves in fact dealing exclusively with certain continental channels." Letter, Farquhar to Malozemoff, Rio, Jan. 23, 1939, Malozemoff File, BN. For supporting evidence: Memorandum of Conversation, Malozemoff, George Farquhar, and Veatch, Washington, Feb. 14, 1939, DS, 832.6351 It/68. "Mr. Malozemoff had the impression that knowledge of the German offer has been an important factor influencing President Var-

gas to delay ratification of the amended concession [i.e. Farquhar's latest proposal to the Brazilian government, which included the steel plant]."

16. Farquhar, "Confiscatory Decree of the Government of Brazil of 11th August, Cancelling the Itabira Concession Contract. A Short Résumé of the 'Itabira' Case," [Rio, 1939], DS, 832.6351 It/92.

17. *Ibid.*

18. Figures released at the 1910 Stockholm Conference on world ore requirements set Brazilian reserves at three and a half billion tons of a dwindling total world supply of 23 billion tons. From this premise, certain Mineiro experts argued that Brazil, with its large ore reserves, would soon have an overwhelming comparative advantage in world steel production.

19. See debate in Constituent Assembly, *Diário da Assembléia Nacional*, Session of Feb. 1, 1934, p. 509ff.

20. José Américo de Almeida, interview in *Correio da Manhã*, Nov. 8, 1932.

21. Edmundo de Macedo Soares e Silva was the most important tenente on this Commission. Imprisoned for joining the tenente revolts of 1922–24 in Rio and São Paulo, he escaped to France and became a metallurgical expert. After the 1930 revolution, he served under João Mendonça Lima in the tenente government of São Paulo (1931) and established himself as an outstanding Army technocrat. Among other things, he was planner, technical director, and president of the National Steel Company (Volta Redonda), Governor of Rio de Janeiro, a director of Mercedes Benz do Brasil, president of CNI; he is now Minister of Industry in the Artur Costa e Silva government.

22. Góes Monteiro, "Exposição" to President Vargas [mimeo.], (Jan.? 1934), AA. Having been a director of the October Third Club, Góes was the tenentes' candidate for president of Brazil in early 1934.

23. Farquhar cited the intransigent opposition of junior officers to his ore export plans. However, he believed that their more experienced and better informed seniors were prepared to bargain in exchange for the steel plant, which the Army badly wanted. (See Chapter 5.) Letter, Farquhar to Malozemoff, Rio, May 8, 1939, Malozemoff File, BN.

24. These reports are summarized in Brazil, CTEF (Ministério da Fazenda), *A grande siderurgia*. The Revisory Commission under José Américo (1931) wanted Itabira to build the steelworks and assume direct ownership of the Vitória a Minas railroad, of which it had 51 per cent control. See also Gauld, pp. 305ff.

25. Alexandre Siciliano Junior, Articles in *Diário Carioca*, March 11–16, 1933.

26. Consortium Siderurgia Nacional, *Solução brasileira do problema*

da indústria siderúrgica [pamphlet], (Rio, 1937), in CFCE, Processo 702, "Organização da indústria siderúrgica no Brasil," AN.

27. Henrique Lage, *Memorial* to the Conselho Supremo de Segurança Nacional, Rio, Feb. 24, 1938, in CFCE, Processo 702, AN.

28. Figures cited in Baer, "Development," p. 84. The Belgians' success in working with Mineiros, in striking contrast to Farquhar's sometimes tactless maneuvers, also indicates the degree to which the Europeans were able to adapt themselves to Brazilian conditions. French firms, also, were notably successful in Brazilian steel manufacturing.

29. Belgo-Mineira opposed Itabira for two main reasons, according to the *Berliner Lokal-Anzeiger* of April 16, 1937. The ARBED wanted its subsidiary to retain the lead in Brazilian steel production, and also to protect its own mines in Lorraine from being undersold by large shipments of rich Itabira ore. Cited in Ofício 172, Moniz to Pimentel Brandão, Berlin, April 26, 1937, MRE.

30. Companhia Brasileira de Usinas Metalúrgicas, Memorial presented to the Conselho Technico de Economia e Finanças, Rio, May 31, 1938, in CFCE, Processo 702, AN.

CHAPTER 5

1. Letter, Vargas to Aranha, Rio, Oct. 28, 1937, quoted in Bastos, p. 186.

2. Vargas, "Problemas e realizações do Estado Nôvo," Feb. 19, 1938, in *A nova política*, V, 178–81.

3. Letter, Aranha to Vargas, Washington, June 18, 1935, AA.

4. Letter, Aranha to Vargas, Washington, Oct. 6, 1937, AV, no. 45, v. 27 (Aug.–Oct. 1937). Vargas responded to Aranha's point in his letter of Oct. 28.

5. Note by Walmsley, annexed to Despatch 1816, Rio, Oct. 7, 1939, DS, 832.6511/28.

6. *Report*, "O aço no Brasil," drawn up in 1937 and sent from the Brazilian Embassy in Washington in early 1938, AA; also, updated market survey, to accompany the *Report*, by H. C. Winans, who also stressed the Central do Brasil route. Included in Ofício 177, the chargé in Washington to MRE, Washington, April 9, 1938, MRE.

7. Letter, Vargas to Aranha, Rio, Dec. 6, 1937, quoted in Bastos, p. 140.

8. See Azevedo Amaral, pp. 244ff., for a moderate position; see Vivacqua for the exclusionist argument.

9. Mendonça Lima, "*O problema.*"

10. *Report*, by Denizot, presented to the Minister of Transport on January 29, 1938, and accompanied by long summary letter from Men-

donça Lima to Vargas, March 18, 1938. Both documents are in CFCE, Processo 702, "Transporte de minérios, organização da indústria siderúrgica no Brasil," AN.

11. Rache, First Report, May 17, 1938, in Brazil, CTEF, A grande siderurgia, p. 10.

12. Despatch, "Construction of a Steelworks in Brazil," the Reichsminister of Economics (Gustav Schlotterer) to the Foreign Office, Berlin, April 19, 1938, frames 604185–86, roll 3374, microcopy T-120.

13. Ibid.; and Memorandum by Schaumberger of the Reichsministry of Economics, after conference with Demag, Berlin, March 19, 1938, frames 586986–88, roll 84, microcopy T-71.

14. Memorandum by Eisemann of the Reichsministry of Economics, Berlin, April 19, 1938, frames 586992–98, roll 84, microcopy T-71.

15. Letter, Vereinigte Stahlwerke, Raw Materials Division, to the Reichsministry of Economics, Dortmund, May 23, 1938, frame 587000, roll 84, microcopy T-71.

16. Vargas, speech of Feb. 19, 1938, in A nova política, p. 181.

17. Afrânio do Amaral, pp. 282–83. Farquhar thought Ribeiro was subsidized by a prominent Brazilian arms importer and industrialist. Letter, Farquhar to Malozemoff, Rio, May 1, 1939, Malozemoff File, BN.

18. Brazil, CTEF, A grande siderurgia, pp. 263–64.

19. Souza Aranha wrote to Vargas: "A solution of this magnitude [steel-ore-railroads] should not be entrusted to a foreign industrialist who must first of all give satisfaction to his stockholders, who in turn can be very demanding." His alternative to Itabira was a mixed State–foreign private company solution to ore and steel—40 to 50 per cent of the $58 million in capital to come from the government in paper milreis, and the remaining $30 million, for railroad and plant equipment from foreign groups ("preferably more than one country"). Memorial, Souza Aranha to Vargas, Rio, March 8, 1938, in CFCE, Processo 743, AN; and the follow-up letter to Vargas, Aug. 6, 1938, in Processo 702, AN.

20. Courtesy of General Ibá Jobim Meirelles, who in 1938, as a Captain of Engineers, was attached by the General Staff to the Foreign Trade Council.

21. Pacheco.

22. Henrique Novais, "As falhas do projeto Janot Pacheco para exportação de minérios" [mimeo.], Oct. 1938, sent to President Vargas, in CFCE, Processo 702, AN.

23. Assis Chateaubriand, "Siderurgia à Goering," O Jornal, Rio, June 1938.

24. Associação Comercial do Rio de Janeiro, Boletim.

25. Couto, p. 86.

26. Letter, George Farquhar to Percival Farquhar, New York, July 1, 1938, I-8, 20, 16, BN.

27. Brazil, CFCE, "Siderurgia; a indústria nacional de ferro e a exportação de minérios de ferro e de manganês," in *Dez anos de atividade*, pp. 43–50; and CFCE, comissão especial, *Conclusões gerais*, in Farquhar Papers, I-8, 27, 21, BN.

28. Letter, Farquhar to Malozemoff, Rio, May 1, 1939, Malozemoff File, BN.

29. Letter, Farquhar to Malozemoff, Rio, March 3, 1939, Malozemoff File, BN.

30. Minuta para o Exmo. Sr. General Góes Monteiro by Farquhar, Rio, Feb. 29, 1939, I-8, 26, 4, BN.

31. *Missão Oswaldo Aranha, 1939*, Document 9 [typewritten], AA.

32. Demag, Gutehoffnungshuette, and Krupp made definite proposals in 1940 (see Chapter 6).

33. Letter, Macedo Soares to Mendonça Lima, New York, May 10, 1939, AV no. 70, v. 31 (Jan.–June 1939).

34. *Missão Oswaldo Aranha, 1939*, Document 9, AA.

35. Letter, Bouças to Vargas, New York, March 15, 1939, AA; also, Memorandum of conversation between Bouças and Mr. Laurence Duggan [in March?], Washington, June 8, 1939, DS, 832.51/1482.

36. Telegram, Farquhar to Malozemoff, Rio, April 15, 1939, I-8, 18, 21, BN.

37. Letter, Macedo Soares to Mendonça Lima, New York, May 25, 1939, AV, no. 79, v. 31 (Jan.–June 1939).

38. Letter, Macedo Soares to Mendonça Lima, New York, May 10, 1939, AV, no. 70, v. 31 (Jan.–June 1939).

39. Letter, Macedo Soares to Mendonça Lima, New York, May 25, 1939, AV, no. 79, v. 31 (Jan.–June 1939).

40. Memorandum, "United States Steel Corporation Committee's Report on the Steel Industry in Brazil and on the Feasibility of Building a Modern Steel Plant in Conformity with the Wishes of the Brazilian Government," Washington, Jan. 22, 1940, DS, 832.6511/64. Consult also the "Relatório apresentado pelas Comissões Brasileira e Americana sôbre a indústria siderúrgica no Brasil," Oct. 20, 1939, filed as Protocolo Geral 20.169–40 in MVOP.

41. Memorandum of Conversation with Heman Greenwood, Duggan, Donnelly, and Walmsley, Washington, Dec. 14, 1939, DS, 832.6511/45.

42. *Ibid.*

43. Despatch 2014, William C. Burdett for the Ambassador to the Secretary of State, Rio, Nov. 3, 1939, DS, 832.6511/36.

44. *New York Times*, Jan. 18, 1940, and Leon Pearson in the *Washington News*, Jan. 18, 1940.

45. Memorandum by the Adviser on International Economic Affairs, H. F[eis], Washington, Jan. 17, 1940, DS, 832.6511/51.
46. Memorandum, H. F[eis] to Sumner Welles, Washington, Jan. 29, 1940, DS, 832.6511/53.
47. Telegram, Vargas to Ambassador Carlos Martins, Rio, Jan. 18, 1940, AV, no. 18, v. 33 (Jan.–June 1940).

CHAPTER 6

1. Letter, Ambassador Martins to Vargas, Washington, Dec. 5, 1940, AV, no. 76, v. 34 (July–Dec. 1940); United Nations, Department of Economic Affairs, p. 28.
2. Urgent Despatch, The Reichsministry of Economics to the Foreign Office, Berlin, Aug. 3, 1940, frames 604202–3, roll 3374, microcopy T-120.
3. Memorandum of Conversation, The Brazilian Ambassador, Feis, Briggs, Walmsley, in Washington, Feb. 23, 1940, DS, 832.6511/79. Bastos, p. 189. Telegram, Vargas to Martins, Feb. 23, 1940, AV, no. 39, v. 33; letter, Martins to Vargas, Washington, Feb. 27, 1940, AV, no. 41, v. 33.
4. Bastos, p. 221, p. 238.
5. Telegram EC/161, Martins to Aranha, Washington, May 31, 1940, MRE. The Export-Import Bank committed $10 million and was open minded about the remainder. Martins considered the negotiations successful.
6. To reassure Jones the Brazilians agreed to hire a specialized United States construction firm, which would also manage the plant initially, in conjunction with an American training team of some 85 engineers and foremen. What finally won Jones over was the promise to set up an executive office, composed of four eminent American experts and the Brazilians, to oversee all phases of the project. Letter, Macedo Soares to Vargas, New York, Oct. 12, 1940, AV, no. 58, v. 34 (July–Dec. 1940).
7. The loan, payable in twenty semiannual installments at 4 per cent, was later supplanted with several large United States credits. As Langer and Gleason point out (pp. 614–20 and p. 702), the related security negotiations were successful. The September agreement allowing Pan American Airways to stockpile aviation fuel and parts, to improve existing Brazilian airfields in the Northeast, and to construct new airfields was followed by a military accord on October 29, which governed United States Army troop dispositions in Brazil during wartime.
8. Urgent Despatch, The Reichsministry of Economics to the Foreign Office, Berlin, Aug. 3, 1940, frames 604202–3, roll 3374, microcopy

T-120; also Urgent Despatch by Pheiffer of the Reichsministry of Economics to the Foreign Office, Berlin, Oct. 1, 1940, frame 604212.

9. Memorandum, "United States Interest in Brazilian Steel Plant," Washington, April 25, 1941, DS, 832.6511/195. See also United States Congress, Arey study, p. 98.

10. "Realidade que chega," *Diário de Notícias*, Sept. 28, 1940.

11. Vivacqua, p. 337.

12. Brazil, Comissão Executiva, p. 19.

13. *Ibid.*, p. 21.

14. *Ibid.*, pp. 23–24.

15. Macedo Soares e Silva, "Volta Redonda," p. 22.

16. Brazil, Comissão Executiva, p. 26.

17. White, p. 464. Also consult Baer, "Development," p. 186ff.

18. Brazil, Comissão Executiva, p. vii.

19. *Ibid.*, p. 18.

20. United Nations, Economic Commission for Latin America, I, 96. Baer, "Development," especially pp. 155–58.

21. Long, p. 126.

22. Report of remarks by opposition politicians linked to Antônio Carlos (ousted regional leader), by Captain Baptista Teixeira of the Delegacia Especial de Segurança Política e Social to the Police Chief (Felinto Müller), Rio, Nov. 4, 1940, AV, no. 69, v. 34 (July–Dec. 1940). Mineiros were still bitter in the Constituent Assembly debates six years later; see Brazil, Assembléia Constituinte, *Anais*, April 29, 1946, VII, 444, and May 15, 1946, IX, 130–31, in which PSD leader Amaral Peixoto said that the decision had been Macedo Soares's, not his.

23. Macedo Soares, "Volta Redonda," pp. 18–19.

24. United Nations, Economic Commission for Latin America, II, p. 354. Baer in his "Development of the Brazilian Steel Industry," p. 195, concludes that Volta Redonda is not at a cost disadvantage in comparison with more recent plants when rail services are used. In the mid-1960's, the state of Guanabara eyed Santa Cruz for its projected COSIGUA steel complex, while the Hanna Mining Company hoped to develop the port for ore exports.

25. Interview with Guilherme Guinle, *Diretrizes*, Ano IV, No. 42 (April 10, 1941), pp. 8–9. The Army General Staff's suggestion that officers and public functionaries might purchase stock against their monthly wages was rejected as impractical. Letter, Guinle to Mendonça Lima, Rio, Nov. 18, 1940, Protocolo Geral 39149-40, MVOP.

26. Brazil, Comissão Executiva, pp. xvi–xix; see Amaral, p. 325, for discussion of finance and the Pension Funds, and private participation.

27. Macedo Soares, "Volta Redonda," p. 25. Expanded capacity

meant lower costs, so that by 1965 Volta Redonda had reached production levels (1,400,000 ingot tons) where economies of scale were making themselves felt. Baer, "Development," p. 158.

28. *Ibid.*, p. 18.

29. Remarks by Eduardo Jafet (Director of the Centro das Indústrias do Estado de São Paulo, and a textile manufacturer with metallurgical interests) in FIESP, p. 129.

30. *Ibid.*, pp. 6–7.

31. Speech by Morvan Dias de Figueiredo of FIESP, in *ibid.*, p. 114.

32. Amorim, pp. 74–79.

33. Interview with Luis Simões Lopes, President of the Fundação Getúlio Vargas, Rio, March 22, 1965.

CHAPTER 7

1. Although there is yet no book-length history of Brazil's oil industry, see the concise historical summary by Fróes Abreu, Vol. II, especially p. 161. Peter S. Smith is completing his history doctoral dissertation on the industry at the University of New Mexico. Extensive documentation and debates are reprinted in Congresso, Câmara dos Deputados, *Petróleo* (hereafter cited as *Petróleo*). See also Vaitsman. Articles on special subjects are cited in other notes, below.

Gabriel Cohn's excellent monograph, *Petróleo e nacionalismo*, came to my attention too late for incorporation in the text. Cohn makes skillful use of published documents (most of which are familiar) to show how Petrobrás resulted not from the clash of rigidly defined policy options, but from the actions taken by various social groups in different situations since the 1930's. His emphasis on the process of policy-making is close to my own approach, and I agree substantially with his historical narrative and chronology. Perhaps because of his sociological perspective, however, Cohn finds more internal consistency in group actions and positions than I would support. Moreover, Cohn's tendency to view the acts of these groups as reflections of the total situation leads him to emphasize integration and consensus. As a result, Cohn sees Petrobrás as a dynamic synthesizing of several attitudes that made up the social, political, and economic context of the early 1950's: Vargas's nationalism, the technocrats' economic perspective, the petroleum mobilization campaign, and the political motives of the "middle-class UDN intellectuals," all brought out in his conclusion. By contrast, I interpret Petrobrás as the result of a conflictual situation in which the UDN and the radical nationalists joined to defeat the government's petroleum program. The result was a labored compromise that was also a severe blow to Vargas's style of consensus politics and to his use of nationalism. But readers will want to draw their own conclusions. Gabriel Cohn's stimulating monograph should be read.

2. Lacking a modern refinery, there was no need to increase production beyond the minimal amount needed for firing the boilers of two drilling rigs and for experimentation.

3. In 1930, Jersey Standard founded Cia. Geral de Petróleo Pan-Brasileira S.A., an American-owned subsidiary, to acquire petroleum leases and develop them. At one time Pan-Brasileira held as many as 96 private leases on prospective petroleum properties, but these were canceled following the enactment of the 1934 Mining Code, which made all subsoil wealth the property of the nation. Pan-Brasileira was dissolved in 1941 when foreign-owned subsidiaries organized for exploration purposes were declared illegal under Decree Law 2627 (Oct. 1, 1940). Letter, T. R. Armstrong of Standard Oil to the Secretary of State, New York, Jan. 18, 1941, DS 832.6363/334.

4. Oligopoly agreements limited competition under an industry-wide system of administered prices and shared markets. Pricing in the 1930's is discussed briefly in Hartshorn, pp. 131–32. The other companies were the Atlantic Refining Company, the Texas Company, and the Caloric Company.

5. Brazil, IBGE, Ano XVII, p. 351. Percentage increase is given in Brazil, Presidência da República [Rômulo de Almeida], p. 8. (Hereafter cited as Almeida.)

6. The companies protected their dollar earnings, for example, by invoicing gasoline exports at double the real cost to themselves and then demanding full exchange cover for the padded invoices. Letter, Aranha to Vargas, Washington, Feb. 12, 1935. AA.

7. In 1938, gasoline retailed for 1$200 per liter in Rio. Of this, the average CIF price was $350 (milreis) including profits on production, refining, and transportation. After deducting federal and municipal taxes of $420 and $195, the distributing subsidiaries were left with $324.5 to cover port expenses, distribution costs, and dealer discounts and bonuses. After local expenses, an estimated $109.3 remained for amortization and profits. CNP estimates are cited in "Exposição de motivos no. 1777," Horta Barbosa to Vargas, Rio, July 18, 1939, reprinted in Brazil, CNP, Análise dos preços de venda, p. 31.

8. Voto do Conselheiro Euvaldo Lodi, Sept. 1935, in CFCE, Processo 257, "Preço da gasolina na praça do Rio de Janeiro," Vols. 1 and 2, AN.

9. Despatch 929, Ambassador Gibson to Secretary of State, Rio, Jan. 23, 1936, DS, 832.6363/161. The four American companies said they intended to discourage the promoter from obtaining a loan in New York.

10. Leite articles. Also, Simões Lopes, "Petróleo nacional," and his lecture to the Sociedade Nacional de Agricultura, "O petróleo brasi-

leiro," May 23, 1936, reprinted in *Petróleo*, II, 197–200. Extensive documentation on the 1920's is contained in Volume III of *Petróleo*.

11. See Brazil, CNP, Parecer do Consultor Geral. Monteiro Lobato's nationalist campaign was a device to sell stock. See Café Filho, II, 456–57. Later, Monteiro Lobato came out openly for unrestricted access to all comers, the only way, he said, to get an oil strike (see note 17, Chapter 8).

12. The literature is extensive. See Monteiro Lobato's *O escândalo do petróleo*, which went through four editions before the Estado Nôvo banned it; the views of one of his associates, Edson Carvalho; and the account of his biographer, Cavalheiro. The government's case is presented in Brazil, Ministério da Agricultura, Odilon Braga, *Bases*.

13. For their report, see Fróes Abreu et al.

14. Paiva and Amaral, "Rumos novos em sondagens profundas."

15. Memorandum, "O petróleo e a defesa nacional," Colonel Horta Barbosa to Minister of War [General Eurico Gaspar Dutra], Rio, Jan. 30, 1936, in *Petróleo*, II, 6.

16. See Mosconi. See also Frondizi's account of the YPF.

17. Typewritten memorandum, "Petróleo (refinarias)," by General Horta Barbosa, sent under signature of General Góes Monteiro to the Secretary General of the National Security Council [General João Pinto], Rio, Jan. 7, 1938, AM.

18. Domingos Fleury da Rocha, *Relatório*, "Comércio e indústria da refinação do petróleo," CFCE, March 16, 1938, AM. He was assisted by Secretary General Antônio Barbosa Carneiro, of the CFCE, and Captain Ibá Jobim Meirelles who, as the General Staff's representative on the Council, had been detailed by the National Security Council to safeguard military and security interests.

19. The following account is from Fleury, *Relatório*.

20. CFCE, Processo, "Petróleo, refinação, e comércio," n.d., AM.

21. Letter, Ambassador Mário de Pimentel Brandão to Vargas, Washington, Oct. 28, 1938, AV, no. 54, v. 30 (June–Dec., 1938).

22. Fleury, *Relatório*, pp. 34–35, and Horta Barbosa, opening address to CNP, Sept. 12, 1938, "Sessões realizadas," in CNP *Relatório, 1° triênio, 1938–41*, p. 4. Also Freire, "O petróleo no Brasil," p. 5. Much has been written about the subsequent history of Brazilian-Bolivian negotiations, which continue. The best published source is Guilherme's. See also President João Café Filho's memoires, II, 441–58.

23. See the excellent summary by Antônio Chagas Meirelles. For documents on the tax, see Brazil, CNP, *Relatório, 1° triênio*, including *Anexos 1 and 2*, as well as the CNP's *Análise dos preços de venda*.

24. All Uruguayan oil was imported from abroad. In 1940, Veigh

Garzón proposed the South American Institute of Petroleum, a continental organization to encourage economic nationalism and the exchange of technical information and price lists among Latin Americans. For ANCAP (Administración Nacional de Combustibles, Alcohol y Portland) and the Institute, consult Pérez Prins; also *World Petroleum*, Vol. 11, No. 12 (Nov. 1940), pp. 62–63.

25. "Relatório do General J. C. Horta Barbosa ao Presidente da República, sôbre sua viagem ao Prata, em abril de 1939," *Petróleo*, II, 279–303.

26. The draft decree, along with Horta's "Exposição de motivos no. 1.745," of July 17, 1939, and other documents, is in *Anexo 2* of Brazil, CNP, *Relatório, 1° triênio.*

27. The rumors of Mexican government finance for Corrêa e Castro in 1938 were highly exaggerated, and in any case the major foreign distributors in Brazil would have resisted any PEMEX imports, considering this recently expropriated oil as "pirated." Despatch 864, Scotten to Secretary of State, Rio, Sept. 6, 1938, DS, 812.6363/209. In 1939, Corrêa e Castro allegedly formed a company with Monteiro-Aranha for the Niteroi refinery, for which the crude oil would come from Standard Oil of California. Despatch 1927, Burdett to Secretary of State, Rio, Oct. 20, 1939, DS, 832.6363/279. Horta's comments on Lodi et al. are in his confidential ofício to Vargas, Rio, Jan. 3, 1939, AM.

28. Foster-Wheeler was to have furnished the equipment (approximately two million dollars) to Alves and was planning to ask for Export-Import Bank financing. Despatch 1777, Burdett to Secretary of State, Rio, Sept. 22, 1939, DS, 832.6363/271. See also Drault Ernanny's Senate speech of May 16, 1952, in *Diário de Notícias*, May 21, 1952, p. 7.

29. O. B. A., "As refinarias de petróleo projetadas para o Estado do Rio de Janeiro, e para o Estado de S. Paulo," Rio, Nov. 11, 1942, memorandum in file Correspondência geral, AS. Originally (Oct. 1938), the Export-Import Bank had agreed to finance refinery equipment for Foster-Wheeler, but later (spring 1939) deferred to the oil companies' strong protests and let the loan authorization expire. Memorandum by RFW, "Export-Import Bank Credits for Refinery in Brazil," Washington, Aug. 16, 1939, DS, 832.6363/260-1/2. The majors' subsequent change of heart regarding Brazilian-operated refineries was such that Horta considered the state plants to be fronts for their plans.

30. Decree Law 2615 (Sept. 9, 1940). Horta's proposed ten-year limit on refinery concessions was dropped in the long intra-governmental debates that preceded this decree.

31. Ministerial reports in Brazil, CNP, *Relatório, 1° triênio, Anexo 2.* Oliveira Vianna's *Report*, dated Oct. 12, 1939, is a classic.

32. CTEF reports by Romero Estrellita and debates, Oct. 1939, pp. 314–19, 333, and Mário de Andrade Ramos, Jan. 1941, pp. 486–88, all in Brazil, CTEF, *Atas*.

33. Horta Barbosa, "Exposição dos motivos no. 2.664" of July 10, 1941, to Vargas, in Brazil, CNP, *Relatório, 1° triênio, Anexo 2*.

34. Kemnitzer's report for the Morris Cooke economic mission, on which he served in late 1942, appeared in January 1943 as Board of Economic Warfare Publication AH-161-6, AS. Consult also his chapter on petroleum in the Cooke Mission report, pp. 164–90.

35. Valentim Bouças informed an embassy official that "Vargas and other government officials favor private ownership. . . . Although [they] believe the foreign companies and capital are not necessary for this industry [refining], the government would be pleased to study proposals." Despatch 1989, Burdett to Secretary of State, Rio, Oct. 30, 1939, DS, 832.6363/281. At the same time, Standard advised that "in view of the European situation, the company has decided to suspend negotiations looking to a join agreement with the government for the installation and operation of petroleum refineries." Despatch 1706, Burdett to Secretary of State, Rio, Sept. 8, 1939, DS, 832.6363/268. As with U.S. Steel, so with Standard; interest in joint operations resulted from Aranha's early 1939 mission to the United States (see Chapter 5).

36. Horta Barbosa, Ofício to Vargas, July 18, 1941, in *Petróleo*, II, 317.

37. [Simonsen], *Sugestões para uma política econômica panamericana*.

38. Primeiro Congresso Brasileiro de Economia [Nov. 26–Dec. 18, 1943], *Anais*, I (1943), 131. Memorandum by Sindicato dos Engenheiros do Rio de Janeiro to Vargas, May 4, 1943, in *Jornal de Debates*, Sept. 17, 1948, p. 9.

39. Aluizio de Lima Campos, "Suggestões no propósito de atrair o capital estrangeiro," report for the CTEF, Aug. 18, 1942, reprinted in *Diário Carioca*, Sept. 27, 1942, p. 4. Horta Barbosa, Ofício to Vargas, Oct. 20, 1942, in *Petróleo*, II, 323.

CHAPTER 8

1. Fuel derived from burning blocks of wood and other carbonaceous material in a mechanism ordinarily installed in the vehicle's trunk.

2. Letter, A. A. Barros Penteado [FIESP technical expert] to Simonsen, São Paulo, May 19, 1945, AS.

3. Barreto to Vargas, Exposição de motivos 2.588, May 5, 1945, in *Petróleo*, III, 209–10.

4. Barreto to Vargas, Ofício 17.884, Oct. 17, 1945, in Brazil, CNP, *Resoluções do plenário*, pp. 2–5.

5. On hearing of the competition, Drault had hastily called together a group of supporters including Veigh Garzón, designer of the 1939 Salvador project, Colonel Ibá Jobim Meirelles, Horta's former aide at the CNP, and Elyeser Montenegro Magalhães, who had worked at Argentina's YPF and was the younger brother of Juracy Magalhães, the prominent União Democrática Nacional party leader from Bahia.

6. The great postwar Canadian oil rush and more Middle Eastern discoveries were in part responsible for Standard's cooling interest in Brazil. Canada was where the real money was. Contemporaries on the scene believed that Standard pulled out because it could not control all the private groups, because the new CNP demands for a cash deposit and prospecting agreement made the União deal less attractive, and because in any case Standard expected to begin operating without a domestic intermediary once the oil laws were changed.

7. The official outline of these events is in the CNP *Relatórios*; the private refiners' story is recounted by Drault in his Senate speech of May 15, 1952, reported in *Diário de Notícias*, May 21, 1952, pp. 7–8. See the sensationalist account by journalists Lourival Coutinho and Joel Silveira, *O Petróleo*, pp. 409ff, which is based on the *Livro Negro* (AM), a "black book" of revealing documents on the concessionary struggle arranged by the Manguinhos group to be seen by military officers and congressmen.

8. Brazil, CNP, *Relatórios* for 1946, pp. 72–73; 1948, p. 60; and 1950, p. 73.

9. The official name of the commission was Comissão Elaboradora do Anteprojeto do Estatuto do Petróleo. Included were President Odilon Braga, a former Minister of Agriculture and a leader of the União Democrática Nacional, Glycon de Paiva Texeira, who had helped reorient the government's drilling program ten years before, and Colonel Arthur Levy of the Army General Staff. A good short summary of this legislation is Paiva's "Característicos do projeto do 'Estatuto do Petróleo.'"

10. Exposição do Relator, Odilon Braga to Barreto, Nov. 11, 1947, *Petróleo*, III, 285–86. Braga's report prefaced the official *Relatório* of this Commission.

11. Some of the statute's provisions were unworkable, such as one for dividing a petroleum deposit into private and government zones, with the government half remaining in reserve. Misunderstandings and disputes would have been inevitable as the drilling went on.

12. *Petróleo*, III, 211, 264–70; and Herbert Hoover, Jr., and Arthur A. Curtice, "Comentários sôbre o anteprojeto do Estatuto do Petróleo,"

and "Discussão detalhada dos dispositivos pertinentes ao anteprojeto do Estatuto do Petróleo," in *Petróleo*, III, 392–455. The quotation is from p. 412. Both men were acting as consultants to the Brazilian government.

13. Interview, under the title "Refinarias de petróleo," *Correio da Manhã*, July 12, 1949, p. 1.

14. Ofício, Barreto to Dutra, Nov. 19, 1947, accompanying the draft statute, *Petróleo*, III, 204.

15. Exposição do Relator, Odilon Braga to Barreto, *Petróleo*, III, 226, 234–38.

16. *Ibid.*, p. 213. The Investment Commission, entrusted by President Dutra to Minister of Agriculture Daniel de Carvalho, an old Farquhar partisan, submitted a draft that was more liberal toward foreign capital than the Statute was.

17. Monteiro Lobato, "Mensagem de Monteiro Lobato à mocidade do Brasil sôbre o problema do petróleo," *Diário de Notícias*, May 23, 1948, p. 7.

18. PCB bill no. 3,259 was introduced as an amendment in the Constituent Assembly, June 24, 1946. Osório Borba, a Socialist, tells the story in *Diário de Notícias*, May 4, 1952, p. 4.

19. For a highly critical article that purports to show how the oil companies made high profits on operations and accumulated assets in Brazil from 1942 to 1948 while bringing in almost no new capital from abroad, see "O comércio do Petróleo no Brasil."

20. Távora's lectures (April 24, June 19, and September 16), and Horta's (July 30 and Aug. 6 before the Military Club, and Oct. 16 in São Paulo) are reprinted in *Petróleo*, II, 324–469.

21. *Jornal de Debates* (1946–53) followed the democratic-left editorial policy of its directors, of whom two, Matos Pimenta, an old-line nationalist, and Plínio Catanhede, a CNP engineer, were founders of the Brazilian Socialist Party (February 1947). Mário de Brito was the third director. Lourival Coutinho was editor-secretary.

22. General E. Leitão de Carvalho wrote the CEDP's official history of the struggle against the Statute, *Petróleo! Salvacão ou desgraça do Brasil?* A Positivist and a former member of the wartime Joint United States–Brazil Military Mission, General Leitão de Carvalho was made an Honorary President of the Centro in order to refute by his presence the charge of Communist domination. On CEDP origins see the conflicting testimony of Matos Pimenta, "A campanha de petróleo e os comunistas," *Jornal de Debates*, Dec. 17, 1948, pp. 1, 10, and the Tijuca Anti-Fascist League's rejoiner in *Diário de Notícias*, Jan. 21, 1949, p. 4.

23. PCB bill 383, of June 25, 1947, allowed native and juridical Bra-

zilians (i.e. foreign companies operating and organized under Brazilian law) to hold stock, but in its follow-up bill 422, of July 7, foreigners were excluded. These bills were tabled when the Statute reached the floor.

24. Carlos Marighella, "Nossa Política," *Problemas,* Ano I, No. 3 (Oct. 1947), pp. 3–5; the quotation is from the November issue, p. 6.

25. Resolutions of the Federal District Conference, printed in *Diário de Notícias,* Oct. 1, 1948, p. 1. The *Diário* under Orlando Dantas was the only major Rio newspaper to report regularly on Centro and UNE affairs.

26. "A rainha do petróleo brasileiro," *Jornal de Debates,* Jan. 1, 1949, p. 1.

27. See, in *Diário de Notícias,* the extensive analyses by the Socialist Rafael Corrêa de Oliveria, "O petróleo e a política," Oct. 26, 1948, p. 4, "Crise no Centro Nacional de Petróleo," Jan. 23, 1949, p. 4, and "Os comunistas e o petróleo," Feb. 29, p. 4; the letters of resigning Honorary President Matos Pimenta to Orlando Dantas for Jan. 22, p. 5 and Feb. 1, p. 5; and the Centro's defense for Jan. 21, 1949. At first the PCB, with its organizing talents, had been welcomed in order to broaden the movement. But when this collaboration became increasingly one-sided, they balked, arguing that there was no effective or independent check on the Secretary General.

28. Brasil Gerson, "Os grandes partidos favoràveis ao capital estrangeiro," *O Jornal,* April 12, 1948, p. 3, and Carlos Lacerda, "A opinião do governo," *Correio da Manhã,* May 6, 1948, p. 2.

29. Interview, by Daland with Sampaio, May 28, 1963, cited in Daland, p. 49.

30. By 1951 consumption was increasing 20 per cent a year and had reached 120,000 b/day, rather than the 80,000 b/day forecast by the DASP. By the late 1950's, Brazil's modest tanker fleet became more expensive to operate as crude costs declined, and as the industry turned to tankers of over 30,000 tons with greater economies of scale. Exploration costs had soared far above the cr$1.5 billion ($75 million) projected, but never fully allocated, for SALTE, when Vargas abandoned the whole plan in 1951.

31. Letter, Sampaio to Dutra, Rio, n.d., in *Diário de Notícias,* Sept. 22, 1948, p. 4. On União see [Samuel Wainer] "É nas maõs do estado que está a chave das refinarias," *Diário de São Paulo,* Oct. 27, 1948, p. 4.

32. Comments by J. E. de Macedo Soares, "Medidas acertadas," *Diário Carioca,* Oct. 1, 1948, p. 1, and Barreto's interview in *Diário de Notícias,* Oct. 13, 1948, p. 4.

33. The projected SALTE plan refineries would not give profits for

several years, and in fact would constitute a hard currency drain (Cubatão excepted) until completed. Furthermore, since consumption was increasing rapidly, net profits would have to be plowed back into the same refining sector, not exploration.

34. Matos Pimenta, "Histório da solução Dutra ao problema de petróleo nacional," *Jornal de Debates*, Oct. 15, 1948, pp. 1, 5; Drault Ernanny interview, *Diário de São Paulo*, April 17, 1949, p. 2; "O dilema do govêrno," in *O Globo*, April 24, 1949, p. 10; and "As refinarias," in *Correio da Manhã*, April 22, 1949, p. 8.

35. Letter, Oswaldo Aranha to Matos Pimenta, April 20, 1949, in *Jornal de Debates*, April 22, 1949, pp. 1–2; Vargas's interview at Itú, in *ibid.*, May 20, 1949, pp. 1, 2; and his campaign speech at Salvador, Bahia, Aug. 30, 1950, in Vargas, *A campanha presidencial*, p. 256.

CHAPTER 9

1. To date, the best inside account of these events is Jesus Soares Pereira's short but important *Depoimento* [Aug. 24, 1964], in Vargas's *A política nacionalista*, pp. 39–52. Until participants publish their accounts, and until more documentation is available, researchers must rely heavily (as I did) on newspaper reportage, the copious parliamentary documents and debates in the excellent *Petróleo* volumes, and interviews.

2. Vargas, speech at Candeias oil field, Bahia, June 23, 1952, in *Correio da Manhã*, June 24, 1952, p. 5.

3. Rômulo de Almeida's testimony to Congress, March 5, 1952, in *Petróleo*, V, 364–65. In Vargas's words: "The exchange drain represented by petroleum has already reached 13 per cent of our import charges and tends to grow ever larger—without an analogous long-term growth in our capacity to export." This will constitute a major problem, he said, "until national production increases substantially." Mensagem ao Congresso Nacional [Jan. 1952] in Vargas, *A política nacionalista*, p. 104.

4. Several ministers were prepared to consider opening the way for the majors to come into the industry. Láfer (PSD-Finance), João Neves (PSD-Foreign Affairs), Negrão de Lima (PSD-Justice), Souza Lima (PSP-Transport), and João Cleofas (UDN-Agriculture) were reportedly in favor of doing so; Danton Coelho (PTB-Labor) and General Estillac Leal (War) opposed. Rafael Corrêa de Oliveira, "Os mistérios de petróleo," *Diário de Notícias*, May 16, 1951, p. 4. João Neves was a Standard Oil shareholder.

5. Robert Bellamy (for France-Presse) from London on FIESP, "Capitais britânicos e petróleo brasileiro," *Correio da Manhã*, May 9,

1952, p. 2; "Prospecção ingleza do Petróleo no Brasil," *Diário de Notícias*, July 7, 1951, p. 1; and *O Jornal*, quoted in the *New York Times*, May 7, 1951, to cite some of the many articles on this theme appearing in the Brazilian press during 1951.

6. "Proposto pelas companhias estrangeiras, 'New Deal' petrolífero para o Brasil," *Diário de São Paulo*, July 7, 1951. The Amapá analogy was false; laws governing iron ore and manganese concessions had been liberalized since the early 1940's, but the 1938 oil laws were still in force.

7. Speech by State Deputy Romeiro Neto to the State Assembly of Rio de Janeiro, Dec. 9, 1951, reported by *O Jornal*, Dec. 18, 1951; *O Jornal* editorial, "Empreendimento Patriótico," reprinted in *Diário de Notícias*, May 16, 1951, p. 4.

8. Café Filho, II, 464-65.

9. Interview with Rômulo de Almeida, Rio, Nov. 21, 1967. Hélio Jaguaribe, a junior member of Vargas's staff at the time, provides supporting evidence (*O nacionalismo*, p. 138): When the major companies were asked by Almeida whether they were prepared to carry out a sufficiently extensive exploration program, they replied that in view of the inherent risks of exploration and the fact that they considered their investments globally rather than in terms of a specific area they could not make a rigid advance commitment to invest such large sums in a determined region.

10. Skidmore, p. 99.

11. One new group slipped under the wire before Petrobrás was decreed in 1953. This was the powerful I. B. Sabbá e Cia.,which in March 1952 was authorized by the CNP to found the Cia. de Petróleo de Amazonia (COPAM) and to proceed with a 5,000 (later 7,000) b/day refinery at Manaus as part of the Amazon Development Plan.

12. The following analysis of Petrobrás is based on Vargas's message and the original bill, both in *Petróleo*, V, 5-38; Almeida's unsigned defense, Brazil, Presidência da República, *Os fundamentos da "Petrobrás,"* and his testimony to Congress, in *Petróleo*, V, 364-65; and my interview with Almeida, Rio, Nov. 21, 1967.

13. Soares Pereira, in Vargas, *A política nacionalista*, p. 43.

14. "Petróleo," *Correio da Manhã*, Dec. 8, 1951, p. 4; "O projeto do petróleo," *Diário de Notícias*, Dec. 15, 1951, p. 4.

15. "Que pensa o nosso povo sôbre a questão de petróleo brasileiro?," *Jornal de Debates*, Dec. 28, 1951, p. 5.

16. Besides Bernardes (Partido Republicano-Minas), the other leading petroleum nationalists were Euzébio Rocha (PTB-São Paulo), Lobo Carneiro (Partido de Representação Trabalhista-Federal District), General Lima Figueiredo (PSD-São Paulo), Hermes Pereira da Souza

(PSD–Rio Grande do Sul), Augusto Meira (PSD-Pará), and Orlando Dantas (Partido Socialista Brasileiro–Sergipe).

17. Letter, Horta to Matos Pimenta, Dec. 12, 1951, reprinted in *Jornal de Debates*, Dec. 21, 1951, p. 10.

18. As discussed in Chapter 7, foreigners were explicitly excluded from directing or holding stock in refining companies (Decree Law 395), or from obtaining permits to prospect for oil (Decree Law 3,236).

19. There were 19 members on this Petroleum Study Commission including General Horta Barbosa as President, General Raimundo Sampaio (Centro Honorary President), General Artur Carnaúba (Centro Director and Interim President of the Military Club from January to August 1951), General Felicíssimo Cardoso (Second Vice-President of the Military Club and President of the Centro), General Antônio José Henning (on the Centro Directorate), General Jonathos Moraes Correia, several colonels, and officers of lesser rank. See Clube Militar, *Revista*, p. 134.

20. General Felicíssimo Cardoso, Statement of Dec. 14, 1951, on Petrobrás, reprinted in *Petróleo*, VI, 35–36. In 1949 the Centro was renamed Centro de Estudos e Defesa do Petróleo e da Economia Nacional (CEDPEN). General Cardoso served as president through 1954, when the Centro merged with the Liga da Emancipação Nacional, and on to 1957, when President Kubitschek ordered the Liga dissolved. Fernando Luis Lobo Carneiro, "O projeto Vargas sôbre o petróleo," *Jornal de Debates*, Dec. 28, 1951, pp. 1–2. Family bonds reinforced this circle: Cardoso's younger brother was married to Horta's daughter; Lobo Carneiro, an ex–CNP official, was Horta's cousin.

21. Euzébio Rocha's Bill 1,595 in *Petróleo*, V, 49–55.

22. Rocha in floor debate of Jan. 25, 1952, in *Petróleo*, VI, 5.

23. Bernardes in floor debate of Feb. 1, 1952, in *Petróleo*, VI, 97–98.

24. General Lima Figueiredo, *Report* for Bernardes's Committee on National Security, March 7, 1952, *Petróleo*, VI, 535–46.

25. Sampaio's testimony to Congress in Feb. 1952, *Petróleo*, V, 245–311; see also Almeida's rebuttal, *Os fundamentos*, pp. 46–56.

26. This rump of the PSD followed ex-President Dutra, whom Vargas had assailed during the 1950 presidential race for mismanaging the inflation and monetary policy and for supporting the old Petroleum Statute. Furthermore, Vargas repudiated Dutra's SALTE plan.

27. The PSP Committee extended the management and stock ownership provisions governing the parent holding company to cover any future subsidiaries, for which Almeida had stipulated only 51 per cent State control. A broad spectrum of congressional opinion could support this change, given the state of public opinion, the nationalists' views on subsidiaries, and the Congress's genuine desire to eliminate any chance

for foreign penetration that might have existed in the original bill. That PSP leader Adhemar de Barros hoped to inherit the presidency from Vargas in 1955 was an additional reason for staying on the right side of populist issues like petroleum. *Parecer e emendas do P. S. P.* [Typewritten, March 1952] summarized in *Tribuna da Imprensa*, March 14, 1952, both courtesy of Dr. Castilho Cabral.

28. PSD Petroleum Study Committee, *Resolution*, by Senator Francisco Galoti, President, and Deputy Daniel Faraco, Secretary, in *Folha da Manhã*, March 28, 1952.

29. Estillac's speech of May 9, 1952, cited in *O Estado de São Paulo*, May 10, 1952, p. 5; "Parecer da Commissão de Estudo do Petróleo do Clube Militar," May 13, 1952, in Clube Militar, *Revista*.

30. General Nelson Werneck Sodré, the Marxist major under whose authority the pro–North Korean article was issued, makes this point on election tactics (p. 359).

31. In his speech one month after the Club elections, General Lima Figueiredo, a dutrista deputy who was influenced by petroleum nationalists in the Military Club, reckoned that 80 per cent of the military favored a State monopoly (Session of June 17, 1952, in *Petróleo*, VII, 319). On Juarez see "Pronunciou-se o general Juarez Távora a favor da 'Cruzada democrática,'" *O Estado de São Paulo*, May 17, 1952, p. 3. In 1947 it was Távora who insisted in speaking out on petroleum over Horta's objections. With stubborn honesty he continued to discuss the options in public in the early 1950's, and was called an entreguista by the extreme nationalists who could accept nothing less than a total State monopoly. But when Petrobrás was signed into law Távora dutifully supported it.

32. The vote was 8,288 (64.9 per cent) for Etchegoyen to 4,489 (35.1 per cent) for Estillac, more than double the 1950 turnout when Estillac had defeated General Cordeiro de Farias, 3,883 to 2,721. The huge 1952 vote was above all a repudiation of Estillac. However, some radical nationalists were purged or assigned to distant garrisons; the hard-liners wanted blood.

33. UDN bill, printed in full in *O Estado de São Paulo*, May 11, 1952, p. 4. Others who signed it were Prado Kelly, Ferreira de Sousa, and Maurício Joppert. When this substitute bill was submitted officially on June 6, it bore the following symbolic signatures: Bilac Pinto, Luis Garcia, Ernani Satiro, and Aliomar Baleeiro, all of the UDN, Artur Bernardes (PR), Euzébio Rocha (PTB), Orlando Dantas (PSB), Lima Figuiredo and Hermes Pereira de Sousa (PSD), and Joaquim Viegas (PST). In short, the nationalists joined forces with the UDN.

34. Almeida, in his interview with me, recalled that unlike the doctrinaire Rocha and the rigid Bernardes, these men were well-connected

lawyers with business sense. In mid-1952 Mineiros were the only delegates to oppose association with foreign private capital at a petroleum roundtable discussion sponsored by the Federation of Commercial Associations. (*World Petroleum,* Vol. 23, No. 7, p. 45.) And in November 1952 the Minas Gerais Commercial Association submitted a pro-monopoly ofício during the Senate debates on Petrobrás. (Alves, p. 163.)

35. This discussion of parliamentary maneuvers is based on daily political reports appearing in *Diário de Notícias, Correio da Manhã,* and *O Estado de São Paulo,* as checked against the debates and reports reprinted in *Petróleo,* vols. VI–XII.

36. Dutra, interview in *O Globo,* May, 17, 1952, p. 5; Lobo Carneiro in June 16, 1952 session, *Petróleo,* VII, 266; editorial, *O Estado de São Paulo,* May 17, 1952, p. 3; and editorial "A estrutura da Petrobrás," *Correio da Manhã,* July 22, 1952, p. 4.

37. A relatively unimportant special luxury tax on consumer items was abandoned in response to PTB criticism, but the government applied pressure successfully to retain the major finance provisions.

38. If it came to a power play, Capanema estimated he could obtain 190 votes (compared to 110 opposition votes), based on his control over 90 PSD, 24 PSP, 3 PR [Republicans], 3 Integralistas [followers of Plínio Salgado], virtually all the PTB, and 15 UDN deputies, including Flôres da Cunha, who were bolting the UDN monopoly position. *O Estado de São Paulo,* July 26, 1952, p. 3.

39. Almost all the PTB delegation accepted Lúcio Bittencourt's "nationalist" amendment that would limit private stockholders to natives, citizens naturalized more than five years, and Brazilians not married to foreigners. The effects were moral and political, rather than practical. However, Bittencourt's maneuver enabled his colleagues to bypass Rocha's bill, making the government's new position less politically dangerous to them. Bittencourt was a deputy from Minas.

40. "Novo formula do imposto único sôbre combustíveis," *Última Hora* [São Paulo], Sept. 6, 1952. São Paulo contributed about cr$748 million to the national Highway Fund, of which it received about cr$320 million in reallocated funds. Under Baleeiro's plan this would have fallen to cr$233 million. (These figures cover the total non-federal quota given to São Paulo, that is, 48 per cent of reallocated imposto único revenues to the state, and 12 per cent to its local governments.)

41. Baleeiro's amendment no. 21 carried, 102 to 75, on September 2. A less drastic reallocation formula by Saturnino Braga (PSD–Rio de Janeiro) lost narrowly, 103 to 112, on September 18, in voting that pitted the North against the South regardless of party affiliation. *Petróleo,* VIII, 220, 630.

42. FIESP, in a telegram to the Senate, maintained that the "exclusion of private initiative [was] prejudicial to the highest interests of national economy." (Cited in *World Petroleum*, Vol. 24, No. 4, p. 49.) Although he had fallen out with Vargas politically, Pasqualini agreed to defend the government-backed Chamber bill and was advised by Soares Pereira of the President's Technical Staff. Soares Pereira, in Vargas, *A política nacionalista*, p. 46.

43. FIESP, Primeiro Reunião de Indústria, May 27–June 3, 1953, in *Correio da Manhã*, June 9, 1953, p. 4; also Memorandum by a Commission under Horácio de Mello, published by the São Paulo Commercial Association, cited in *ibid.*, Nov. 22, 1952, p. 6.

44. In his article "Um alvitre," p. 12, Souza Dantas recalled that both Vargas and Aranha had supported his scheme because they feared Petrobrás would be inflationary. Later, Carlos Medeiros Silva in a lecture to the Confederação Nacional do Comércio reported that motor vehicle owners had subscribed cr$400 million in stock, more than cr$150 million above expectations. Having organized the Corporation juridically, Medeiros Silva urged that it be given a chance to prove itself despite the current exchange and political crises. Lecture reprinted in *Jornal do Comércio*, Oct. 29, 1954.

45. Both Juracy and Juarez Távora of the UDN urged the public to support Petrobrás now that it was written into law, and Vargas's successor, João Café Filho, did not revise the Corporation, contrary to expectations.

46. For three informed, favorable views see Lima Rocha; Beltrão; and Gilberto Paim, "Objetivos em petróleo," *Jornal do Brasil*, July 9, 1967, p. 5 [caderno especial].

47. Hartshorn, p. 227; see also the pessimistic geophysical report by Arthur Link, summarized in "Petróleo no Brasil e o relatório Link," *Correio da Manhã*, Feb. 19, 1967, p. 3 [segundo caderno]. According to Link, Petrobrás spent more than $150 million exploring unproductive areas from 1954 to 1960.

48. Cited in "Quem é quem na economia brasileira."

49. "Concedido o aval para petroquímica," *Jornal do Brasil*, Dec. 18, 1968.

50. Senators Plínio Pompeu (UDN), Othon Mäder (UDN) and Apolônio Sales (PSD) sponsored the Senate bill (no. 1 of 1955). "Apresentado ontem à mesa do Senado um projeto de lei modificando a Petrobrás," *O Jornal*, Jan. 26, 1955. Their project to allow foreign capital into general development contracting was defeated 32 to 5. *New York Times*, April 1, 1955, p. 37.

51. Skidmore, pp. 180 and 385 n.35.

BIBLIOGRAPHY

UNPUBLISHED DOCUMENTS

Official Archives

Brazil, Conselho Federal do Comércio Exterior. Processos, 1934–42. Arquivo Nacional, Rio.

Brazil, Ministério das Relações Exteriores. Arquivo, 1934–40. Telegrams and ofícios, Rio–Washington–Berlin. Palácio Itamaraty, Rio.

Brazil, Ministério da Viação e Obras Públicas. Arquivo, 1939–40. Protocolos gerais. Ministério da Viação e Obras Públicas, Rio.

Brazil, Presidência da República. Presidential Papers, 1934–40. Arquivo Nacional, Rio.

Germany, Foreign Office. Unpublished Documents. "The Steel Works in Brazil, 1939–1940." Correspondence between the Foreign Office and the Ministry of Economics, roll 3374, microcopy T-120. United States National Archives.

――――. "Barter Transactions and Compensation Agreements Between Germany and Brazil." Economic Department, roll 4465, microcopy T-120. United States National Archives.

――――. "Financial Agreements Between German and Brazilian Institutions in 1934." Economic Department, roll 4463, microcopy T-120. United States National Archives.

――――. "Political Relations of Brazil with Germany, 1936–40." Roll 3155, microcopy T-120. United States National Archives.

Germany, Reichsministry of Economics. Unpublished Documents. "Mining in Brazil, 1938–1942." Roll 84, microcopy T-71. United States National Archives.

United States, Department of State. Unpublished Documents. "The Brazilian Steel Project," 832.6511.

――――. "Itabira Iron Ore Company," 832.6351 It.

――――. ["Petroleum" 1936–43], 832.6363. United States National Archives.

Private Papers

Oswaldo Aranha Archive. 1930–42. Rio.
Percival Farquhar Collection. Biblioteca Nacional, Rio.
Ibá Jobim Meirelles Archive. 1936–58. Rio.
Roberto Simonsen Archive. 1936–48. São Paulo.
Getúlio Vargas Archive. 1936–42. Rio.

PUBLISHED DOCUMENTS, BOOKS, AND ARTICLES

Almeida. Fundamentos. *See* Brazil, Presidência da República.
Alves, Senator Landulpho. Atividades parlamentares. O problema brasileiro do petróleo. Rio, 1954.
Amaral, Afrânio do. Siderurgia e planejamento econômico do Brasil. São Paulo, 1946.
Amora, Paulo. Bernardes: O estadista de Minas na República. São Paulo, 1964.
Amorim, Deolindo. "O plano social de Volta Redonda e a transformação do capitalismo," *Digesto Econômico*, Ano X, No. 110 (Jan. 1954), pp. 74–79.
Andrade, Almir de. Contribuição à história administrativa do Brasil na República até 1945. Vol. II. Rio, 1950.
Assis Barbosa, Francisco de. JK. Uma revisão na política brasileira. Vol. I. Rio, 1960.
Associação Comercial do Rio de Janeiro. *Boletim Semanal*, Ano IV, No. CXXXIV (May 27, 1938), pp. 2894–99.
Azevedo Amaral, [Antônio José]. O estado autoritário e a realidade nacional. Rio, 1938.
Baer, Werner. The Development of the Brazilian Steel Industry. Unpublished manuscript.
————. Industrialization and Economic Development in Brazil. Homewood, Illinois, 1965.
Barbosa Lima Sobrinho, [Alexandre José]. Alcool-motor. Rio, 1943.
————. Desde quando somos nacionalistas? No. 24 in the series Cadernos do Povo. Rio, 1963.
Bastos, Humberto. A conquista siderúrgica no Brasil. São Paulo, 1959.
Beckett, Grace. The Reciprocal Trade Agreements Program. New York, 1941.
Beltrão, Helio. Os seis equívocos fundamentais sôbre a Petrobrás. Rio, Dec. 1957.
Bernardes, Artur da Silva. Discurso pronunciado na sessão de 18 de junho de 1937 sôbre a Itabira Iron. Rio, 1948.
Bouças, Valentim F. História da dívida externa. Rio, 1946.
Brazil, Assembléia Constituinte de 1934. Diário. Session of Feb. 1, 1934.

Brazil, Assembléia Constituinte de 1946. Anais. Vols. V, VII, IX. Rio, 1947–48.

Brazil, Comissão Executiva do Plano Siderúrgico Nacional. Relatório. Rio, 1940–41.

Brazil, Comissão Nacional de Siderurgia. Relatório final in Boletim 75 of Serviço Geológico e Mineralógico. Rio, 1935.

Brazil, Congresso. Câmara dos Deputados. Annaes. Vols. 15–16. Rio, 1935.

————. ————. Petróleo, Documentos parlamentares. 12 vols. Rio, 1957–59.

Brazil, Conselho Federal de Comércio Exterior. Atividades (1934–1940). Rio, 1940.

————. O Conselho Federal de Comércio Exterior em São Paulo, maio de 1938. São Paulo, 1940.

————. Dez anos de atividade. Rio, 1944.

Brazil, Conselho Nacional do Petróleo. Análise dos preços de venda, no mercado interno de petróleo e seus derivados. Rio, 1950.

————. Legislação do petróleo. Rio, 1964.

————. Parecer do Consultor Geral da República no recurso que a Companhia Matogrossense de Petróleo interpôs de decisão do Conselho Nacional do Petróleo para o senhor presidente da República. Rio, 1941.

————. Relatório, 1° triênio, 1938–41, and Anexos 1 and 2 [typewritten]. Rio, 1941.

————. Relatórios, 1943–50. Rio, 1943–

————. Resoluções do plenário, 1945 a 1961 [mimeo]. Rio, n.d.

Brazil, Conselho Técnico de Economia e Finanças. Valentim F. Bouças, ed. Atas e pareceres, 1937–42. Vol. XII in Finanças do Brasil. Rio, n.d.

————. A grande siderurgia e a exportação de minério de ferro brasileiro em larga escala. Rio, 1938.

Brazil, Departamento Nacional de Propaganda. Francisco Campos. Os problemas do Brasil e as grandes soluçoes do novo regime. Rio, 1938.

Brazil, Instituto Brasileiro de Geografia e Estatística. Conselho Nacional de Estatística. Anuário estatístico do Brasil. Rio, 1935–55.

Brazil, Ministério da Agricultura. Odilon Braga. Bases para o inquérito sôbre o petróleo. Rio, 1936.

————. Departamento Nacional de Produção Mineral. Código de minas (decreto-lei 1.985 de 29-1-40). Rio, 1940.

————. Juarez Távora. O ministro da agricultura perante a assembléia nacional constituinte. Rio, 1934.

Brazil, Ministério da Viação e Obras Públicas. José Américo de Almeida. O ministério da viação no governo provisório. Rio, 1933.

Brazil, Presidência da República. [Rômulo de Almeida.] Os fundamentos da "Petrobrás." Rio, 1952.

Brazil, Superintendência da Moeda e Crédito. "Notas relativas à evolução do sistema cambial brasileiro," Boletim, I, No. 4 (1955), 12–20.

Bulhões, Octavio. "Comércio exterior em 1939," O Observador Econômico e Financeiro, Ano V, No. 50 (March 1940), pp. 97–102.

Burns, E. Bradford. Nationalism in Brazil: A Historical Survey. New York, 1968.

Café Filho, João. Do sindicato ao Catete. Vol. II. Rio, 1966.

Carvalho, Edson. O drama da descoberta do petróleo brasileiro. São Paulo, 1958.

Cavalheiro, Edgard. Monteiro Lobato: Vida e obra. Vol. II. 2d ed., rev. São Paulo, 1956.

Clube Militar. "Parecer da Comissão de Estudo do Petróleo do Clube Militar," May 13, 1952, Revista do Clube Militar, No. 120, (March–April–May 1952), pp. 134–47.

Clube 3 de Outubro. Esbôço do programa revolucionário de reconstrução política e social do Brasil. Rio, 1932.

Cohn, Gabriel. Petróleo e nacionalismo. São Paulo, 1968.

"Comércio exterior do Brasil," Observador Econômico e Financeiro, Ano I, No. 4 (May 1936) and No. 7 (Aug. 1936).

"O comércio do petróleo no Brasil," Conjuntura Econômica, Ano III, No. 8 (Aug. 1949), pp. 13–18.

[Cooke Mission]. A missão Cooke no Brasil. Portuguese version, ed. Fundação Getúlio Vargas. Rio, 1949.

Coutinho, Lourival, and Joel Silveira. O petróleo do Brasil, traição e vitória. Rio, 1957.

Couto, Roberto M. A questão de ferro. Rio, 1938.

Daland, Robert T. Brazilian Planning: Development Politics and Administration. Chapel Hill, N.C., 1967.

Diebold, William, Jr. New Directions in Our Trade Policy. New York, 1941.

Dix, Robert. Colombia: The Political Dimensions of Change. New Haven, 1968.

Dulles, John W. F. Vargas of Brazil: A Political Biography. Austin, Texas, 1967.

Farquhar, Percival. Contracto Itabira, resposta do discurso do deputado Arthur Bernardes de 6 de março de 1937, publicado em 18 de março no "Correio da Manhã." Rio, [1937?].

———. A verdade sôbre o plano Raul Ribeiro da Silva. Rio, 1939.

Federação Industrial do Estado de São Paulo. A cidade do aço, impressões de Volta Redonda. São Paulo, 1943.

Freire, Floro E. "O petróleo no Brasil," *Brasil Mineral*, Ano 1, No. 1 (Jan. 1940), pp. 1–9.

Fróes Abreu, Sylvio, et al. Contribuições para a geologia do Recôncavo (Bahia). Rio, 1936.

Fróes, Abreu, Sylvio. Recursos minerais do Brasil. Vol. II. Rio, 1962.

Frondizi, Arturo. Petróleo y política. 2d ed. Buenos Aires, 1955.

Frye, Alton. Nazi Germany and the American Hemisphere, 1933–41. New Haven, Conn., 1967.

Furtado, Celso. The Economic Growth of Brazil. Berkeley, 1963.

Gardner, Lloyd C. Economic Aspects of New Deal Diplomacy. Madison, Wis., 1964.

Gauld, Charles A. The Last Titan, Percival Farquhar. [Special issue of the *Hispanic American Report*.] Stanford, 1964.

Góes Monteiro, General [Pedro Aurélio]. A revolução de 30 e a finalidade política do exército. Rio, 1933.

Gordon, Wendell C. The Political Economy of Latin America. New York, 1965.

Great Britain, Department of Overseas Trade. Report on Economic and Commercial Conditions in Brazil. London, 1930–39.

Guilherme, Olympio. Roboré: A luta pelo petróleo boliviano. Rio, 1959.

Guinle, Guilherme. Interviewed in *Diretrizes*, Ano IV, No. 42 (April 10, 1941), pp. 8–9.

Hartshorn, J. E. Politics and World Oil Economics. New York, 1962.

Hexner, Ervin. The International Steel Cartel. Chapel Hill, N.C., 1943.

Hirschman, Albert O. Journeys Towards Progress. New York, 1964.

Hull, Cordell. The Memoirs of Cordell Hull. Vol. I. New York, 1948.

"Indústria siderúrgica brasileira," *Revista* do Conselho Nacional de Economia, Ano 2, Nos. 9–10 (Jan.–Feb. 1953), pp. 30–54.

Jaguaribe, Hélio. Economic and Political Development. Cambridge, Mass., 1968.

———. O nacionalismo na atualidade brasileira. Instituto Superior de Estudos Brasileiros. Rio, 1958.

Jobim, José. O Brasil na economia mundial. Rio, [1938].

Johnson, Harry G. "A Theoretical Model of Economic Nationalism in New and Developing States," *Political Science Quarterly*, LXXX, No. 2 (June 1965), 169–85.

Johnson, John J. "The New Latin American Nationalism," *Yale Review*, LIV, No. 2 (Dec. 1964), 187–204.

Labouriau, Ferdinand. O nosso problema siderúrgico. Rio, 1924.

Langer, William L., and S. Everett Gleason. The Challenge to Isolation, 1937–1940. New York, 1952.

Leão, Josias. Mines and Minerals in Brazil. Rio, [1939].

Leff, Nathaniel H. Economic Policy-Making and Development in Brazil, 1947–1964. New York, 1968.

Leitão de Carvalho, General Estêvão. Petróleo! Salvação ou desgraça do Brasil? Centro de Estudos e Defesa do Petróleo e da Economia Nacional. Rio, 1950.

Leite, Solidonio. O petróleo e o dever do Brasil [Series in *Jornal do Brasil*, reprinted by the Ministry of Agriculture]. Rio, 1927.

Liga Naval Brasileira. O contracto do Itabira Iron Ore: sua repercussão sôbre a economia brasileira em geral, sôbre o desenvolvimento da siderurgia nacional, em particular, parecer da Liga Naval Brasileira. Rio, 1937.

L[ima] R[ocha] H[eitor]. "Política do petróleo," *Cadernos do Nosso Tempo*, No. 4 (April–Aug. 1955), pp. 35–56.

Lindblom, Charles E. "The Science of 'Muddling Through,'" *Public Administration Review*, XIX, No. 2 (Spring 1959), pp. 79–88.

Link, Walter. "Petróleo no Brasil e o relatório Link," Segundo Caderno, *Correio da Manhã*, Feb. 19, 1967, p. 3. Resumé of Report to General Idálio Sardenberg, President of Petrobrás.

Lobo Carneiro, Fernando Luis. "A política petrolífera que mais convem aos interesses do Brasil." Lecture, Sept. 3, 1947, in São Paulo. *Engenharia*, Ano VI, No. 62 (Oct. 1947), pp. 61–66.

Long, Roberto G. "O Vale do Médio Paraíba," *Revista Brasileira de Geografía*, Ano XV, No. 3 (July–Sept. 1953), pp. 53–139.

McCann, Frank D. "La Lucha por el comercio brasileño, 1935–1939," *Foro Internacional*, IX, No. 2 (Oct.–Dec. 1968), 182–93.

Macedo Soares, José Carlos de. Discursos, rumos da diplomacia brasileira. Rio, 1937.

Macedo Soares e Silva, Edmundo de. "O ferro e o carvão no história, na economia e na civilização do Brasil," *O Jornal do Comércio* (Oct. 18, 1952).

———. *O movimento da indústria pesada e o progresso econômico do Brasil*. Rio, May 1955.

———. "Volta Redonda, gênese da idéia, seu desenvolvimento, projeto, execução e custo," *Revista do Serviço Público*, Ano VIII, Vol. IV, No. 2 (Nov. 1945), pp. 5–27.

Manoilescu, Mikail. O século do corporativismo. [Brazilian translation.] São Paulo, 1938.

———. Theoria do proteccionismo e da permuta international. [Brazilian translation for the Centro das Indústrias do Estado de São Paulo.] São Paulo, 1931.

Marighella, Carlos. "Nossa política," *Problemas*, Ano I, No. 3 (Oct. 1947), and No. 4 (Nov. 1947).

Meirelles, Antônio Chagas. "Imposto único federal sôbre os combustíveis e lubrificantes líquidos minerais," *Indústria Automotiva*, Ano IV, No. 47 (Jan. 1963), pp. 53–60.

Mendonça Lima, Colonel João. "O problema do transporte do minério," *Revista do Clube de Engenharia*, Ano III, No. 36 (Sept. 1937), pp. 1556–60.

Monteiro Lobato, José Bento. O escândalo do petróleo. São Paulo, 1936, 1959.

Mosconi, Enrique. El petróleo argentino. Buenos Aires, 1936.

Oil and Gas Journal. Tulsa, Oklahoma: The Petroleum Publishing Company. 1950–68.

Oliveira, Avelino I. de. "Tentativas de pesquisa de petróleo no Brasil e pesquisas atuais," *Mineração e Metalurgia*, XIII, No. 78 (March–April 1949), 302–3.

Oliveira Vianna, F. V. Problemas de política objectiva. Rio, 1930.

Pacheco, J. Junot. Exportação de minério de ferro e siderurgia. Conferência realisada na Associação Comercial de Minas em 6 de Julho de 1938 e lida perante o Conselho Director do Clube de Engenharia do Rio de Janeiro e a Sociedade Mineira de Engenharia. Belo Horizonte, 1938.

Paiva, Glycon de. "Característicos do projeto do 'Estatuto do Petróleo,'" *Digesto Econômico*, Ano II, No. 49 (Dec. 1948), pp. 45–52.

Paiva, Glycon de, and Irnack C. do Amaral. "Rumos novos em sondagens profundas," *Boletim do Departamento Nacional da Produção Mineral*, No. 36 (1939), pp. 1–15.

Peláez, Carlos Manoel. "A balança comercial, a grande depressão e a industrialização brasileira," *Revista Brasileira de Economia*, Ano 22, No. 1 (March 1968), pp. 15–47.

Penteado, Antônio Augusto de Barros. *Projeto de revisão do código de minas*. . . . São Paulo, [1944].

Pérez Prins, Ezequiel. "La refinaria de petróleo de la ANCAP," *Boletin del Instituto Sudamericano del Petróleo*, I, No. 1 (April 1943), 15–36.

Pereira, Jesus Soares. Depoimento. See Vargas, A política nacionalista.

Petróleo. See Brazil, Congresso.

Pimenta, Dermeval José. Implantação da grande siderurgia em Minas Gerais. Belo Horizonte, 1967.

Pinheiro, Alcides. Direito das minas: Comentários à legislação. Rio, 1939.

Primeiro Congresso Brasileiro de Economia [Nov. 26–Dec. 18, 1943]. Anais. Vol. I. Rio, 1943.

"Quem é quem na economia brasileira," *Visão*, 33, No. 5 (Aug. 30, 1968), 222.

Rache, Athos de Lemos. Contribuição ao estudo da economia mineira. Rio, [1957].

Reichard, Ernst. "El comercio de Alemania con los países Ibero-Americanos, sobre la base de la compensación natural," in *Alemania y el mundo Ibero-Americano*, pp. 161–67. Ibero Amerikanisches Institut. Berlin, 1939.

Rocha Diniz, Osório da. O Brasil em face dos imperialismos modernos. Rio, 1940.

Rogers, Edward Jonathan. "A Study of the Brazilian Iron and Steel Industry and Its Associated Resources." Unpublished doctoral dissertation, Stanford University, 1957.

Santa Rosa, Virgínio. O sentido do tenentismo. Rio, 1933.

Sayre, Francis Bowes. The Way Forward: The American Trade Agreements Program. New York, 1939.

Scalapino, Robert A. "Ideology and Modernization—The Japanese Case," pp. 93–127 in *Ideology and Discontent*, David E. Apter, ed. Glencoe, Ill., 1964.

[Siciliano Junior, Alexandre.] Articles on the steel problem in *Diário Carioca* (March 11–16, 1933).

Simões Lopes, Ildefonso. "Petróleo nacional," *Revista do Clube de Engenharia*, Ano III, No. 36 (Sept. 1937), pp. 157–82.

Simonsen, Roberto. Aspects of National Political Economy. Translation of speech in Chamber of Deputies, Sept. 11, 1935. São Paulo, 1935.

———. Níveis de vida e a economia nacional. São Paulo, Sept. 1940.

[———]. Sugestões para uma política econômica panamericana: Problemas do desenvolvimento econômico latino-americano. Conselho Economico da Confederação Nacional da Indústria. Rio, 1948.

Skidmore, Thomas E. Politics in Brazil, 1930–1954. New York, 1967.

Snyder, Richard C. "Commercial Policy as Reflected in Treaties from 1931 to 1939," *American Economic Review*, XXX, No. 4 (Dec. 1940), 787–802.

Souza, Egídio Câmara de. "Legal Incentives to Investment Abroad: Foreign and Domestic Statutes and Policies." Remarks to the International Investment Law Conference, session of Feb. 25, 1965. Typewritten, courtesy of Dr. Cleantho de Paiva Leite.

Souza Dantas, Marcos de. "Um alvitre para maior rapidez na solução do problema do petróleo brasileiro," *Digesto Econômico*, Ano XI, No. 121 (Jan.–Feb. 1955), pp. 11–14.

———. "História verdadeira dos 'marcos de compensação,' " in *Correio da Manhã*, July 1, 1937, p. 8.

Stein, Stanley J. The Brazilian Cotton Manufacture. Cambridge, Mass., 1957.

Távora, General Juarez. Petróleo para o Brasil. 2d ed. Rio, 1955.

Tendler, Judith. Electric Power in Brazil: Entrepreneurship in the Public Sector. Cambridge, Mass., 1968.

Tôrres, Alberto. O problema nacional brasileiro. Rio, 1914.

Truda, Leonardo. "Reflexões sôbre o problema do ferro," Boletim do Ministério do Trabalho, Indústria e Comércio, Ano V, No. 32 (Dec. 1938), pp. 135–59.

United Nations, Department of Economic Affairs. World Ore Resources and Their Utilization with Particular Reference to the Use of Iron Ores in Underdeveloped Areas. New York, 1950.

United Nations, Economic Commission for Latin America. A Study of the Iron and Steel Industry in Latin America. 2 vols. New York, 1954.

United States, Congress. History of the Operations and Policies of the Export-Import Bank of Washington, by Hawthorne Arey. Printed in Study of the Export-Import Bank and World Bank, Part I, Hearings, Senate Banking and Currency Committee, 83rd Congress, 2nd Session. Washington, 1954.

United States, Department of Commerce. Bureau of Foreign and Domestic Commerce. Statistical Abstract of the United States. Washington, D.C., 1930–42.

United States, Department of Interior. Bureau of Mines. World Petroleum Statistics. Washington, 1951–68.

United States, Department of State. Documents on German Foreign Policy. Series D, Vol. X. Washington, D.C. 1957.

————. Foreign Relations of the United States, 1933–40. Volumes for "The American Republics." Washington, D.C., 1950–61.

United States, Tariff Commission. Digest of Trade with Respect to Products on which Concessions Were Granted by the United States in the United States–Brazilian Trade Agreement. . . . [mimeo.] Washington, D.C., May 1935.

————. The Foreign Trade of Latin America. Part II, Report No. 146, Vol. I, Second Series. Washington, D.C., 1942.

————. Foreign-Trade and Exchange Controls in Germany. Report No. 150, Second Series. Washington, D.C., 1942.

————. The International Petroleum Cartel. Washington, D.C., 1952.

————. Mining and Manufacturing Industries in Brazil. Washington, D.C., 1949.

Vaitsman, Maurício. O petróleo no Império e na República. Rio, 1948.

Vargas, Getúlio. A campanha presidencial. Rio, 1951.

————. A nova política do Brasil. Vols. V and X. Rio, 1939 and 1944.

————. A política nacionalista do petróleo no Brasil. Includes the excellent Depoimento by Jesus Soares Pereira. Rio, 1964.

Veliz, Claudio, ed. The Politics of Conformity in Latin America. London, 1967.

Vilela Luz, Nícia. A luta pela industrialização do Brasil. São Paulo, 1961.

"Vinte anos decisivos, o romance da siderurgia," *Diretrizes*, Ano III, No. 31 (Nov. 1940), pp. 3–22.

Vivacqua, Attilio. A nova política do sub-solo e o regime legal das minas. Rio, 1942.

Werneck, Sodré, General Nelson. Memórias de um soldado. Rio, 1967.

White, C. Langdon. "Water—A Neglected Factor in the Geographical Literature of Iron and Steel," *The Geographical Review*, XLVII, No. 4 (Oct. 1957), 463–89.

Wirth, John D. "A German View of Brazilian Trade and Development, 1935," *Hispanic American Historical Review*, XLVII, No. 2 (May 1967), 225–35.

————. "Tenentismo in the Brazilian Revolution of 1930," *Hispanic American Historical Review*, XLIV, No. 2 (May 1964), 161–79.

Wood, Bryce. The Making of the Good Neighbor Policy. New York, 1961.

World Petroleum. New York. 1952–53. Vols. 23 and 24.

INTERVIEWS

Almeida, Rômulo de. Director, Technical Advisory Staff in Vargas's second presidency; economist. Rio, Nov. 21, 1967.

Amaral Peixoto, Alzira Vargas do. Daughter of Getúlio Vargas; aide to President Vargas in the 1940's; lawyer. Rio, Sept. 19, 1967.

Amaral Peixoto, Admiral Augusto do. Secretary, Clube 3 de Outubro; Guanabara State Deputy. Rio, Jan. 4, 1965.

Berle, Adolph A., Jr. United States Ambassador to Brazil, 1945; professor of law. New York, July 14, 1966.

Cardoso, General Felicíssimo. President, Center for the Study and Defense of Petroleum and the National Economy in the early 1950's; now retired. Interviewed with Henrique Miranda. Rio, Dec. 8, 1967.

Castilho Cabral, Carlos. Leader, Partido Social Progressista bloc in the Chamber of Deputies during Petrobrás debates; lawyer. Rio, Sept. 11, 1967.

Feis, Herbert F. Director of Economic Affairs for the Department of State; historian. The Orchard, Maine, July 9, 1966.

Fróes Abreu, Sylvio. Petroleum pioneer; Director, National Institute of Technology. Rio, July 13, 1967.

Kemnitzer, William J. Member of the Morris Cooke Mission to Brazil, 1942–43; petroleum geologist. Stanford, 1967–68.

Meira, Admiral Lúcio. Deputy Chief of Military Household in Vargas's second presidency; industrialist. Rio, Nov. 29, 1967.

Meirelles, General Ibá Jobim. Chief Aide to General Horta Barbosa in the CNP, and petroleum pioneer; retired. Rio, 1967–68.

Miranda, Henrique. Secretary General of the CEDP (after 1949, CEDPEN) for many years; professor of literature. Interviewed with General Felicíssimo Cardoso. Rio, Dec. 8, 1967.

Paiva Teixeira, Glycon de. Petroleum pioneer; Director of the National Economic Council. Rio, Sept. 18, 1967.

Pedreira, Fernando. Secretary, the National Union of Students 1947–48; journalist. Rio, Sept. 14, 1967.

Simões Lopes, Luis. DASP Director, 1938–45; President, the Getúlio Vargas Foundation. Rio, March 22, 1965.

Stolear, Smaia. Chief, CNP Economic Section. Rio, Sept. 20, 1967.

Teixeira, Cipriano. Long-time CNP functionary; now Chief, CNP Juridical Section. Interviewed with Alfredo Valdetario da Fonseca. Rio, Sept. 18, 1967.

Valdetario da Fonseca, Alfredo. Long-time CNP functionary; lawyer for the CNP. Interviewed with Cipriano Teixeira. Rio, Sept. 18, 1967.

Vicq de Cumptich, Vincente de. Director, Standard Oil of Brazil in the 1950's; semi-retired. Rio, Sept. 21, 1967.

INDEX

Abbink, John, 179
Acesita (steel company), 110
Aciéries Réunies de Burback-Eich-
  Dudelange (ARBED), 87
Administración Nacional de Com-
  bustibles, Alcohol y Portland (AN-
  CAP), 152, 248 n.24
Alencastro Guimarães, Napoleão,
  157, 210
Almeida, Aristides de, 161
Almeida, José Américo de, 83
Almeida, Rômulo de, 185, 191, 195–
  201 passim, 205
Alves, Landulfo, 153, 210
Amaral, Irnack Carvalho do, 142f,
  191
Amaral Peixoto, Ernani do, 123, 153,
  188
Amazonas Commercial Association,
  55
Amazon Development Plan, 181n,
  255 n.11
ANCAP (Administración Nacional
  de Combustibles, Alcohol y Portland), 152, 248 n.24
Anderson, Wingate Man, 167
Anglo-Mexican Oil Company, 136–
  37, 137n, 139, 144
Anti-Comintern Pact, 52
Anti-Fascist League, 173
Aranha, Oswaldo: remedies for bal-
  ance-of-payment crisis, 10–11;
  trade policy, 18, 61, 63f; biograph-
  ical sketch, 24–25; negotiations for
  U.S. trade treaty, 27, 33–40 passim; and the steel industry, 80,
  91ff, 106–7, 108, 127, 250 n.35;
  and oil policy, 148, 156, 183, 207,
  250 n.35; as Finance Minister,
  211–12. See also Aranha Plan
Aranha Plan, 10–11, 28, 41, 48, 62,
  231 n.18
ARBED (Aciéries Réunies de Burback-Eich-Dudelange), 87
Argentina, 32, 59, 134, 146, 149

Argentine National Petroleum Company, see YPF
Army, see Military
Arrojado Lisbôa, Joaquim Miguel de,
  109n
Arthur G. McKee and Company, 114,
  126
ASKI marks (Auslander-Sonderkonto-fuer-Inlandszahlungen), 38. See
  also Compensation marks
A. Thun and Company, 96, 121
Atlantic Refining Company, 137n,
  139

Balance-of-payments problem, 4, 9–
  11, 186–87, 189; in 1935, 40–44,
  48–49. See also Aranha Plan
Balbo, Gen. Italo, 21
Baleeiro, Aliomar de Andrade, 197,
  204–10 passim
Bank, government savings (Caixa
  Econômica), 115, 171
Bank of Brazil, 87, 164, 179f; and for-
  eign trade, 27, 31, 40f, 44, 62n
Barbosa Lima Sobrinho, A. J., 23
Barreto, Col. João Carlos, 161–64,
  167, 179, 180–82, 188, 220
Barros, Adhemar Pereira de, 206
Behr & Co. (German firm), 29
Belgo-Mineira Company, 81, 87f,
  118n, 241 nn.28 & 29
Beltrão, Helio, 191, 195
Berle, Adolf A., Jr., 162
Bernardes, Artur da Silva, 77n, 139,
  207; and the steel industry, 77, 81,
  81n, 87; nationalism of, 82, 199–
  200, 222; and the Centro, 173, 177;
  and oil policy, 178, 197, 199, 206
Bethlehem Steel Company, 79, 115,
  188
Beutner, Wilhelm, 236 n.3
Bilac Pinto, Olavo, 204f, 207
Bittencourt, Gen. Amaro Soares, 103
Bittencourt, Lucio, 258 n.39
Boavista Bank, 162